COMPUTER SIMULATION IN FINANCIAL RISK MANAGEMENT

COMPUTER SIMULATION IN FINANCIAL RISK MANAGEMENT

A Guide for Business Planners and Strategists

Roy L. Nersesian

QUORUM BOOKS
New York • Westport, Connecticut • London

Library of Congress Cataloging-in-Publication Data

Nersesian, Roy L.
  Computer simulation in financial risk management : a guide for
business planners and strategists / Roy L. Nersesian.
      p.   cm.
  Includes index.
  ISBN 0-89930-578-4 (alk. paper)
  1. Risk management—Computer simulation.   2. Corporations—
Finance—Computer simulation.   I. Title.
HD61.N46   1991
658.15—dc20   90-45146

British Library Cataloguing in Publication Data is available.

Library of Congress Catalog Card Number: 90-45146
ISBN: 0-89930-578-4

First published in 1991

Quorum Books, 88 Post Road West, Westport, CT 06881
An imprint of Greenwood Publishing Group, Inc.

Printed in the United States of America

∞

The paper used in this book complies with the
Permanent Paper Standard issued by the National
Information Standards Organization (Z39.48-1984).

10 9 8 7 6 5 4 3 2 1

Copyright Acknowledgment

Extracts from Richard W. Stevenson's "Where Savings Crisis Hits Hard," *The New York Times*,
January 16, 1990, copyright © 1990 by The New York Times Company. Reprinted by
permission.

TO
MY MOTHER
AND
IN MEMORY OF
MY FATHER

Contents

Introduction   ix

1 Bridging the Cultural Gap   1

2 A Businessman's Assessments   17

3 The Equity Decision   55

4 The Loan Decision   85

5 Self-Insuring a Loan Portfolio   123

6 Determining the Safe Load of Debt   155

7 Hedging and the Futures Market   199

Index   223

Introduction

The management of risk is a contradiction in terms. Management implies control. Sales managers who decide to cut prices by 10 percent do so on the basis that they control those prices. They direct supervisors to lower the prices on goods by 10 percent. They manage price by virtue of the fact that they can come to a decision about price and then exert control over price by means of an instruction or by changing the price themselves. This is management, particularly if managers order someone else to go around the store marking down prices rather than doing it themselves.

Production managers determine the quantity of output in a factory. They review what has to be reviewed, meet, talk, discuss, contemplate, and act. They issue an instruction, orally or in writing, for production to be increased or decreased by a certain amount. Since they are controlling the output of the factory, they are deemed managers. Managers are managers by virtue of the fact that they exert control over situations.

Can we manage risk in the same way we determine prices on goods or the output of a factory? If the answer is affirmative, then the implication is that we have control over future events. And this is demonstratively not so. We have no control over future events, but simply do the best we can dealing with the unfathomable.

Yet we can take actions to reduce the chances of something terrible happening. For instance, if someone insists on driving over a wet, slippery mountain road in the midst of fog in the dead of the night with the accelerator pressed to the floor and the brakes disconnected, there is a certain risk of plunging over a cliff. If, on the other hand, the driver exercises a great deal of caution, there is certainly less risk of finding oneself in free fall. And if the driver waits for the sun to lift the fog and dry the road, there is an even greater chance of surviving the trip. Certainly, risk management is involved in deciding how to undertake this trip. There is no certainty that survival is guaranteed by waiting until the sun has lifted the fog and dried the road. The chances of survival, however, are far higher than if the driver should careen around steep embankments with no visibility or brakes.

We have some ability to manage risk: we can behave in such a fashion that we enhance our chance of survival. Survival can be taken in a broader context than the safe completion of an automobile trip. Survival can mean that a company has not been forced to declare bankruptcy to protect itself from creditors, while its competitors continue to conduct business as usual. The company may have survived if its management had not taken on projects of such a magnitude of investment that the failure of one spelled doom for the company.

Survival can be viewed from a lending perspective. A loan to a company might not have to be declared worthless if the lender had not been so eager to make a loan to a company which had been even more eager to overburden itself with debt. Perhaps if the management of the company had not been so optimistic about everything going its way, and if the lender had more realistically appraised the chances that business would remain robust for the borrower, the company or the loan would have survived.

Management of risk need not deal exclusively with survival. Risk management may mean that managers have less reason not to lose sleep over adverse changes in commodity price affecting the value of their inventories, or over the possibilities of fire, wind, or storm creating a situation that may financially cripple a firm for years. There is certainly an element of being able to rest easy, or at least easier, at night when home, property, and self are protected by insurance.

MANAGEMENT BY REWARD

Most decisions are made on the basis of reward, that is, on the basis of some measure of profitability. The greater the degree of profitability in an investment, the greater the chance of it being approved for funding by a company. Suppose that a conglomerate has many manufacturing subsidiaries that collectively make many diverse products. The conglomerate's capital budget for the year is limited to a given amount. Two subsidiaries propose major expansions of their productive capacity, and there is sufficient capital to fund only one proposal. A decision will eventually have to be made as to which of these two proposals will be funded.

Proposal A is from a subsidiary that makes plastic fad items. Its proposal is to construct a factory that has the potential of making enough plastic fad items (say, hoola hoops) to inundate the market before the fad passes. The rationale of the proposal, as adduced by management, is to position the company with the capacity to satisfy worldwide demand for a fad item before the fad expires. Several examples of plastic fad items whose market demand was not satisfied before the fad passed from view are cited. By having this capacity "upfront," so to speak, the company can satisfy the burgeoning demand while it is still burgeoning, rather than risk waiting for a factory to come on line to satisfy demand for a product that may have already passed its zenith. Management, in its presentation, gives several salient examples of factories built for a market which had already evaporated by the time the first shipment was made. By having a versatile plastic goods factory capable of making nearly any fad item imaginable, and by having a capable marketing team poised to exploit any development in the plastic fad market, management is confident that its cash flow projection can be realized.

Proposal B is from a subsidiary that has negotiated to make mundane steel parts for an automobile assembly plant. The contract is for ten years; the subsidiary priced its product very competitively in order to obtain the contract. Management is confident that other similar contracts will be awarded, but only after the new factory has successfully demonstrated its ability to handle the first contract. The economy of scale of a large-sized factory in being able to deliver component parts at a low cost of production dictates building a factory far larger than the initial contract can justify. Given time to demonstrate the factory's efficient and reliable operation, management is confident that its cash flow projections can be realized.

The management of each subsidiary presents to the parent organization a cash flow projection that can be analyzed to obtain a rate of return on the investment. The subsidiary presenting proposal A has no fad business in hand, and can only point to the past where fad items have generated enormous profits for their manufacturers. In the absence of a market for fad items, management proposes that the factory be dedicated to making nonfad plastic products. The factory will be poised to shift production to fad items as soon as its marketing department detects the emergence of a potential fad product.

The subsidiary presenting proposal B has a contract in hand that will generate a certain amount of revenue on the very day the factory opens. The state of the art plant envisioned in this proposal is much too large for this single contract. Yet a factory of this size has to be built in order to obtain sufficient economy of scale to reduce unit costs to a point where the plant output can be competitively priced. Management believes that the demonstrated efficiency and reliability to make a competitively priced high quality product would be such that follow on contracts are inevitable.

MANAGEMENT BY RISK AND REWARD

Although the two proposals are ranked by reward, that is, by some measure of profitability, in analyzing their relative merits no board of directors worth its salt is going to decide which one should be approved using profitability as its sole criterion. Pertinent questions are going to be asked, such as how proposal A management knows that future fad items will be made out of plastic. The hoola hoop fad might be followed by the pet rock fad that would make a shambles out of their business plan. If proposal A management retorts that they intend to manufacture ordinary plastic products until the next plastic fad item appears on the horizon, a member of the board is probably going to point out that conventional plastic goods are well served by Hong Kong, Taiwan, and other Far Eastern manufacturers. Their low cost of operation have made this facet of the plastic goods market extremely competitive, which is another way of saying that profit margins are as thin as a sheet of plastic. And what about the possibility of unsold inventories of hoola hoops becoming obsolete somewhere in transit from the factory to retailers? Someone in top management will ask these questions— particularly someone who does not like hoola hoops!

Proposal B is different than proposal A. Proposal A is oriented to the transient market with the potential of high profit margins while proposal B is oriented to the most mundane of markets where profit margins are modest. Proposal B has a contract that guarantees a minimum rate of utilization for the new factory. This is the worst-case scenario, which is far better than the worst-case scenario of proposal A where plastic fad items become nonplastic. On the other hand, questions can be fielded as to why the plant has to be so large in relation to the initial contract and on the reality of the assessment that the plant will perform to specifications such that follow on contracts are sure to follow. Again, such questions will inevitably be posed, particularly by those members of the board who like hoola hoops.

Thus management does address new ventures and expansion plans in terms of risks and rewards, and they do so with a listing of proposals ranked in order of magnitude of reward. And management does exercise judgment in weighing the relative risks of each proposal. But they do not exercise impartiality. Individuals on the plastic novelties side of the conglomerate have an appreciation for the risks inherent in proposal A and tend to focus their tough questions on proposal B. Individuals whose professional experience is in the more conventional automotive parts business will follow the same behavior pattern. Their salvos will tend to be directed against the proposal that they least understand. Their perception of the risks attendant on the "factory of the future" will be far less in scope than the risks associated with the plastic goods proposal. They will have a natural aversion to fad plastic throwaways and will aim all their guns at proposal A.

If this is the case, then management of risk becomes a political matter. Is the majority of votes in the final deliberating body proplastic or prosteel? And if this body is deadlocked on the extent of the risks of each of these proposals, then the one with the higher rate of return will probably be declared the winner.

THE QUANTIFICATION OF RISK

Reward has long been quantified. Net present value, internal rate of return, and payback period are common measures of reward. Risk is sometimes quantified in the sense of measuring the reward for the worst, best, and most likely scenarios. Then some judgment is made as to the relative likelihood of these events occurring, and a decision is made whether to approve or reject a proposal.

Frequently, however, risk is relegated to a qualitative judgment independent of the quantitative analysis of potential return. If decision makers are unfamiliar with the basic aspects of a business, they tend to be much more risk averse than when they have had first-hand experience. A railroad or a steel company that owns a subsidiary in the oil business usually tends to be more cautious in approving proposals associated with the oil business than in approving proposals associated with the parent industry. An executive who has been involved with the manufacturing of parts for the automotive industry, who is familiar with and sensitive to trends in manufacturing technology, will perceive much less risk associated with proposal B than with proposal A. On the other hand, an executive who has marketed trinkets to a fickle public will sense a much smaller degree of risk with proposal A because of familiarity with this facet of business. He will perceive a much greater degree of risk with proposal B and will doubt management assertions that they will be able to obtain follow on contracts for the manufacture of automotive parts.

Reward has been quantified, and in so doing, the degree of speculation on the nature of the reward has been reduced. If management agrees to the basic parameters used to generate the reward, there is no argument over which proposal is the most profitable. Therefore, proposals can be ranked in terms of reward or profitability. The final decision as to which proposals are to be approved can be made by bringing risk into the discussion of those proposals that are at the top of the reward list. It must be admitted, however, that proposals at the bottom of the reward list may be selected for strategic reasons.

Risk, on the other hand, is measured by perceptions, and perceptions vary widely. Thus the nature of the final decision is ultimately linked to a qualitative feeling about the inherent risk of the project. The purpose of this book is to develop a quantitative method for analyzing risk in order to reduce the wide variations in the perceptions of risk. By quantifying risk, it may be possible to rank projects by the degree of risk much as they can be ranked by the degree of profitability and thereby reduce the speculative element in the final decision.

Ranking proposals by reward, however, does not mean that the perceived reward actually materializes. It is extremely rare for management to review the actual profitability of a project and compare it to its projected profitability indicated at the time when it was an idea, not a reality. Were management to do so, there would probably be a wide disparity between perceptions and reality. Management calculates reward assuming a certain price and volume of sales in the presentation of a proposal. Usually this magic price and volume remain unchanged over a twenty-year period for the calculation of reward.

Experience has shown otherwise: Price and volume assumed for projection purposes do not materialize when exposed to the sunlight of reality. Furthermore, constancy of either is a statistical fluke. The price for selling the goods and the volume of production change with time. Perceived reward and actual reward rarely coincide because expectations and reality are never the same.

Ranking proposals by risk will have the same consequence. If management perceptions of reward do not always materialize—maybe never materialize—then the same fate awaits the quantification of risk. Therefore, management perceptions of risk must be treated just as gingerly as perceptions of reward. The essential problem is not a management problem. The essential problem is that no one knows what the future will bring. Perceptions of risk may turn out to be entirely wrong just as perceptions of reward may miss the mark by a mile.

Given these circumstances, we might conclude that the thing to do is to put all the proposals in a hat, reach in, and let random selection be the deciding factor. There is nothing wrong with this approach other than having highly paid executives reaching into the hat. This act can be done by a monkey. Management needs something more than a hat from which to select proposals that are to be approved for funding. Management already has quantitative tools to aid them in their decision-making process on reward. The purpose of this book is to attempt to give management a quantitative handle on risk.

This, obviously, is a tough assignment. Otherwise, proposals would be routinely ranked in terms of risk just as they are ranked in terms of reward. Whether simulation can provide a method to analyze risk, or act as a substitute for the mathematical complexity of modeling risk, remains to be seen. Readers will have to come to that conclusion themselves.

I wish to take this opportunity to thank the faculty and staff of Monmouth College, my family, and my friends for their support and encouragement. Naturally, they are not to be blamed for the fact that I may not have lived up to my own expectations. Not only can I not escape that responsibility, I accept the challenge. In a way, I am venturing out on a journey in the dark of the night and in the midst of a fog. The road is slippery and wet and meanders over a mountain range. I cannot wait for the sun to rise to clear the fog and dry the road. However, I have checked the brakes and intend to drive at a snail's pace. That does not necessarily mean that I will survive the journey.

1

Bridging the Cultural Gap

Risk management entails the evaluation of a set of circumstances which, if they were to occur, would be costly for an individual or a firm. Risk management also includes the investigation of various ways to minimize the possibility of occurrence of these circumstances and their consequent costs. Simulation can quantify the cost and provide an inexpensive and bloodless evaluation mechanism for addressing a particular risk. A comparative analysis of the simulations of various courses of action can aid in the management of risk by determining an optimal approach to a particular set of circumstances.

Simulation has been put to good use in engineering and science, but has not made a major impact in business. Although simulation has been incorporated in various management simulation games, it has not been incorporated into the business decision evaluation process. In fact, the existence of management simulation games may well impede the adoption of simulation in a business environment. Managers may associate simulation with a modeling of a contrived situation for educational and training purposes and not as a possible means of analysis of actual business problems. This is one gap that has to be bridged. To help bridge this gap, the application of simulation focuses on obtaining a measure of reward and risk in the decision-making process for new investments. There is no more practical application of simulation in the business environment than this because no firm, no matter what its function or size, can avoid financial risk management.

While engineers and scientists have adopted simulation to a much greater extent than businessmen,* engineers and scientists are more apt to sense the

*As a business professor whose classes are half female, I appreciate the role of women in the field of business. The term "businessmen" should be viewed in its androgynous context referring either to both sexes, or neither sex, as the reader prefers.

potential contribution of simulation to their evaluation process. Not only is this a result of their natural inclination to quantitative analysis, but it is also the result of their introduction to simulation as something other than a game. In addition to having a similar mind set, computer specialists, engineers, and scientists speak the same language. Technicians, engineers, and scientists can sit around a table and converse with one another with words, phrases, and sentences having a common meaning to all. Some may have a deeper appreciation of what is being said, but none of them require an interpreter.

This is not true when businessmen and computer specialists sit around the same table. It is easy for businessmen to make broad generalities that are as incomprehensible to computer specialists as the jargon of computerese is to businessmen. For simulation to make serious inroads into those business decisions that are open to quantitative analysis, businessmen and computer specialists must learn to speak the same language. The principles of simulation must be comprehensible to those sitting on both sides of the table. The language describing simulation must be understood by those who have had no specific training in computers and computer technology. Words, phrases, and sentences cannot be selected on the basis of protecting the mysteries of simulation from the uninitiated. If the discussion of simulation is shrouded in esoteric terminology that keeps others from learning an arcane craft, then the experts will maintain exclusive control over their domain. Maintaining an inner sanctum prohibits the application of simulation to a new field of endeavor. It is an extremely high cost to pay for ensuring the privacy of a club of specialists.

There are cultural differences that have to be bridged between managers, who are primarily generalists, and specialists who design, build, run, and evaluate simulations. Unless the different perspectives of generalists and specialists are reconciled, simulation cannot contribute to the decision-making process. Businessmen have enough to worry about without having to become programmers, or to acquire a greater in-depth knowledge of mathematics, or to learn the jargon of simulator designers, builders, and evaluators. The businessman's appreciation of the possible role of simulation in the decision-making process with regard to providing a measure of reward and risk in a venture must be won in a battle fought on their turf. It is, fortunately, a bloodless battle. It can be won by raising the level of consciousness of businessmen with regard to the existence of simulation and its possible contribution to the measurement of the risk of proposals in addition to the conventional means of measuring the reward. No more than this is required.

Specialists in simulation have to realize that most businessmen are not quantitatively oriented in the sense of having a natural inclination toward mathematics. In fact, many business students are business students because they have a natural aversion to mathematics. Indeed, the world of business does not require much in mathematics beyond arithmetic calculations. One does not have to be a mathematical genius to recognize the economic consequences of buying a piece of cloth for $3, cutting it into four parts, and selling each for $1. Businessmen operate primarily in a world where they must make qualitative judgments steeped in intuition and experience with little in the way of quantitative analysis. Success in business does not depend on quantitative expertise in juggling numbers as much as on qualitative, or intuitive, interpretation of events. Success in business lies largely in the nature of an individual's response to these events. Success stories in business usually hinge on an individual's reaction to a commercial opportunity. Horatio Alger did not have an enormous talent in mathematical manipulations.

However, qualitative feelings may not help managers convince their superiors that a major portion of a firm's capital should be dedicated to certain projects. Someone—and that someone may be an outsider in the form of a banker—will demand a cash flow projection. It would be nice if the projection of cash inflow can at least match the anticipated outflow of cash. It would be even nicer if there is a little surplus cash to provide some degree of profit in the venture. The proposing of a venture for either approval within a firm, or the seeking of capital support outside a firm, demands that a manager or a businessman exercise quantitative skills to obtain a measure of reward. And with a little more effort, he may as well obtain a measure of risk.

The problem is that profit, the measure of reward, requires, as a minimum, a pencil, the back of an envelope, and some degree of skill in arithmetic calculations. Can a businessman, steeped in intuitive reactions in an ever-changing world, rise to the occasion? Of course, he can. In fact, the pencil-pushing exercise may be a welcome break from having to deal with the choice of a marketing plan, a demand for a large discount from an important customer, a labor dispute down on the shopfloor, a shipment of goods that has been sent to a customer or received from a supplier that has been manufactured with a defective part, pilferage in the warehouse, an unpaid invoice, and a personal problem with a close business associate.

In the last few decades, more sophisticated means of measuring reward than cash inflow exceeding cash outflow, or the payback period necessary to recoup the initial investment, have been introduced. The projection of cash flow is discounted to obtain either the net present value or the internal rate of return. These methodologies demand more than a back of an envelope to handle the calculations. They also require the knowledge of exponents in addition to the rudiments of addition, subtraction, multiplication, and division. Being calculations, these methodologies could be, and have been, incorporated in computer programs. Managers have turned to computer software packages to perform the calculations for obtaining the net present value or the internal rate of return with relatively little knowledge of computers and even less in the way of computer programming.

MANAGERS AS GENERALISTS

Effective managers are good personnel managers. Managers know more than anybody that they cannot operate every facet of an enterprise. Even if they have all the requisite skills, experience, and expertise, they do not have enough hours in the day to deal with the myriad of problems that human endeavors seem to generate. Therefore, they must select people to act on their behalf to keep the firm running on a continual and regular basis. How do general managers with a marketing background know that the accounting department is operating satisfactorily? They made a personnel decision with regard to the person heading the accounting department. Obviously, an element of trust entered the decision. Trust is an intuitive act not amenable to quantitative analysis. Trust, however, is tested everyday in interactions between the general manager and the accounting department. The annual audit by an outside accounting firm confirms, or deconfirms, that trust. Be that as it may, general managers can manage something they themselves are not proficient in doing. Although a conductor of an orchestra does not have to be proficient in playing every instrument, the ability to recognize a good player from a bad one is crucial. The same is true for general managers. They acquire the requisite talent to run an organization through personnel decisions. And, like a conductor hearing a string of sour notes, they replace those employees who do not measure up to expectations.

General managers with a background in law usually feel comfortable about the use of computers in the operation of a firm. After all, the information system staff is capable of overseeing the operation. Nor do they feel uncomfortable about the computer being programmed to perform specific functions such as handling the financial accounts or printing out orders to replenish inventory. Businessmen, being practical and possessing a finely honed "show-me" attitude, have found it possible to incorporate the computer in the operation of their firms once they have been shown the practicality and utility of computer technology in performing certain functions. Nor have they shied away from having the computer perform the necessary calculations for measuring the potential reward of a venture. Nor have they failed to see the utility of being able to compare computer outputs of the measure of reward of one project with another as an aid in the decision-making process. They must now become aware of the possibility of the computer performing certain calculations which, if properly programmed, and if the inputs are reasonably on target, might aid in their dealing with the imponderable nature of future events by providing an output that brackets risk.

CONVERSATION AS COMMUNICATION

Leaving aside body language, oral and written communication are the primary ways assignments are given and results are submitted. Everyone is told of the importance of a well-written report, but conversation, the oral delivery of a report, must be given equal consideration. Much of business is conducted orally and expressing simulation in a conversational format can go a long way in bridging the gap between simulator builders as specialists and managers as generalists.

The need to express simulation in a conversational manner is a necessary prerequisite for considering the use of simulation in the business planning process. Businessmen cannot be expected to attend language school so that they can understand the stylized lingo of computer specialists. Businessmen simply do not have the time to attend the Blitz Computer Technical Language School so that they can communicate effectively with computer specialists. It is the computer specialist who designs simulation models who must learn a new language—a language known for its conciseness, clarity, and simplicity.

Explaining the concepts of simulation must be done on the basis of a businessman having limited knowledge of computer technology and quantitative skills. Conversation is the primary means of communicating the information that is required of the individual responsible for planning, designing, building, running, and interpreting the simulation. The simulator model builder must be able to sit down with a businessman, and through the media of conversation, extract all the salient facts and pertinent points of the situation under consideration. Some degree of probing is necessary because a businessman does not always communicate subconscious thoughts, assuming that these must be obvious to the most casual observer. Were the simulator builder exposed to these circumstances, these thoughts would indeed be obvious. Because a simulator model builder lacks the ten to thirty years of extensive, and intensive, experience in a field of business, some probing is necessary to bring the subconscious to the conscious level for identification. Otherwise the model builder risks credibility when a businessman or manager realizes that a salient fact has been left out of the model.

Conversation is the prelude to a written report. When a financial analyst is given the task of evaluating the potential profitability of a proposed project, the source of the information concerning the salient details is generally not a written four-page report from a harassed manager. Usually a harassed manager calls in the analyst and provides a brief summary of the project. Salient points flow one after the other with the analyst feverishly writing them down or storing them in memory. Then there is the pregnant pause. This is the opportunity for the analyst to ask for information or elaborations on key points that have just been delivered staccato style.

The analyst does not dare to pause until all the points are covered because that signals the end of the session. This is the famous two-pause assignment session that planners and analysts must learn to cope with in a world where managers are generally pressed by events and short on time. The financial analyst has long learned to cope in this world of harassed executives. The financial analyst presents, or at least should present, findings in a way that leaves no doubt as to what was assumed in the performance of the analysis. Usually underlying assumptions are explicitly stated to provide the manager with the opportunity to rethink the situation, to correct initial misjudgments, or to suggest an alternative set of assumptions for comparison with the initial set.

The simulator designer or builder as the risk analyst has to learn to operate in the business world in a fashion similar to a financial analyst. It is the simulator designer or builder who must adapt to the ways of business, who must understand the principles of financial analysis as they relate to measuring reward, and who must assume the burden of being a risk analyst. The simulator builder, as risk analyst, must learn to glean all the salient facts in the few precious minutes of a manager's time.

The manager does not make the trek to the analyst's desk—that is not how the system works. The analyst does the walking, and the analyst bends his knees when he sits down in a manager's office. And the flow of information is primarily through oral communication. The first pause in the meeting gives the analyst the opportunity to ask the right questions and to confirm points which may have been alluded to in vague terms. An analyst must be able to pick up the innuendoes and subconscious thoughts that need to be identified and realized. The manager will patiently respond to all those matters right up to the first pause by the analyst. That signals the end of the two-pause meeting.

Bridging the gap between specialists and generalists is not entirely a one-way trip. Businessmen and managers have to adapt to the world of simulation by realizing its existence, having some appreciation of its advantages and disadvantages, and being able to understand the mechanism of communicating the results of a simulation. Even here, the task is not that great. Businessmen do not have to use such terms as "discrete probability distributions" and "cumulative probability distributions." They do have to become accustomed to results being expressed in terms of a probability of meeting, or not meeting, a goal.

Terminology is not the problem. Businessmen have become accustomed to the terminology of conventional methods of evaluating profit: net present value, internal rate of return, discount and hurdle rates. The real challenge that a manager is going to have to face is the concept of an outcome not being expressed in concrete terms, but in terms of a probability or a chance that an outcome will or will not be desirable.

THE COMMUNICATION OF RESULTS

One way for risk to be measured is in terms of a lower than desired rate of return on an investment. All that is required for this measure of risk is to run a simulation of an investment proposal and let the computer perform the calculation of reward. The computer is basically a simple calculator that can be programmed to perform the same sequence of calculations thousands of times over in a very short period of time. Simulation permits the variables determining profit, which can then be related to return on investment, to change on a daily, weekly, monthly, or yearly basis. The key variables determining profit (price, volume, and fixed and variable costs) are assigned values within a prescribed range with a tendency for the value to be somewhere around the most likely value within the range. As the price, volume, and fixed and variable costs change each time the calculation is made, so does the annual profit, (or lack thereof). The various levels of profit over the life of the project can then be compared to the initial investment to obtain the rate of return.

The consequence of performing the same sequence of calculations where the variables take on different values is a differing rate of return each time the sequence of calculations is repeated. We can expect ten thousand individual rates of return if we decide to repeat a simulation ten thousand times. This must come about when the outcome is a measure of profitability and the variables determining profit—price, volume, and costs—are not single discrete values, but a businessman's assessments of most and least likely values.

The end product of a simulation run is a family of returns that has been generated by repetitive calculations of profit whereby the key variables are forever changing within their prescribed ranges. With ten thousand possible outcomes, the question becomes how we can best analyze and communicate the results. We should not look upon the selection of a probability distribution as the best way to display ten thousand outcomes of a simulation. We might be better off realizing that the selection of a probability distribution as a means to communicate and analyze data is a default condition. There is no other way to express ten thousand numbers than by means of a probability distribution.

A probability distribution describes the rate of return of an investment in terms of an expected value and an associated measure of the spread of the returns around the expected return. The description of the results would most likely include the possibility of a certain criterion either being exceeded or not being satisfied. This usually takes the form of a probability of not meeting a minimum hurdle rate. Not meeting the minimum hurdle rate of a company is a measure of risk, not reward. For illustration purposes, suppose that a simulation is run on an investment possibility ten times and the following rates of return have been generated:

SIMULATION	RATE OF RETURN
1	16%
2	12
3	15
4	18
5	18
6	16
7	15
8	19
9	16
10	13

Reviewing the results, we note that there is a tendency for the numbers, or data, to concentrate around 15 or 16 percent. In statistics, this is known as the center of a distribution of data, which in this case, has a range of values between twelve and nineteen. Statistics can measure the tendency of data to concentrate around a point. The question is what single number best describes the results without having to recite all the individual outcomes.

Unfortunately, as in everything else in life, there is a choice. There is the mode, the median, and the mean as ways of describing the center of a distribution of data. Listing the returns in ascending or descending order allows us to select the mode and the median.

$$12 \quad 13 \quad 15 \quad 15 \quad 16 \quad 16 \quad 16 \quad 18 \quad 18 \quad 19$$

The mode is the value that occurs most frequently (in this case 16, which occurs three times). The median is the middle point, where half of the distribution of values is above and half is below. With an even number of data points, convention dictates taking the average of the two middle values (the fifth and sixth numbers in this case). The median has a value of 16, the same as the mode. The average is simply the summation of the ten returns divided by ten, or 15.8 percent.

We often see or hear the term "expected value" in the description of probability distributions and may be tempted to think that it is something other than the mode, median, or mean. Its derivation deserves clarification.

A return of 12 percent occurred once. Ten simulations were run. The chance of a return of 12 percent is 10 percent. There is 10 percent discrete probability of a return being 12 percent. The discrete probability for a return of 13 percent is also 10 percent. The discrete probability for 14 percent is 0 percent because none of the ten runs resulted in a return of 14 percent. The discrete probability for a return of 15 percent is 20 percent because there were two runs out of ten with a return of 15 percent. The cumulative probability that the return is 15 percent or less is the summation of the discrete probabilities associated with all returns including, and below, 15 percent. This includes the 20 percent for the probability that the return will be 15 percent, 0 percent that the return will be 14 percent, and 10 percent each that the return will be 12 and 13 percent, for a total of 40 percent. The cumulative probability that the investment will bear a rate of return below, and equal to, the minimum objective of 15 percent is 40 percent. The following table illustrates the nature of the discrete and cumulative probabilities:

RATE OF RETURN	DISCRETE PROBABILITY	CUMULATIVE PROBABILITY
12%	10%	10%
13	10	20
14	0	20
15	20	40
16	30	70
17	0	70
18	20	90
19	10	100

The total of the discrete probability column must equal 100 percent, representing the entirety of outcomes. The last entry in the cumulative distribution column must be 100 percent for the same reason. The expected return is the summation of the discrete probability distribution multiplied by the associated rate of return.

Expected Return = 10% × 12% + 10% × 13% + 0% × 14% + 20% × 15% +
30% × 16% + 0% × 17% + 20% × 18% + 10% × 19%

Expected Return = 1.2% + 1.3% + 0% + 3.0% +
4.8% + 0% + 3.6% + 1.9%

Expected Return = 15.8%

The expected return is the same as the mean. It represents the fulcrum point about which the various outcomes would be balanced were they represented as weights on a see-saw. The weights represent the number of times each particular result of the simulation has occurred. The distance for placing the weights from the fulcrum point in order to balance the see-saw is the difference between the particular return and the expected return.

Suppose that each return is represented by a one-pound weight. The fulcrum point is at 15.8. Twelve percent is 3.8 units to the left of the fulcrum of the see-saw. Twelve percent happened once. Place a one-pound weight 3.8 feet to the left of the fulcrum. Thirteen percent occurred once. Place a one-pound weight 2.8 feet to the left of the fulcrum. A two-pound weight 0.8 units to the left of the fulcrum represents the two times that the result was 15 percent. The mass times distance of the weights to the left of the fulcrum point is as follows:

$$1 \times 3.8 + 1 \times 2.8 + 2 \times 0.8 = 8.2$$

These are units of torque which, if exerted on a see-saw, would cause a predictable movement. To counteract this, a three-pound weight is placed 0.2 feet to the right of the fulcrum point representing the three times that the return was 16 percent. A two-pound weight placed 2.2 feet to the right of the fulcrum takes care of the two occurrences of a return of 18 percent, and a one-pound weight placed 3.2 feet to the right of the fulcrum finishes the job. The torque in the opposite direction is calculated as follows:

$$3 \times 0.2 + 2 \times 2.2 + 1 \times 3.2 = 8.2$$

This counteracts the torque being exerted on the opposite end of the see-saw. Thus the see-saw is perfectly balanced at the fulcrum point. This is the physical meaning of the expected value, which is the mean or average of the distribution of data.

The mode is usually not used as a measure of a center of a distribution. A mode can be misleading as an indication of the center of a distribution if the distribution is sufficiently askew. For instance, suppose that the range of outcomes on return varies between 0 and 100 percent, with 0 percent being the most common value. The mode is then 0 percent—hardly a measure of the center point of the distribution of data that varies from 0 to 100 percent.

The median does not represent the fulcrum point of a set of data as well as the expected value, or mean. In this example, the highest return is 19 percent and the median is 16 percent. The median would still be 16 percent if the highest return was 190 percent. The median would remain at 16 percent because 16 percent still represents the middle point where half the data has higher values and half has lower values. While the median value remains the same after changing the highest return from 19 to 190 percent, the expected return, which is the average of all the returns, would be affected by such a change. For this reason, the expected return, calculated as illustrated, has been selected as the best indication of the center of a distribution of outcomes. The expected value is nothing more than the mean, or average, of the data making up the distribution.

The center of the data is only half of the description of the distribution of outcomes. Equally important is the spread, or the variation, in the data about the center of the distribution. Statisticians favor the standard deviation as the way to represent the spread in a distribution of data. Although this can be incorporated into the description process of the outcomes of running a simulation ten thousand times, it might be just as well, from the point of view of communicating results, to remain with the range and with the cumulative probability distribution to signify the failure to achieve a corporate goal of satisfying some minimum objective on the return of the investment.

Suppose that management has a minimum rate of return on making investments of more than 15 percent. This is sometimes referred to as the hurdle rate. Investments are supposed to beat the hurdle rate because the hurdle rate represents the cost of capital to the company. We can then describe the result of the ten simulations, which, in reality may be ten thousand, or a hundred thousand, or a million simulations, in terms of less than a half-dozen figures. One figure indicates the center of the distribution of a million outcomes, another two figures indicate the possible range of the outcomes, and another two figures are needed to state the minimum acceptable return and the chance of not satisfying this objective. A million outcomes can be summarized by stating that the average, or expected, return is 15.8 percent with a range between 12 and 19 percent and with a 40 percent chance that the minimum hurdle rate of a return over 15 percent will not be satisfied. This tells management that they can expect, on average, a return on the investment close to 16 percent. However, the return could be as low as 12 percent or as high as 19 percent. Furthermore, there is a 40 percent chance that the investment will not satisfy their minimum objective (the so-called hurdle rate) of over a 15 percent return. The probability of failing to satisfy the hurdle rate is the conventional measure of risk.

BRIDGING THE GAP

The expected return, a measure on the range of returns, and the chance that a minimum level of return is not achieved, may be all that a manager is burdened with from running a simulation. This information is part of the process of arriving at a decision. The final decision, however, entails more than the quantitative output of a financial analysis as to the likely return or a measure of the probability of failure from a simulation. This point is generally misunderstood by specialists.

Computer specialists, along with engineers and scientists, often have trouble understanding the role of qualitative judgments and intuition in the business decision-making process. One does not build a bridge with an intuitive insight that the steel needs to be of a certain thickness. Most decisions in engineering and science are quantitatively supported, if not determined. Engineers and scientists sometimes have trouble mastering the art of management precisely because it is an art. They must bridge the cultural gap by recognizing that business decisions are primarily qualitative rather than quantitative. This is a common stumbling block for specialists taking on the mantle of management. They also have trouble playing the managerial role because of their reluctance to let go of direct responsibility for performing a task. A good manager delegates the authority for performing a task while retaining responsibility for ensuring that it is accomplished properly.

Managers have to be convinced that measuring risk in terms of the chance of not meeting a goal is useful to them. They also have to be convinced that providing more information to permit the measurement of risk is easier, in some respects, than conventional means of measuring reward. Conventional methodologies force a manager to come up with a single value for key variables that remain unchanged over the life of a project. A range of numbers is a lesser commitment in assessing the unknowable. Suppose that a manager is put on the line to assess the next year's volume of sales, and determines that it will be 500. If actual sales turn out to be 480, the manager will be called on the carpet to explain why sales were lower than projected. If future volume in terms of sales is assessed at 500, with upper and lower limits of 600 and 400, who is going to challenge a sales volume of 480? And the lesser commitment to assessing future values is what is required for risk/reward analysis.

There is going to be a natural reluctance to change—here defined as the incorporation of simulation in the decision-making process concerning major investments. Reluctance to change, however, can be overcome. Once the barrier of introducing a new concept has been penetrated, the old can fall away very fast and be replaced by the new. Human ways of doing things appear immutable, and seemingly desirable changes can be bottlenecked for long periods of time. Then, in a flash of time, the transition from old to new is completed, and everyone wonders why the change had not been made years before.

In some respects, simulation has already penetrated the business planning process. A single value for revenue over twenty years of a new venture's economic life has already been recognized as an unsatisfactory way of looking at things. The imponderable nature of the future is handled by "What If" analysis where a number of cases are scrutinized, each of which to some degree may be a likely outcome. How many cases can be examined in "What If" analysis?

Actually a fair number can be scrutinized. A proposal for a project can be laid out on an electronic spreadsheet in a manner where it is convenient to change key variables and generate a measure of reward or degree of profitability for each case.

In "What If" analysis on a spreadsheet, the manager would first look at a volume of 500 and measure the reward. Then sales would be reduced by units of 10; the manager would consider each "what if volume were reduced by another increment of ten" scenario. If this becomes too depressing, a "what if volume blossomed to 600" scenario can restore emotional balance. Spreadsheets contain a random number function that permits simulation of the financial performance of a project for as many times as the operator can press the appropriate function key. Macroinstructions effectively incorporate programming in a spreadsheet environment. There are software packages available that run simulations on a spreadsheet providing a variety of displays and options for the ease and comfort of the operator. An example of a spreadsheet software package tailored for risk analysis is @RISK (Palisade Corporation, Newfield, New York).

"What If" analysis is part of risk management. "What If" analysis consists of looking not only at the most likely, from which one derives a measure of reward, but also certain unlikely cases where the events of business life do not follow the most likely script. What if the "What If" script is examining the unlikely script of less than anticipated revenues or more than anticipated costs? The measure of reward diminishes with respect to the measure of reward for the most likely case. At some point, the measure of reward becomes the measure of risk. A measure of risk is a low degree of reward that is insufficient either to meet expenses or to provide a minimum return on investment. Risk, in a business environment, can be looked upon as an unsatisfactory level of reward where the wisdom of proceeding with the project must be questioned.

There is one aspect of conventional "What If" analysis that is unrealistic. If the performance of "What If" analysis assumes one price for a product, or one volume, or one revenue figure that does not change over the projection period, then we can question the adequacy of the model in reflecting reality. A free market economy simply does not stand still for twenty years, which is an implicit assumption every time the volume, price, or revenue remains unchanged for two decades of time.

Simulation of reality should include the best of times along with the worst of times. This is in recognition of the fact of life that businesses do not generally operate in a state of euphoria, or a state of mediocrity, or a state of depression for long periods of time. Over the twenty-year life of a project, we can expect all types of business conditions. If an appraisal is being made on the outcome of an investment, should not the good times be as much a part of the picture as bad times? And good times, and bad times, and mediocre times for that matter, do not come in twenty-year lumps. The chance of bankruptcy must be balanced with the chance of making huge profits. One bad year does not spell doom to a company that has just tucked several good years under its financial belt.

THE VALIDITY OF ASSESSMENTS

Computer simulation permits a modeling of reality where the most likely is balanced by the least likely of the best and worst of times. It takes into account the imponderable nature of the future with the basic assumption that the assessments of the businessman are fairly realistic—an assumption that will not stand up under close scrutiny. There is little point in analyzing the validity of a businessman's assessments of the future after the future has revealed itself. It is conceded right here and now that they cannot be validated before the fact.

The time is the late 1970s when the price of crude oil is $35 per barrel and the marginal tax rate is 70 percent. Tax-shielding participations in drilling programs are the in-thing. You find a promoter—or rather, a promoter finds you—who offers the following deal: a 100 percent immediate writeoff for tax purposes in a drilling program where the driller has the finest reputation in the area. The promoter's brother is the drilling supervisor. The promoter is investing his own money, his friend's money, his family and his wife's family money into the drilling program. The salespeople are taking their commissions in participations, not cash. Question: What is the minimum return we would expect in purchasing a participation in terms of a limited partnership? How about a simple return of investment—$1,000 back over the ten-year life expectancy of the well for every $1,000 invested. The entire return on the investment is locked into the substantial tax savings. This is the minimum assessment of return. The most likely assessment is that there will be some modest profit in real cash terms. The maximum assessment is that the profit may not be that modest.

Isn't this a reasonable set of assessments under the circumstances? What is wrong with the least likely minimum return given the situation at the time the decision is being made? Can't wells that made money with oil at $10 and $20 per barrel do well when oil is at $35 per barrel? From every point, the investment appears reasonable: the reputation of the driller is excellent, the promoter's brother is on the scene as a safeguard, and most important of all, the promoter has tapped his wife's family pocketbook. What can possibly go wrong? How could an investor expect to receive less than what was invested in the project when the promoter suggests that the most likely case is a 40 percent return on investment after the first full year's operation of the well ($400 for every $1,000 invested)?

These are the assessments made before the wells are drilled, when the check is written. The validity of these assessments becomes apparent only with the passage of time. The reality of the situation as revealed with the unfolding of events is the final arbiter on the validity of the assessments. The driller is highly reputable from the point of view of drilling and operating his own wells. But he turns out to be less than reputable when it comes to drilling wells for a New York promoter. The drilling supervisor, carrying out the instructions to drill wells that maximize the return for the driller while minimizing the return for the owners of the wells, tells his brother, the promoter, that all is not going according to plan.

The driller, as fleecer, does not notice the slight similarity in the last names of his drilling supervisor, who is carrying out his instructions, and the New York promoter, as fleecee. Nor does he notice any family resemblance between the two. The driller is intent in fulfilling his obligations to the New York promoter for the least amount of money, profiting as much as he can from the fixed contractual price for drilling the wells. The New York promoter instructs his brother to carefully document the shenanigans in preparation for a lawsuit. The investors begin to recognize a possible problem concerning the validity of their initial assessments when the first check from the operation of the wells is just sufficient for paying the phone bill to the promoter to ask about the prospects of the promised 40 percent return on the investment.

At this point, what is the minimum likely assessment of the return from the investment? Obviously, it is less than the assessment made when the check was handed over to the promoter. It may be raised a bit when the promoter tells you that it is an open and shut case of fraud with the potential of triple damages because of the weight of evidence that has been garnered by a certain drilling supervisor. The years drag by; the wheels of justice grind exceedingly slowly. Triple damages lose their flavor when it is realized that the subsequent fall in the price of oil has placed the driller himself on the list of potential financial casualties of the crash in the oil industry. To cut an agonizingly slow process short, the promoter obtains a settlement for a batch of wells that is supposed to make him whole. Naturally, they don't. Through each step of this degenerating situation, the minimum assessment of some sort of return keeps getting smaller and smaller with always some residual hope of something positive. It is finally recognized that the present value of the future income from all the wells cannot pay the legal costs of the litigation. The story comes to its sad conclusion when the promoter hands over a batch of wells to lawyers as settlement for their legal fees, and the investors, including the parents-in-law, are left with nothing.

The moral of this story is not a criticism of the business acumen of the promoter, the driller, or the investors. The purpose is to illustrate the difficulty of judging the potential reward of an investment. What was initially judged to be the least likely minimum assessment of an outcome turned out to be wildly optimistic. The unfolding of events, the revealing of reality, can destroy the most conservative assessment of outcomes. Every personal bankruptcy, every corporate bankruptcy, every bad loan, in short, every financial headache in life, is vivid testimony to the limitations of businessmen, as humans, to assess the future with any degree of accuracy.

Discussing the validity of assessments need not be confined to the lower end of the scale. Queen Isabella of Spain rejected the advice of her experts and decided to finance Columbus's iconoclastic venture. Her assessment of the minimum return would presumably have been a total loss of investment as Columbus sailed off the edge of a flat world to be deservedly swallowed up by the awaiting monsters. Her assessment of the maximum return was probably some undefined advantage to Spain in finding a shorter route to India. Needless to say, her assessment of the best was substantially surpassed.

Another example of the least likely being greatly exceeded is Thomas Watson, Sr., of IBM fame. He was incensed over the fact that his tabulating equipment was thrown out by the U.S. Census Bureau in favor of a new-fangled computer manufactured by Sperry Rand. This government decision pushed him into the computer age kicking and screaming all the way with his best assessment that six computers would satisfy the entire market demand. Of course, at the time that he made his assessment the government made up the entire market. Watson's best estimates were exceeded by five or six zeros when his company discovered another continent of a market known as business.

COPING WITH THE IMPOSSIBLE

The act of validating assessments is an exercise not only in futility, but in uselessness. The money is already spent. What purpose is there in validating that the assessments on minimum and maximum outcomes, and most likely outcomes for that matter, are all wrong? What matters are the assessments which form the basis for making a decision. Once the decision is made and the check is written, all the judgments, discussions, assessments, and studies that went into the making of the decision become irrelevant. Now it is a matter of making good on what may turn out to be a wrong decision, or making better on what may turn out to be a right decision.

Human beings are limited in their ability to perceive future outcomes. This is most obvious when we look at the accuracy of year-end predictions of stock and commodity market experts. The essential problem for those who pose as experts in stock and commodity price movements is that their predictive powers, their assessments of the future price of stock and commodities, can be easily verified. Wait a year, open up the financial pages, and judge for yourself. In performing this exercise, we should not be surprised to find that:

1. The experts' assessments on price movements vary considerably among the experts. In other words, there is no consensus.
2. If there is something approaching a consensus, events will have probably proven them all wrong.
3. The validation check on the outcomes of their assessments would be better handled by the selection of those who were less wrong rather than on the basis of those who were more correct.
4. Those who were less wrong in one year may not be able to repeat their performance the next year.

This is the basic human predicament. We stumble blindly despite our heroic attempts to do otherwise. In the world of business, it must be conceded that some do a better job at assessing the future than others, either in terms of being less wrong or in being better able to cope with a changing business environment. It has been said that a successful general is one who has made less mistakes than his counterpart on the other side of the battlefield. Successful businessmen and successful managers are selected from the vast pool of aspirants by virtue of their demonstrated ability to more accurately guage the future. Successful businessmen and managers plan their actions and then adapt these plans in the face of unforeseen, or unforeseeable, events. Then they carry their ever-evolving plans to fruition better than those who are deemed less successful. It is not just businessmen who have problems perceiving the future. Politicians, rulers, and futurists face the same problem with the same likelihood of error. There have been a few occasions, such as after the invention of the steamboat, when it was proposed to close the U.S. Patent Office because it was eminently clear to the most casual observer that nothing more could possibly be invented! In the economic realm, a businessman's assessments are the best mortal man can do and they are all that is available for decision making.

The adoption of simulation in a business environment setting requires managers to provide information beyond the most likely sequence of events. Even though it has been maintained that having to provide a range of values is less onerous for a manager than conventional methods of analysis where a manager is forced to think in terms of single values, simulation does demand more information. Assessments have to be made not only for the most likely value for key variables, but also on an associated range of values surrounding the most likely value that serve as demarcation points for the least likely values.

Providing an assessment of a range of values is easier than the assessment of a single value because a range represents a lesser commitment in foretelling the future. It might be compared to betting on a horse to show or place rather than to win. It is easier to pick a horse to place first, second, or third than to pick a horse to place first. We might note that the proceeds of a bet on picking a horse to show or place is less than picking a horse to win. In simulation, it might be quite the opposite. We might end up with a greater payoff in making a lesser commitment in picking the horse to place rather than to win. A range of values permits the measurement of risk along with the measurement of reward.

Whether simulation is better, or easier, will not determine whether it will be incorporated in the decision-making process of businessmen. Their measure is strictly one of utility. If simulation is helpful in the pursuit of their objectives, then there is a chance that simulation may become part of the process. If it is not useful, or is not perceived as being useful, then it is not a matter of little hope. There is no hope at all.

2

A Businessman's Assessments

The perception of risk and reward is the result of a businessman's thought processes. Let us say that the businessman speculates that a new factory will be able to produce V volume of goods that can be sold for P price. The question is: Where do V and P come from? Some say that V and P spring from the imagination while others maintain that V and P are a result of a deliberate cognitive process of logic and dispassionate judgment. Perhaps these, and other conjectures concerning the thought process of the human mind, are all part of a businessman's assessments of the projected values of price and volume. These values, when properly manipulated with costs, provide the businessman with an estimate of the profitability of an investment. This is the quantification of reward.

The quantification of risk entails obtaining additional assessments from a manager. Reward is based on the most likely assessment of outcomes. Risk requires assessing the least likely outcomes—not just the worst outcome, but also the best. This should not be too much of a burden to place on the mental shoulders of a manager who must assess the most likely of outcomes. When a manager is attempting to assess the most likely, high volumes and equally high prices and low volumes and equally low prices come to mind.

Suppose that a manager has assessed the reward of a proposal to build a new factory on the basis of a volume of sales of 500 units per year (bearing in mind that a unit may represent hundreds or thousands of an individual item). This volume is the most likely assessment of what sales will be for the purpose of calculating profit over the twenty-year life of the factory. This assessment of sales of 500 units does not mean that the manager expects the factory to produce, and sell, 500 units without any variation over the next twenty years. Nor does the manager expect that the price used to calculate reward will also remain unchanged for the entire twenty-year projection period. Yet these two key variables are held constant in order for a financial analyst to calculate what is presumed to be the most likely return on investment.

In attempting to gauge the profitability of the investment, the analyst may take a higher volume and a higher price and consider this to be the best of all possible worlds. To complete the picture, a lower volume and a lower price than the most likely volume and price are selected for the worst of all possible worlds. This then provides measures of profitability for the most likely, the best, and the worst of all possible worlds—yet these are all measures of impossible worlds. There has never been a time in history when a factory operated in a free market environment with the price of the goods, and the volume of goods produced, remaining exactly at one value for twenty years. The one thing that can be said about the most likely of worlds is that it fairly represents the manager's best assessment of average volume and average price over a long period of time.

"Mr. Manager, you used a projected sales volume of 500 units per year for the next twenty years in the presentation of your proposal for consideration by the board of directors."

"Good, at least someone has read my proposal."

"Well, I have to. It's my job to perform an evaluation of all proposals. Would you object to my saying that the figure of 500 means that half the time sales will be above 500 and that half the time sales will be below 500?"

"No, that's exactly what that figure means. Average sales will be 500 units per year."

"Not to be a stickler for detail, but I do mean half the time sales will be above or below 500, not the average sales."

"Alright, if you insist. I don't see any difference."

"Well, there is a difference between the two that is of critical importance to me. Let me ask the question one more time. Your assessment of sales being 500 units per year—does that mean that half the time sales will be 500 or more units and half the time sales will be 500 or less units?"

"I think I better answer 'yes' to your question."

"Then what is your estimation of the best and worst of all possible worlds— possible worlds being interpreted to mean that the world today is in existence tomorrow in roughly the same shape."

"You mean no volcanoes destroying the United States, or revolutions sweeping away our system of government."

"Yes, things like that."

"Well, I have given some thought to that just in case you, or someone like you, asked me that question. I think that it is not realistic to assume sales below 400 units per year for the reasons cited in my report."

"Four hundred units is rock bottom assuming that the world hasn't stopped turning, at least in an economic sense."

"Yes."

"And at the top of the rock?"

"I guess I can dream about selling 800 units per year. That number is physically close to maximum possible capacity working three shifts, deferring maintenance and doing everything else to push the plant and the workers to the hilt."

"Under these circumstances, you're assuming you can also sell this volume, not just produce it."

"Sure, in an exceptionally strong year."

"Now, I am going to need a little more information from you, Mr. Manager, and I hope I'm not wasting your time in getting this information from you."

"How can you be wasting my time when this proposal depends to some degree on the conclusions of your study? My time is your time unless I detect you're about to pour gasoline on my pet project and strike a match."

"I assure you that that's hardly the case. Before I ask for more information, I do need a little time to prepare some exhibits. Do you mind if we reconvene in a little while?"

"Of course not."

"Back already?"

"Yes, the miracle of the laptop computer! You see, the problem I have is this. You expect to see sales around 500 units. Sales at 400 or 800 are rare events. That is, you would be surprised to see sales as low as 400 and as high as 800. I need your opinion on how rare sales around 400 and 800 units are. To do that, I would like you to first examine the following exhibits."

"Shoot."

"The first exhibit [Exhibit 2.1] is a demand simulator. The fact that a sales volume of 500 units corresponds to a random number of 50 means that half the time sales will be less than 500 and half the time sales will be more than 500. I can say this because when I reach into a bag of one hundred numbered ping pong balls, half the time I will draw out a ball with a number of 50 or less and half the time I will draw out a ball with a number of 50 or more. That is why I tend to avoid the word 'average' or 'mean' and use the word 'median.' The median means, excuse my saying 'means,' that half the time your sales will be above 500 and half the time sales will be below 500. That is my understanding of what you meant by a sales volume of 500, right?"

"I guess so."

"This makes 500 the *median,* not the average, of your projection of future sales. The average of your low and high estimates of 400 and 800 is 600. Would you expect sales to be 600 or above 50 percent of the time and sales to be 600 or below 50 percent of the time?"

"No, that is too high."

"How about 500? Would sales be above 500 half the time and below 500 half the time?"

"Yes, that sounds more like it."

"You see, that is the difference between an average and a median. Also notice

Exhibit 2.1
Demand Simulator, Scaling Factor 0.30

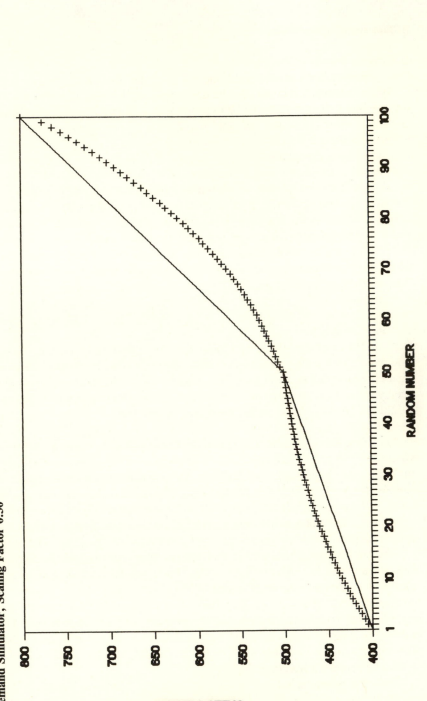

that it is not possible for sales to exceed 800, or to be less than 400, as I can only draw a random number between 1 and 100."

"Well, technically it could. On the one hand, another 1932 might do it on the low side and I guess it might be physically possible to beat 800 if we had to—in support of a war effort or something."

"But you don't expect to exceed either limit, do you? I can reach into a bag of ping-pong balls numbered from 1 to 100, refer to this exhibit, and determine your sales volume, and you wouldn't be upset about the result, would you?"

"No, but it sounds like you're making my proposal into some sort of roulette wheel."

"Good! Now you are beginning to understand how I am going to evaluate your proposal. I am going to use a roulette wheel. Only this roulette wheel is going to be loaded. There are one hundred slots in this roulette wheel and there is an equal probability that the ball will fall into any of these one hundred slots. However, there is not going to be an equal probability that the resulting sales volume will be any number evenly distributed between 400 and 800. I am setting up the roulette wheel in such a way that values around 500 are going to show up more frequently than values near 400 or 800."

"Sounds like a roulette wheel I would like to bet on."

"And if you don't forget that thought, it will be a real help in your understanding what I am trying to do. Let's look at sales below 500. The straight line means that the chance of sales being in the range of, say, 400 to 410, is just as likely as the chance of sales being in the range of 490 to 500. That plainly does not describe your situation."

"No. I would expect sales being near 500 to be much more common than sales near 400."

"Right. Now let's look at sales above 500. Again, the straight line indicates that the chance of sales being between, say, 500 and 510, and being between 790 and 800, is the same. Again, not a true indication of the situation."

"I'd say! The chance of sales near 800 is closer to being a miracle than anything else."

"And sales around 500 is what you would expect in a normal year, so to speak. Now let me tell you a secret. The more the curve bends, the less likely will be sales at the extreme ends of the range. This is the only difference between the three exhibits [Exhibits 2.1–2.3]. Which of these exhibits is the best choice depends solely on how rare a rare event is. In other words, I want your feelings as to how rare sales volumes near 400 and near 800 are with respect to sales around 500."

"I'm not sure if I have any such feelings."

"Let's first examine sales between 400 and 500 units which will occur 50 percent of the time over the life of the project. The straight lines can be considered, as I'll explain shortly, a cumulative probability distribution with a scaling factor of 0.50."

"I don't like the words 'cumulative,' 'probability,' or 'distribution.' "

"I'll use them as sparingly as possible. Let's look at the following table."

SCALING FACTORS

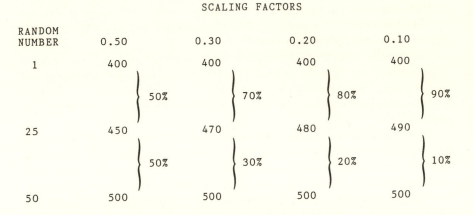

RANDOM NUMBER	0.50	0.30	0.20	0.10
1	400	400	400	400
	} 50%	} 70%	} 80%	} 90%
25	450	470	480	490
	} 50%	} 30%	} 20%	} 10%
50	500	500	500	500

"For now, we are looking only at those times when sales are less than 500. During those times when sales are less than 500, how are these sales distributed? For a scaling factor of 0.50, half the time sales will be between 400 and 450 and half the time they will be between 450 and 500. Sales around 400, or 450, or 500 are all equally probable."

"Like a regular roulette wheel."

"Right. A roulette wheel with one hundred slots where each slot represents one number and where every number is represented one time. No number appears more frequently than others. There are one hundred slots on the roulette wheel, each numbered from 400 to 500 and the chance of any number between 400 and 500 showing up as a winner is the same."

"Actually your wheel must have 101 slots on it to accommodate every number between 400 and 500, including the end numbers."

"Yes, this is a problem that will forever plague me from a programming point of view, but for conversational purposes, let's overlook this point, if you don't mind, and examine the roulette wheel when there is a scaling factor of 0.30. A scaling factor of 0.30 means that 30 percent of the difference between the extreme values of 400 and 500 occurs between the random numbers of 25 and 50 and 70 percent of the difference occurs between the random numbers of 1 and 25. When sales are less than 500, half the time the winning number, or sales volume, will be between 400 and 470 and half the time the winning number, or sales volume, will be between 470 and 500. That makes a sales volume around 400 a rarer event than a sales volume around 500. This is a roulette wheel where the slots do not represent all the numbers between 400 and 500 with equal chance of being declared a winner."

"I'm not sure I am following you."

"Suppose that you have to bet a single number on a roulette wheel that has one hundred slots. Fifty of these slots have numbers between 470 and 500 and will come up just as frequently as the fifty slots that have numbers between 400 and 470. Where are you going to place your bet?"

"Try it again."

"This roulette wheel is loaded in the sense that some numbers are listed more than once whereas others are listed only once, or technically, not at all. If I spin it 100 times, then roughly 50 times the winning number will be between 470 and 500 and roughly 50 times the winning number will be between 400 and 470. You can look at it that a number such as 490 is associated with several slots on the wheel whereas a number such as 410 may be associated with only one. Where would you place your bet?"

"If you are telling me that the 30 individual numbers between 470 and 500 are, in total, listed 50 times and are just as likely to appear as the 70 individual numbers between 400 and 470, I would be a fool not to bet on numbers between 470 and 500."

"That's right. You have the same chance of winning by picking numbers from 470 to 500 as in picking numbers from 400 to 470. Therefore, you may as well bet on the 30 numbers between 470 and 500 than on the 70 numbers between 400 and 470 because the chances of the wheel stopping in either range is the same. Put another way, the chances of winning by betting on the number 472 are higher than betting on the number 402 because the number 472 appears more frequently on the roulette wheel than the number 402."

"You're not saying that operating a business is the same as casting dice or spinning a roulette wheel, are you?"

"Not exactly. Management can take actions to load the dice, so to speak, but how the dice fall is outside the control of management. You can take actions to put your company in a position to take advantage of a future event, but do you control future events?"

"No, businessmen attempt to anticipate future events and plan their actions accordingly."

"But do you know how these events will actually unfold before the fact?"

"Of course not."

"Then, how these events unfold is problematic. They can unfold in a way that is favorable for you—such as sales being around 800. Or they can unfold in a way that is unfavorable for you—such as sales being around 400. So, in trying to quantify how these uncertain outcomes affect you, I could devise a roulette wheel that approximates your situation, give the old baby a spin, and see what happens. In fact, I can spin the wheel twenty times to cover the life of the factory, and analyze the results. Then I can redo the experiment ten thousand, or one hundred thousand, or a million times, and look at the results. The only problem is that I don't have enough years left in my life to spin the roulette wheel a few hundred thousand times and perform all the calculations. But I do have an assistant that loves to crunch through a few million calculations while I'm sipping my coffee."

"Your computer."

"Yes, my computer."

"Let's take the next case for a scaling factor of 0.20 [Exhibit 2.2]. All this means is that 80 percent of the difference between 400 and 500 will occur between the random numbers of 1 and 25, while the remaining 20 percent will occur between the random numbers of 25 and 50. The likelihood of selecting random numbers between 1 and 25 and between 25 and 50 is the same. Therefore, whenever sales are below 500, 50 percent of the time the sales volume will be between 480 and 500 and 50 percent of time sales will be between 400 and 480. So in the spinning of this roulette wheel, half the time the winning number will be between 480 and 500 and the rest of the time between 400 and 480. Therefore, the chance that the winning number will be around, say, 490 is far higher than around 405. Now, Mr. Manager, where would you place your bet, on the number 490 or 405?"

"I would be a fool to bet on number 405."

"Exactly! Your winning with the number 405 will be a rare event compared to winning with the number 490. The roulette wheel can stop at any slot. However, there are more slots containing the number 490 than 405. This being the case, you put your money on the number 490. Now, Mr. Manager, for your final exam, look at this exhibit [Exhibit 2.3] and tell me what a scaling factor of 0.10 means?"

"For a scaling factor of 0.10, whenever sales are lower than 500 units, sales will be between 490 and 500 half the time and between 400 and 490 half the time, so that makes sales around 400 even more remote than with the other scaling factors."

"You passed with flying colors. That's all there is to it. But in viewing the exhibit for a scaling factor of 0.10, the simulator is flat between random numbers of about 30 to 70. That means that the number 500 will occur with alarming frequency—about 40 percent of the time. For the simulators that have been illustrated, I would avoid this particular one. This flattening around the median starts to become a problem for scaling factors less than 0.20. For the record, let's take a look at those times when sales are above 500 units."

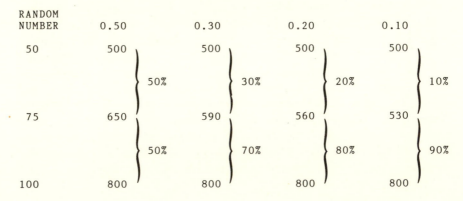

SCALING FACTORS

RANDOM NUMBER	0.50		0.30		0.20		0.10	
50	500		500		500		500	
		50%		30%		20%		10%
75	650		590		560		530	
		50%		70%		80%		90%
100	800		800		800		800	

Exhibit 2.2
Demand Simulator, Scaling Factor 0.20

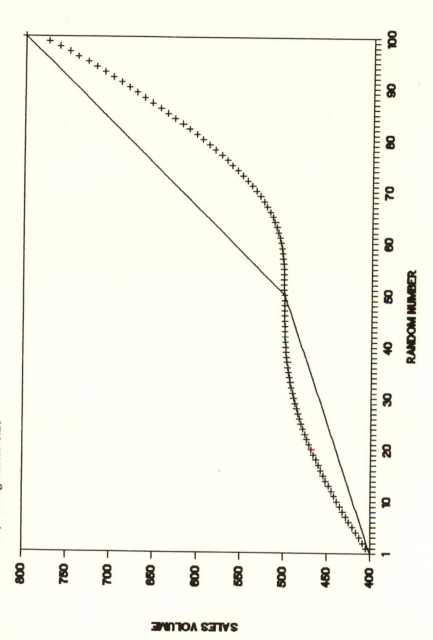

Exhibit 2.3
Demand Simulator, Scaling Factor 0.10

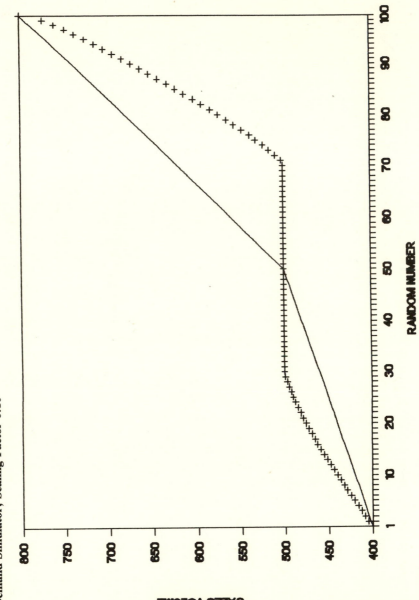

"Sales will be above 500 50 percent of the time. For those times when sales are above 500 with a scaling factor of 0.50, the roulette wheel has a sufficient number of slots such that every number between 500 and 800 is listed once. This means that any number between 500 and 800 will win with equal probability. The chance that the winning number is between 500 and 650 is the same as the chance of the winning number being between 650 and 800. But look at the scaling factor of 0.30. Thirty percent of the difference between the high of 800 and the low of 500 occurs the random number range of 50 to 75. Seventy percent of the difference between the high of 800 and the low of 500 occurs over the random number range of 75 to 100. But the chances of the random number falling between 50 and 75 and between 75 and 100 are the same. Therefore, a sales volume of say, 550, occurs with greater frequency than a sales volume of 750. Using the same logic, a sales volume of 550 will occur even more frequently when the scaling factor is 0.20 than when it is 0.30. And following through with the logic, a scaling factor of 0.10 means that the chance of sales being around 800 is even more remote than with the other scaling factors. Do you understand the meaning of the scaling factor, Mr. Manager?"

"I think I do."

"The concept of probabilities isn't as bad as many people make it out to be."

"But you didn't mention 'probability.'"

"Not much anyway. But we were never off the subject of probability. There may be some who would have taken me to task for not loading up on the terms 'discrete and cumulative probability distributions.' Be that as it may, I would avoid a scaling factor of less than 0.2 because the resulting shape of the simulator makes a sales volume of 500 occur much too frequently, which is not a realistic simulation of sales volume. The fault lies with my simulator program; perhaps a different program can generate 'better-looking' simulators where the extremes are very rare events. But while we are on this subject of the rarity of extreme points, let's take a look at the relative occurrence of sales in the upper and lower regions of the cumulative probability curve, or the tails of the discrete probability curve."

"You told me you weren't going to use those words."

"I lied. Let's look at the range of sales for the random numbers between 1 and 10 and between 90 and 100."

RANDOM NUMBER	SCALING FACTORS			
	0.50	0.30	0.20	0.10
1 – 10	400–420	400–435	400–438	400–440
90 – 100	740–800	693–800	681–800	673–800

"Looking at the extremities, that is, for values of sales close to 400 or close to 800, there isn't that much of a difference between using a scaling factor of 0.20 or 0.30. For random numbers between 1 and 10, which represents the lower 10 percent region of a cumulative probability curve, there is roughly the same chance of sales being between 400 units and 435 units for both scaling factors. The same is approximately true at the upper 10 percent region of the cumulative probability distribution, which is signified by the random numbers of 90 to 100. There is a 10 percent chance of sales being between 693 to 800 for a scaling factor of 0.30 and 681 to 800 for a scaling factor of 0.20."

"I guess you are about to ask me which scaling factor I feel is applicable."

"Yes and no. Yes, I would like to ask you how rare sales are near the extreme points of 400 and 800. But in examining the extremities of both distributions for a scaling factor of 20 and 30 percent, I don't feel that you can differentiate between the two scaling factors. If I asked you whether there was a 10 percent chance that sales would be higher than 693, or 681, do you feel that you could give me a definitive answer?"

"No. But if you pushed, I could say 650, or 700, or 750."

"In which case, I could obtain the appropriate scaling factor. But, somehow, I doubt your ability to so accurately gauge how rare a rare event is. I feel more comfortable merely assuming a scaling factor somewhere between 20 and 30 percent, unless you want to select one for me."

"Look, I'm human. What you don't ask, I don't have to answer. It is true that there is no way to differentiate that the top 10 percent of sales is over 680 or 690, but if you want an opinion of sales being over 650, or 700, or 750, I can give it to you."

"And what is your opinion?"

"I'd say that there is only a 10 percent chance of sales being over 700."

"If that is your opinion, I'll stick to a scaling factor of 0.30. That's good enough for now. The next step in projecting the earnings is to simulate business activity. In this exhibit [Exhibit 2.4], business activity can vary between index numbers of 1 and 100 where the index numbers could represent extremes of what one would expect for the Gross National Product, or some other measure of economic activity, assuming that the world economy continues to operate on an ongoing basis."

"So you are not really simulating reality since, in reality, there could be a nuclear exchange with some country that would end everything."

"Or an earthquake which devastates North America, or a currency collapse, or anything like that. I am essentially suggesting that the ebb and flow of business activity during the post–World War II era will more or less continue into the future. That might not happen. To that degree, I am not simulating reality. But then again, calamities of such a magnitude as a currency collapse affect everybody more or less equally. The rules by which we play the game of business will be suspended under these circumstances. It's a new world and your firm will face the same predicament along with every other firm. I am only simulating a continuation, more or less, of the present world."

"You're right. A general financial panic that bankrupts everybody doesn't really separate businesses that are managed well or managed poorly."

Exhibit 2.4
Business-Cycle Simulator

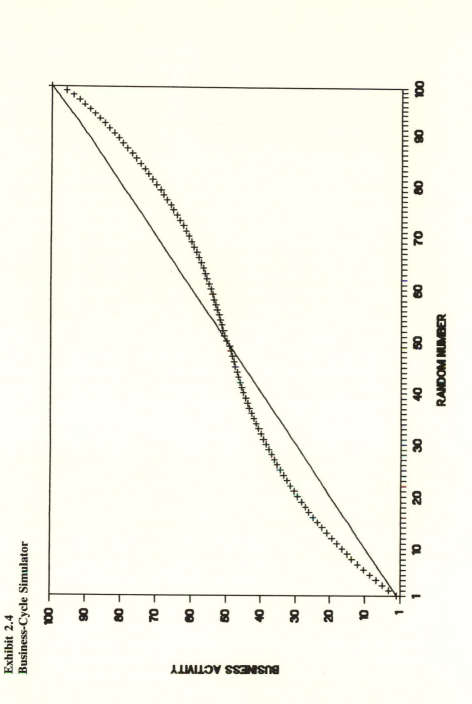

"Right. And in a world where the better-managed firms have a better chance of survival, and poorly managed firms are liquidated, we don't want to find our firm in the latter category. Therefore, we want to have some appreciation for the risk we face when we entertain the idea of doing your proposal in comparison with other proposals. That's all I'm trying to do. And in this exhibit [Exhibit 2.4], all that I'm saying is that there is some cap on how good good times can be and how bad bad times can be and that good times and bad times are relatively rare events in comparison with mediocre times."

"Okay."

"In the next set of exhibits, I am trying to model business activity over a mulityear period. In the first exhibit [Exhibit 2.5], I am modeling the ups and downs of the business cycle where business activity in one year is not affected by the level of business activity in the prior year. That is, I am looking at a purely random pattern of business activity from one year to the next. Notice that business conditions with activity over an index value of 90 or under an index value of 10 are relatively rare. I used a scaling factor of 0.30 to simulate that extremely good and bad times are relatively rare events."

"In the next exhibit [Exhibit 2.6], I introduce bias. If it is a good year, which means that the business activity index is over 50, there will be an 80 percent chance that business will continue to be good. Similarly, the chances that one bad year will follow another is also 80 percent. This models the nature of the business cycle in that both good and bad times tend to last over several years. In other words, the level of business activity in one year does have an impact on what business activity will be like in the next."

"And in the next exhibit [Exhibit 2.7], the bias that one good year will follow another, or one bad year comes after another, is 90 percent."

"Now I can do a comparative analysis of these three business-cycle simulators to select the one I will use. We know for a fact that business activity is cyclical, meaning that good times last for a while before the bad times arrive and vice versa. Therefore, a purely random selection as in the first exhibit [Exhibit 2.5] is not appropriate. Nor is the last exhibit [Exhibit 2.7] where the good times and the bad times are lasting far too long in comparison with the historic fluctuations in business activity. So, by default, a bias of 80 percent, or perhaps another value in that vicinity, would be more appropriate for modeling business activity."

"It looks a bit too bumpy to me."

"This can be taken care of by limiting the degree of swings, so to speak, if that's desirable. For now, I'm more interested in the concept of modeling business fluctuations than in selecting the final model."

"Excuse me for asking dumb questions, but why are you doing this?"

"Because I am going to be looking at your project over a twenty-year period where good and bad years come in bunches. I want to be able to judge whether there is sufficient cash-generating potential in your project during the good times for you to weather the storm of the bad times. Frankly, I want to assess the chances of your going bankrupt. Bankruptcy does not follow one bad year with a

Exhibit 2.5
Business-Cycle Simulator, No Year-to-Year Bias

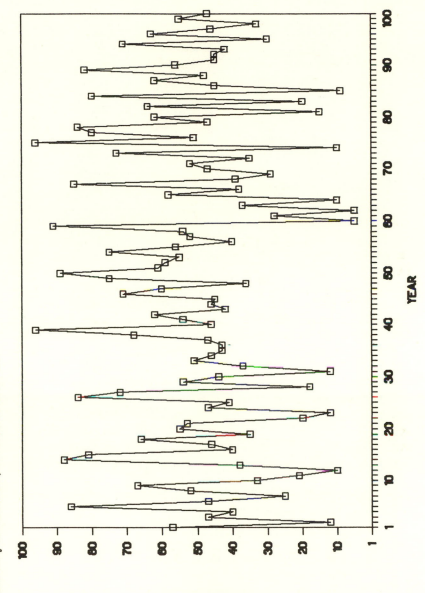

Exhibit 2.6
Business-Cycle Simulator, 80 Percent Year-to-Year Bias

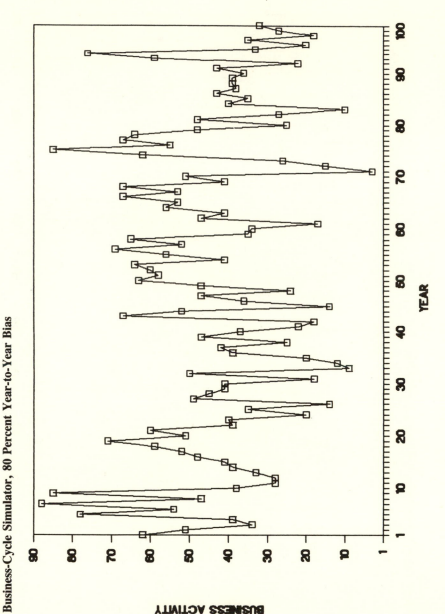

Exhibit 2.7
Business-Cycle Simulator, 90 Percent Year-to-Year Bias

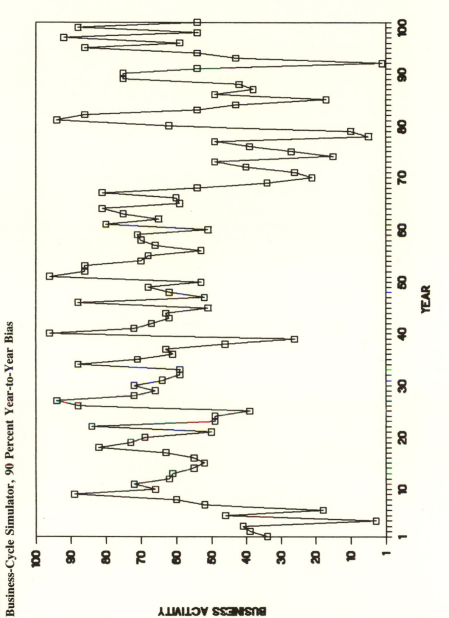

negative cash flow. Bankruptcy does not occur when there are several bad years of negative cash flows if you have accumulated sufficient cash reserves during the good times of the business cycle. The possibility of bankruptcy is present once the cash reserves are gone and you are still hemorrhaging the vital corporate body fluid known as cash."

"Do you know what I think as I look at these business cycles of yours?"

"No, what?"

"I think this whole thing is a game with you. I don't think you are serious. You are having a good time modeling things that you know very little about. You certainly don't know my business."

"I don't have to know your business when I'm evaluating its profit potential and its prospects for not making it. You have your credibility at stake with your superiors who know the business aspects of what you do far better than I. That is why I assume your assessments are realistic, and not 'pie-in-the-sky.' Good financial analysts do not have to be experts in the business that they are analyzing, although it's nice to have some degree of confidence in a manager's assessments and some general appreciation for the business being analyzed. I have already completed the profitability analysis of your proposal without knowing anything about your business. You didn't argue about that, did you?"

"No."

"So now I am going to do a risk analysis of the project from the same comfortable position of relative ignorance about what you make and sell. I did the profitability analysis based on your assessments of what you considered to be the most likely of outcomes. Now I want to do an analysis of risk based on your assessments of the least likely outcomes. Once I can develop a model of all the outcomes of cash flow, then I'll be in a position to make a judgment of risk just as I have already made a judgment of reward. Then I can give top management my evaluation of the reward and risk of this project in comparison with other proposals. That ends my task. It is up to them to decide what to do using my work as a departure point for a discussion on the relative merits of your proposal compared to the others."

"Still sounds like a game you're playing."

"In some respects, you are right. There is an element of gaming in what I'm doing. I will never get away from the roulette wheel which will be spun many times in this exercise. Now let me ask you a few questions."

"Go ahead."

"Didn't you obtain expert engineering advice concerning operational aspects of your proposal? Didn't I see a legal opinion concerning the nature of your product and product safety laws? Correct me if I'm wrong, but wasn't there an expert opinion by a consultant concerning the environmental impact of your waste disposal plan?"

"So?"

"So I'm the expert in assessing risk and I have tools of the trade that are just as fallible as an engineer's ideas that don't pan out when the factory is built, legal opinions that don't stick in court, or environmental waste disposal methods that will have to be dropped at the first public demonstration outside your new plant. And how is the game that I am playing any different than the game the engineers, the lawyers, and the consultants play with the opinions they provide when you are the one paying for their services?"

"Didn't mean to ruffle your feathers."

"Well, you did, a little. You have gone to the trouble of quantifying the reward so that your proposal can be ranked with other proposals and a decision can be made as to what proposals to proceed with and what proposals to reject. I am merely adding one more dimension: risk. If you can quantify reward, why can't I quantify risk? Risk is an imponderable, you say?"

"I'm not sure I said that."

"Well, it is, but no more so than your calculation of reward. You have no more idea of how many units you are going to sell and at what price than the janitor. But you use the best assessments that all your experience and judgment can bring to the table. That is what separates you from the janitor. And you know what?"

"I'm scared to ask."

"Pardon the double negative, but I ain't going to be no more wrong than you!"

"I surrender, if only to get on with it. Please continue."

"Your projection of cash flow assumed a volume of 500 units per year at a price of $12 per unit, I believe."

"Yes."

"I bet you can't guess what I'm about to ask."

"High and low estimates?"

"See? I'm beginning to make an impression on your thinking. When sales are at 500—your assessment of the most likely volume—over what range do you feel price will vary realizing that you have already selected $12 as your most likely price?"

"I feel that price will vary over a somewhat limited range, say, $10 to $14."

"In your wilder dreams of sales being as high as 800 units, what price would you expect to be the most likely price?"

"This is a tougher question . . . maybe $14 per unit."

"How about the range of prices when the sales volume is booming?"

"Well, if $14 is the most likely during the best of times, and $12 is the most likely during the most likely of times, I guess that a price of $12 would be the lowest I would expect during the best of times."

"And the highest?"

"$18."

"Let's concentrate on the worst of times. What is the most likely price you would expect to see during the worst of times?"

"I don't really know . . . perhaps, $10 per unit."

"The upper and lower limits?"

"Well, it's hard for me to imagine breaking $12 on the upside. The down side . . . well, in really bad times, I guess as low as $6 per unit, which is close to the variable cost of production."

"Here are your assessments. Do they look alright to you?"

PRICE RANGE VERSUS BUSINESS ACTIVITY

	WORST	MEDIAN	BEST
LOWER LIMIT	$ 6	$10	$12
MEDIAN	10	12	14
UPPER LIMIT	12	14	18

"Yes, I suppose."

"You're hesitating somewhat. Let me phrase the question differently. Do you want to change any of these numbers?"

"No."

"So by default, they must be your best assessments. Just give me some time to generate two more exhibits for you to examine."

"Ready for another go at it?"

"Shoot."

"In this exhibit [Exhibit 2.8], the lower line represents the worst business activity imaginable. Once business activity is determined to be at that level, then we need another roulette wheel. This wheel has only ten numbers. The lowest price cannot be lower than $6; the highest price cannot be higher than $12; and there is a somewhat higher likelihood that the price will be the median value of $10. The next line up represents the most likely case, where the price can vary between $10 and $14 with a more likely value of $12. And similarly, the upper line represents the best of all possible worlds, where the lowest price is $12, the highest price is $18, and the most likely price is $14."

"Why don't you have one hundred random numbers and curves just like you had before rather than ten random numbers and straight lines?"

"I would if I had more computer capacity, and while we're at it, I would prefer one thousand random numbers for selecting the level of business, not one hundred. But these are programming details that can be handled at another time. I'm still at the conceptual stage in formulating the quantification of risk. Now for the next exhibit."

"I was hoping you were going to say the last exhibit."

"There is a difference between these two exhibits. In this one [Exhibit 2.9], look at the business activity index value of one, which represents the worst you would anticipate for an ongoing world. The low end of the range is $6, the high end is $12, and the median is $10. This is the vertical presentation, so to speak, of the horizontal line in the exhibit [Exhibit 2.8] for the worst business condition.

Exhibit 2.8
Price Variation for Indicated Business Activity

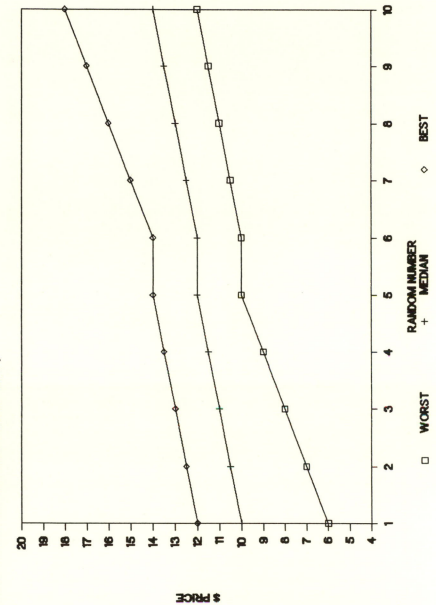

Exhibit 2.9
Price Range versus Business Activity

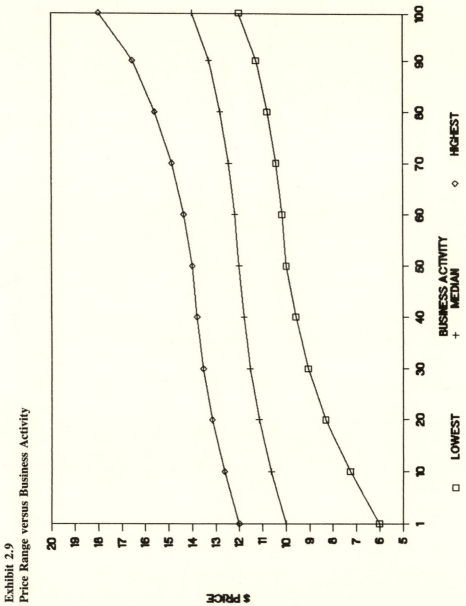

If you move up the business activity scale to an index value of 50, representing your most likely case, the lowest price you would expect to see is $10, the highest $14, and the median value is $12—again, a vertical view of what we had just seen."

"Let me finish. When business is at its best, which has a business activity value of 100, prices will vary between $12 and $18 with a middle value, so to speak, of $14."

"Yes, that $14 represents the point where half the time prices are higher and half the time prices are lower when business is at its very best."

"That famous median of yours."

"Precisely."

"So what does it all mean, if you don't mind my using the word 'mean'?"

"To answer your question, by your giving me the estimates for high, low, and median prices for three separate business conditions representing the best, the worst, and the most likely, I can construct the range of prices for these three business conditions as shown in the first exhibit [Exhibit 2.8]. This represents business conditions when the index value for business activity has a value of 100, 1, and 50, respectively. I can expand this to a tableau of prices for all interim business conditions whose extreme high and low prices and whose median prices are shown in the second exhibit [Exhibit 2.9]. I have taken your nine assessments on prices and expanded it to a tableau of one thousand prices—a range of ten prices for each of the one hundred values of the index of business activity. You can look on this as a two-dimensional simulator. If someone spins a roulette wheel with one hundred numbers on it and tells me what number appears, then I know the business activity index value. With that value, I enter the second exhibit [Exhibit 2.9] and pick off the range of prices and the median. Knowing the upper and lower limits and the median value for prices, another roulette wheel with ten numbers is spun to determine the exact price within the predetermined range of prices. You saw price ranges for just three of the one hundred possible measures of business activity in the first exhibit [Exhibit 2.8]."

"And that exhibit [Exhibit 2.8], which has three lines, in actuality, should have one hundred lines—one for each value of the index of business activity."

"That's right. The exhibit [Exhibit 2.8] shows the price distribution for only three business conditions: the absolute best, the absolute worst, and the most likely business conditions which correspond to business activity index values of 100, 1, and 50, respectively. The two-dimensional simulator is programmed to expand the initial nine assessments of prices to one hundred lines, so to speak, of ten prices each representing a single value of the business activity index."

"Let me see if I have this straight. I gave you nine price assessments, three each for the two extremes of business conditions and three for the most likely business condition, and the computer's programming instructions will generate a total of one thousand prices, ten each for each one hundred values of the business index."

"I think you got it."

"I think I got it!"

"Now if my computer had more capacity and operated with greater speed, there is no reason why I couldn't have, say, one hundred prices for each value of the business activity index. And that index could have one thousand rather than one hundred values. In this case, the tableau of prices would contain one hundred thousand prices rather than one thousand. But, again, relatively minor programming changes can bring this about once the concept of what we are doing has been nailed down."

"And that takes care of price."

"Yes, and now let's move on to volume. You gave me three points on volume: a disaster level of 400, a golden-heights number of 800, and the median number of 500. Suppose I asked you for a range for the median number instead of a discrete or single-valued assessment."

"You mean like 450 to 550 rather than 500?"

"Yes, exactly. The upper limit is 550, the lower is 450, and the median is 500 when business activity has a rating of 50. Isn't it easier for you to give me three numbers rather than one? Don't you get a sense of elbow room in making assessments if you are allowed to work with a range rather than having to select a single number?"

"I guess so, but I'm going to have to end up giving you nine figures whereas I originally gave you only one."

"One figure was sufficient for reward analysis, but more information is required for risk analysis. The additional information is not information that you would not have already thought of—when you contemplate the most likely, isn't it automatically framed by the least likely? You have already given me half the information. All you have to do is complete the following table."

VOLUME RANGE VERSUS BUSINESS ACTIVITY

	WORST	MEDIAN	BEST
LOWER LIMIT	400	450	
MEDIAN		500	
UPPER LIMIT		550	800

"And when I do, what are you going to do with the numbers?"

"Just the same as what I did with prices. The two-dimensional simulator will generate a tableau of volume figures for the high, low, and median for each of one hundred possible business activity index values as you saw in the last exhibit [Exhibit 2.9]. Then for each of these one hundred possible business conditions, ten values for volume will be generated just as you saw in the first exhibit [Exhibit 2.8], again one thousand possible volume figures from your original nine assessments. If you don't mind, why don't you complete the table for me?"

VOLUME RANGE VERSUS BUSINESS ACTIVITY

	WORST	MEDIAN	BEST
LOWER LIMIT	400	450	700
MEDIAN	425	500	750
UPPER LIMIT	450	550	800

"Now what?"

"Take a break for lunch."

"This is what I did with your nine assessments. I first derived the range of volume—the low, the high, and the median for each of the one hundred possible values of business activity as seen in this exhibit [Exhibit 2.10]."

"Notice how the low end of the volume range is simply an interpolated curve constructed from the three lower limits you provided for business activity levels of 1, 50, and 100. This is true for the high end of the volume range. It, too, is an interpolated curve based on the three upper limits you provided for the worst, the most likely, and the best business conditions. The same is true for the median level of volume. The curve is derived from your most likely assessments of volume for the three levels of business activity. From these curves, I created a tableau of volume figures of which I am representing only three: the range of possible volumes for the worst, the median, and the best business conditions as shown here [Exhibit 2.11]."

"This table [Table 2.1] shows the volume figures, to the nearest whole number, for business activity index values of 1, 10, 50, 70, 90, and 100. This should give you a basic idea of how the tableau is developed."

"I see my low, high, and middle estimates."

"The other values are determined by interpolation—equal increments, or steps, between the low and middle values and between the middle and high values. For a business activity index value of one, the low volume is 400 and the middle value is 425. Take the difference and divide by four. That is 6.25. Add 6.25 to 400 in steps up to the middle value and round to the nearest number. Then repeat this process between the middle value of 425 and the high value of 450. And then repeat for each of the one hundred values for the business activity index."

"I see what you are doing."

"I have two roulette wheels, one with one hundred numbers on it and the other with ten numbers on it. I spin the roulette wheel with one hundred numbers. I obtain a number for business activity. I take that number and obtain the appropriate range values, and median value, for volume. Suppose that the number I came up with is 70. Then that range of volume figures has a lower limit of 504, an upper limit of 604, and a middle value of 554. These three were derived from

Exhibit 2.10
Volume Range versus Business Activity

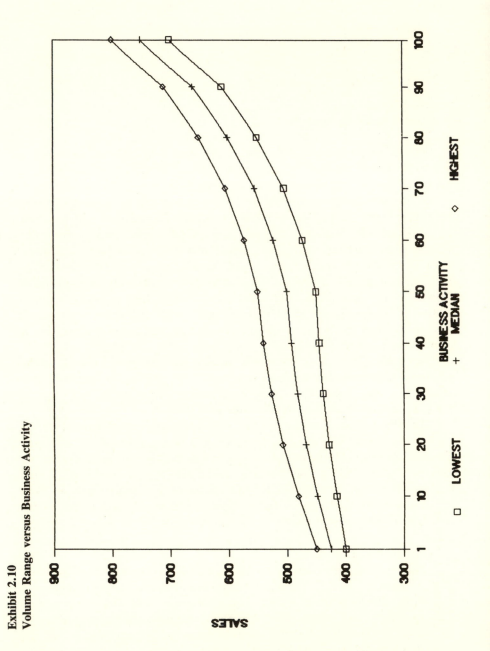

Exhibit 2.11
Volume Variation for Indicated Business Activity

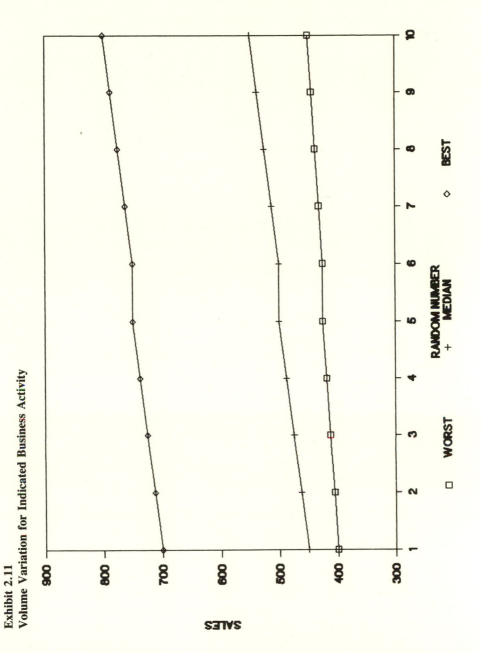

Table 2.1
Sales Volume versus Business Activity

RANDOM NUMBER	1	10	50	70	90	100
1	400	416	450	504	611	700
2	406	424	463	517	623	713
3	413	432	475	529	636	725
4	419	441	488	542	648	738
5	425	449	500	554	661	750
6	425	449	500	554	661	750
7	431	457	513	567	673	763
8	438	465	525	579	686	775
9	444	474	538	592	698	788
10	450	482	550	604	711	800

your assessments of nine values to cover the most and least likely outcomes on volume. Are you with me so far?"

"Do I have a choice?"

"Then I spin the roulette wheel with ten numbers to obtain a value between 1 and 10. Suppose the selected number is 6. What is the resulting volume?"

"Looks like 554."

"And let me give the roulette wheel with one hundred numbers another spin and suppose the number 10 comes up. From the table, I know that the volume ranges between 416 to 482 with a middle value of 449. That comes from your initial assessments. Then I give the roulette wheel with ten numbers a spin, and the winning number is 9. What is the resulting volume?"

"How about 474?"

"The tableau of possible volume figures is generated by a two-dimensional simulator. I only need to select two random numbers: one for business activity and one for the sales volume for the given level of business activity. The roulette wheel for business activity has one hundred numbers on it and the one for sales volume has ten numbers on it. Got it so far?"

"I think so."

"Good. Now let me suggest another idea. Suppose that the roulette wheel with one hundred numbers no longer has each number between 1 and 100 listed with equal probability. Suppose the listed numbers correspond to business activity index values where the numbers between 1 and 10, and between 90 and 100—representing the extremes of bad and good times—are rare events. Therefore, numbers around 50 are going to show up more frequently for normal economic activity. Can't I use this biased set of random numbers representing business activity to enter the volume simulator? And if the roulette wheel is loaded so that the numbers between 1 and 10, and between 90 and 100, don't show up as often as numbers around 50, then the corresponding volume figures close to 400 and 800 will be even more rare than before. I can do this if I want to, can't I?"

"You seem to be doing everything else your little heart desires."

"And now I want to show you the last exhibit [Exhibit 2.12]."

"I cannot express the feeling these words have on me."

"It hasn't been that bad, has it?"

"I'll let that go unanswered."

"I am using two methods to generate sales volume. In one case, I am using a biased set of random numbers which I am denoting as 'business activity.' This set of random numbers has numbers around 50 occurring more frequently than numbers around 1 or 100. If you look carefully, the distribution of sales volume peaks higher for sales around 500 using a biased set of random numbers than when the sales volume has been generated by an unbiased selection of random numbers."

"Yes, I see that."

"An unbiased selection of random numbers means that there is a one-hundred-slot roulette wheel with each slot numbered from 1 to 100. The probability that any given number will appear is the same for all numbers. The reason why the distribution of sales volume generated by the business activity index peaks higher in the middle is a consequence of the roulette wheel associated with business activity having more numbers around 50, and less numbers around 1 and 100. Therefore, the chance that a number around 50 will appear more frequently than numbers near 1 and 100 results in a higher probability of the sales volume being around 500. And if the probability is higher that sales will be in the vicinity of 500, then there is less probability that sales will be in the vicinity of 400 or 800. You can see that, too, in the exhibit."

"Fascinating, but what relevance does that have?"

"It means that if a probability distribution is peaking more in the middle, the tail ends of the distribution have to be smaller. Put another way, using the business activity simulator as a substitute for a random number generator for determining volume of sales results in sales of around 400 or 800 becoming rarer events than if a random number generator is used to determine the sales volume. I have another method in addition to the selection of the scaling factor for increasing the rarity factor of sales being near the extreme ends of the range of possibilities."

"Which method are you going to use?"

"I will be using the business activity simulator to select a random number for business activity. One reason for this is that it is more realistic to have the extremes of business activity—the extremely bad and the extremely good—as relatively rare events. Another reason is that I can introduce year-to-year bias to model the fact that good times and bad times last for a number of years. This way I am in a better position to judge your ability to survive the bad times given the fact that bad times, along with good times, are multiyear phenomena. Also, since I am assuming a scaling factor of 30 percent in the business activity simulator generator, and in the price and volume simulator generators, the probability of the extreme values of price and volume occurring has been reduced. I have, in

Exhibit 2.12
Sales Volume Distribution Generated by Two Methods

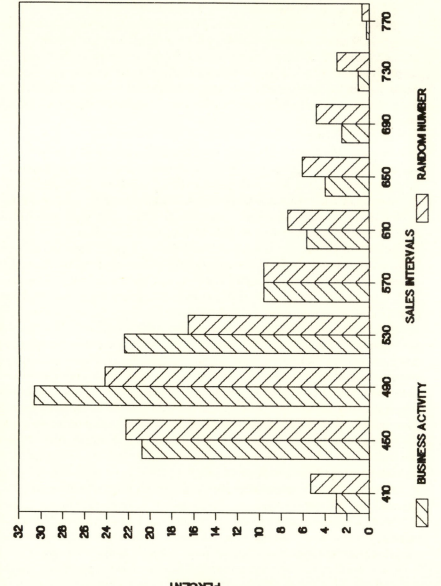

effect, reduced the scaling factor to something less than 30 percent if I use the business activity simulator as a method of generating price and volume values because there is less probability of random numbers near 1 and 100, and greater probability of random numbers around 50, being selected."

"Sounds like you're talking more to yourself than to me."

"I guess I am. But now I am in a position to forecast revenue. I draw one number from the hundred-numbered roulette wheel that represents the business activity simulator. That is the number by which I enter the two-dimensional simulators representing price and volume. Then I can spin the ten-numbered roulette wheel twice—once to obtain a value for price and once to obtain a value for volume from the price and volume ranges of values associated with the selected index value for business activity. I multiply the two and I have a forecast of revenue. I do so for twenty years, and I have your revenue projection. Then I have to take into account fixed and variable costs, taxes, finance charges, and other things. I repeat this exercise until I am in a position to judge both the reward and the risk of the company approving your proposal for funding."

"Sounds like you have a bit more work to do."

"I do, but not right now."

"You know what I sense is the risk in your work?"

"No, what?"

"I think you have a finite probability—how's that for mathematical terminology—to end up with garbage."

"Might if that is the worth of your assessments. In fact, if the quantification of risk is garbage, then the rate of return on your proposal should be thrown into the same garbage can. The quantification of risk is merely an extension of the quantification of reward. But if there is a speck of reality in your assessments of price and volume, and other details that I'll need, then I'll have a spectrum of possible outcomes for your proposal. Comparing this with the initial investment, I may be able to judge both the expected reward and the variation on that reward, which is a measure of risk. I will be able to judge the chances of your not having enough cash, both accumulated and being generated, to meet your obligations. This is the real basis for measuring the risk in your proposal. With both the reward and the risk quantified based on your assessments, I am in a position to compare your proposal with other proposals and, hopefully, add rather than detract from the decision-making process by which proposals are approved, or rejected, for funding."

"Well, I hope my assessments are the right assessments for your sake and mine."

"That's all we have to work on."

APPENDIX

Four programs will be considered in this appendix: SIMONE, SIMTWO, BUSACT, and VOLSIM. SIMONE is a program for generating one-dimensional simulators, and SIM-

TWO for two-dimensional simulators. BUSACT generates a multiyear projection of the business activity index that can also be substituted for an unbiased random number generator to perform a multiyear economic analysis of a proposal. VOLSIM is a special program demonstrating the difference in a simulator for sales volume using biased and unbiased random numbers. All programs are written in GWBASIC language on an IBM compatible personal computer with the MS-DOS operating system.

SIMONE

SIMONE generates simulators on the basis of random numbers with values between 1 and 1,000. A simulator of one hundred random numbers, selected in statements 30 to 50, takes the simulator of one thousand random numbers and stores every tenth value (statements 920–960). Simulators can be generated or changed as selected in statements 60 to 110 and are stored in files named SIM1, SIM2, SIM3, and so on, in statements 850 to 910. It may be advisable to change the file names to reduce the chance of selecting the wrong simulator file through the RENAME command.

The minimum, expected (median), and maximum assessments, and the appropriate scaling factor, are entered in statements 130 to 260. The appendix to chapter 2 of *Computer Simulation in Business Decision Making* (Quorum Books, 1989), describes the mathematics incorporated in SIMONE. Basically, the process involves generating a cumulative probability distribution with probability being represented on the Y-axis and the assumed minimum, median, and maximum assessments of 0, 500, and 1000, respectively (statement 270), being represented on the X-axis. The cumulative distribution curve is created in statements 330 to 460 using the selected scaling factor to determine the 25 and 75 percentile points. The meaning of the scaling factor is described in this chapter. The actual minimum, median, and maximum assessment points are incorporated into the cumulative probability distribution in statements 470 to 490 using an "accordian effect" to stretch or compress the X-axis to fit the actual assessments. The X- and Y-axes are interchanged in statements 500 to 540.

The major difference between this simulator generator and the one contained in *Computer Simulation in Business Decision Making* is in statements 560 to 730. As noted in *Computer Simulation in Business Decision Making,* the simulator did not perform well with a scaling factor of less than 0.3 whereas better-looking simulators could be created using scaling factors of 0.7 or higher.

Programming "sleight of hand" is required to convert an initial cumulative probability distribution with a scaling factor of 0.7 to one with a scaling factor of 0.3. This is done by transferring the cumulative probability distribution to the other side of a straight line connecting the 0 and 50 percentile points and the 50 and 100 percentile points. Thus a simulator with a scaling factor of 0.2 is initially constructed with a scaling factor of 0.8 (statements 190–260) with the resulting simulator transferred to the other side of the straight line segments constructed from a cumulative probability distribution with a scaling factor of 0.5 (statements 280–320). The transfer process is accomplished in statements 570 to 730. Statements 740 to 790 ensure that the cumulative probability distribution increases in value as the probability of occurrence approaches 100 percent. Statements 800 to 830 permit viewing of the cumulative probability distribution prior to its being stored in a file as a one-hundred, or one-thousand, random number simulator.

The exhibits were constructed by adding the .PRN (RENAME SIM* SIM*.PRN) and importing the files into a *LOTUS* spreadsheet with the File Import Numbers command. Standard *LOTUS* (Release 2) graphics were used to create all the exhibits.

```
10 REM NAME OF PROGRAM IS SIMONE
20 DIM X(1000):DIM Y(1000):DIM Z(2,1000):DIM S(6,1000)
30 PRINT:PRINT "RANDOM NUMBER SIMULATIONS"
40 PRINT "ONE HUNDRED:  1"
50 PRINT "ONE THOUSAND: 2":PRINT:INPUT Z6:PRINT
60 PRINT:PRINT
70 PRINT "GENERATE SIMULATORS         : 1"
80 PRINT "CHANGE EXISTING SIMULATORS: 2":PRINT
90 INPUT Z:PRINT:ON Z GOTO 110,100
100 INPUT "ENTER SIMULATOR TO BE CHANGED (1-6): ";D2:D1=D2:GOTO 120
110 INPUT "ENTER NUMBER OF SIMULATORS TO BE GENERATED: ";D2:D1=1
120 FOR D=D1 TO D2
130 PRINT:INPUT "MINIMUM ANTICIPATED VALUE: ";A1
140 INPUT "EXPECTED VALUE (MEDIAN):    ";A2
150 IF A2>A1 THEN 160 ELSE 140
160 INPUT "MAXIMUM ANTICIPATED VALUE: ";A3:PRINT:PRINT
170 IF A3>A2 THEN 180 ELSE 160
180 PRINT "SCALING FACTOR":PRINT
190 PRINT "EXTREMITIES ARE RARER WITH LOWER SCALING FACTORS"
200 PRINT "SCALING FACTOR 10%: 1":PRINT "SCALING FACTOR 20%: 2"
210 PRINT "SCALING FACTOR 30%: 3":PRINT "SCALING FACTOR 50%: 4"
220 PRINT:INPUT Z5:ON Z5 GOTO 230, 240, 250, 260
230 Z9=.9:GOTO 270
240 Z9=.8:GOTO 270
250 Z9=.7:GOTO 270
260 Z9=.5
270 A=0:C=500:B=1000
280 FOR I1=1 TO 2
290 ON I1 GOTO 300,310
300 Z=.5:GOTO 330
310 Z=Z9:IF Z9=.5 THEN 320 ELSE 330
320 I1=2:GOTO 550
330 L=C-Z*(C-A):H=C+Z*(B-C)
340 K1=LOG(.5)/LOG(.75):K2=LOG(.75)/LOG(.25)
350 L1=LOG(K1):L4=LOG(K2)
360 L2=LOG((B-C)/(B-L)):L3=LOG((C-A)/(L-A))
370 L5=LOG((B-L)/(B-H)):L6=LOG((L-A)/(H-A))
380 M=(L1/L3-L4/L6)/(L5/L6-L2/L3)
390 N=(L1/L3)+(L2/L3)*M
400 T1=(B-C)^M:T2=(C-A)^N:T=-LOG(.5)*T1/T2
410 X(1)=A:K=(B-A)/1000
420 FOR I=2 TO 1000:X(I)=X(I-1)+K:NEXT
430 Y(1000)=1:Y(1)=0
440 FOR I=2 TO 999
450 Z1=(X(I)-A)^N:Z2=(B-X(I))^M
460 Y(I)=1-EXP(-T*Z1/Z2):NEXT
470 X(1)=A1:FOR I=2 TO 500:X(I)=X(I-1)+(A2-A1)/500:NEXT
480 FOR I=501 TO 1000:X(I)=X(I-1)+(A3-A2)/500:NEXT
490 Z(I1,1)=A1:Z(I1,1000)=A3:K=1
500 FOR I=2 TO 999
510 FOR J=K TO 1000
520 IF 1000*Y(J)<I THEN 540
530 Z(I1,I)=X(J):K=J:J=1000
540 NEXT:NEXT
550 NEXT:IF Z9=.5 THEN 560 ELSE 570
560 FOR I=1 TO 1000:S(D,I)=Z(1,I):NEXT:GOTO 740
570 S(D,1)=A1:S(D,500)=A2:S(D,1000)=A3
580 FOR I=2 TO 499
```

```
590 Y=Z(1,I)-Z(2,I)
600 IF Y>0 THEN 610 ELSE 620
610 S(D,I)=Z(1,I)+Y:GOTO 630
620 S(D,I)=Z(2,I)
630 IF S(D,I)>A2 THEN 640 ELSE 650
640 S(D,I)=A2
650 NEXT
660 FOR I=501 TO 999
670 Y=Z(2,I)-Z(1,I)
680 IF Y>0 THEN 690 ELSE 700
690 S(D,I)=Z(1,I)-Y:GOTO 710
700 S(D,I)=Z(2,I)
710 IF S(D,I)<A2 THEN 720 ELSE 730
720 S(D,I)=A2
730 NEXT
740 K=10:FOR I=10 TO 1000 STEP 10
750 IF S(D,I)<S(D,I-10) THEN 760 ELSE 770
760 K=1
770 NEXT
780 IF K=1 THEN 790 ELSE 800
790 PRINT:PRINT "IMPROPER CUMULATIVE DISTRIBUTION":PRINT
800 PRINT "CUM PROBABILITY"
810 PRINT "DISTRIBUTION","VALUE":PRINT 1,S(D,1)
820 FOR I=50 TO 1000 STEP 50:PRINT I/10,S(D,I):NEXT
830 INPUT "FILE DATA  YES-1  NO-2: ";Z
840 ON Z GOTO 850,130
850 ON D GOTO 860,870,880,890,900,910,920,940
860 OPEN "O",#1,"SIM1":GOTO 920
870 OPEN "O",#1,"SIM2":GOTO 920
880 OPEN "O",#1,"SIM3":GOTO 920
890 OPEN "O",#1,"SIM4":GOTO 920
900 OPEN "O",#1,"SIM5":GOTO 920
910 OPEN "O",#1,"SIM6":GOTO 920
920 ON Z6 GOTO 930,970
930 Z(1,1)=S(D,1):Z(1,100)=S(D,1000):Z(1,50)=S(D,500)
940 FOR I=2 TO 49:K=10*(I-1):Z(1,I)=S(D,K):NEXT
950 FOR I=51 TO 99:K=10*I:Z(1,I)=S(D,K):NEXT
960 FOR I=1 TO 100:WRITE #1,Z(1,I):NEXT:CLOSE #1:GOTO 980
970 FOR I=1 TO 1000:WRITE #1,S(D,I):NEXT:CLOSE #1
980 NEXT:END
```

SIMTWO

SIMTWO generates a two-dimensional simulator. It is an adaptation of the SIMONE program. Only one simulator can be generated at a time and its file name is entered in statement 40. The minimum, median, and maximum assessments for the worst, most likely, and best business conditions are entered in statements 50 to 240. A scaling factor of 0.30 is assumed in generating two-dimensional simulators (statement 340).

SIMONE is used to generate the lower, median, and upper range limits for the one hundred possible business activity values. Statements 250 to 290 direct the creation of one-dimensional simulators for the three lower limits, the three median values, and the three upper limits as inputs for SIMONE. Statements 80, 100, 130, 150, 170, 200, 220, and 240 are necessary to ensure ascending values for proper operation of the SIMONE program contained within the SIMTWO program (statements 300–730).

The three single simulators are shown in statements 740 to 790 for viewing as each is generated. The tableau of ten values to be assigned to each of the one hundred possible levels of business activity is accomplished in statements 800 to 920, and statements 930 to 940 direct the storing of the resulting tableau under the selected name.

```
10 REM NAME OF PROGRAM IS SIMTWO
20 DIM X(1000):DIM Y(1000):DIM Z(2,1000):DIM S(3,1000):DIM P(10,100)
30 PRINT:PRINT "TWO DIMENSIONAL SIMULATOR GENERATOR":PRINT
40 INPUT "FILE NAME FOR SAVING RESULTS: ";F$:PRINT
50 PRINT "FOR THE WORST BUSINESS CONDITION, ENTER:"
60 INPUT "    LOWER LIMIT: ";L1
70 INPUT "    MEDIAN:      ";M1
80 IF M1<L1 THEN 70
90 INPUT "    UPPER LIMIT: ";U1:PRINT
100 IF U1<M1 THEN 90
110 PRINT "FOR THE MEDIAN BUSINESS CONDITION, ENTER:"
120 INPUT "    LOWER LIMIT: ";L2
130 IF L2<L1 THEN 120
140 INPUT "    MEDIAN:      ";M2
150 IF M2<M1 THEN 140:IF M2<L2 THEN 140
160 INPUT "    UPPER LIMIT: ";U2:PRINT
170 IF U2<U1 THEN 160:IF U2<M2 THEN 160
180 PRINT "FOR THE BEST BUSINESS CONDITION, ENTER:"
190 INPUT "    LOWER LIMIT: ";L3
200 IF L3<L2 THEN 190
210 INPUT "    MEDIAN     : ";M3
220 IF M3<M2 THEN 210:IF M3<L3 THEN 210
230 INPUT "    UPPER LIMIT: ";U3:PRINT
240 IF U3<U2 THEN 230:IF U3<M3 THEN 230
250 FOR D=1 TO 3
260 ON D GOTO 270, 280, 290
270 A1=L1:A2=L2:A3=L3:GOTO 300
280 A1=M1:A2=M2:A3=M3:GOTO 300
290 A1=U1:A2=U2:A3=U3
300 A=0:C=500:B=1000
310 FOR I1=1 TO 2
320 ON I1 GOTO 330,340
330 Z=.5:GOTO 350
340 Z=.7
350 L=C-Z*(C-A):H=C+Z*(B-C)
360 K1=LOG(.5)/LOG(.75):K2=LOG(.75)/LOG(.25)
370 L1=LOG(K1):L4=LOG(K2)
380 L2=LOG((B-C)/(B-L)):L3=LOG((C-A)/(L-A))
390 L5=LOG((B-L)/(B-H)):L6=LOG((L-A)/(H-A))
400 M=(L1/L3-L4/L6)/(L5/L6-L2/L3)
410 N=(L1/L3)+(L2/L3)*M
420 T1=(B-C)^M:T2=(C-A)^N:T=-LOG(.5)*T1/T2
430 X(1)=A:K=(B-A)/1000
440 FOR I=2 TO 1000:X(I)=X(I-1)+K:NEXT
450 Y(1000)=1:Y(1)=0
460 FOR I=2 TO 999
470 Z1=(X(I)-A)^N:Z2=(B-X(I))^M
480 Y(I)=1-EXP(-T*Z1/Z2):NEXT
490 X(1)=A1:FOR I=2 TO 500:X(I)=X(I-1)+(A2-A1)/500:NEXT
500 FOR I=501 TO 1000:X(I)=X(I-1)+(A3-A2)/500:NEXT
510 Z(I1,1)=A1:Z(I1,1000)=A3:K=1
520 FOR I=2 TO 999
530 FOR J=K TO 1000
540 IF 1000*Y(J)<I THEN 560
550 Z(I1,I)=X(J):K=J:J=1000
560 NEXT:NEXT:NEXT
570 S(D,1)=A1:S(D,500)=A2:S(D,1000)=A3
580 FOR I=2 TO 499
```

```
590  Y=Z(1,I)-Z(2,I)
600  IF Y>0 THEN 610 ELSE 620
610  S(D,I)=Z(1,I)+Y:GOTO 630
620  S(D,I)=Z(2,I)
630  IF S(D,I)>A2 THEN 640 ELSE 650
640  S(D,I)=A2
650  NEXT
660  FOR I=501 TO 999
670  Y=Z(2,I)-Z(1,I)
680  IF Y>0 THEN 690 ELSE 700
690  S(D,I)=Z(1,I)-Y:GOTO 710
700  S(D,I)=Z(2,I)
710  IF S(D,I)<A2 THEN 720 ELSE 730
720  S(D,I)=A2
730  NEXT
740  ON D GOTO 750,760,770
750  PRINT "LOWER":GOTO 780
760  PRINT "MEDIAN":GOTO 780
770  PRINT "UPPER"
780  PRINT "POINTS","VALUE":PRINT 1,S(D,1)
790  FOR I=50 TO 1000 STEP 50:PRINT I/10,S(D,I):NEXT
800  Z(1,1)=S(D,1):Z(1,100)=S(D,1000):Z(1,50)=S(D,500)
810  FOR I=2 TO 49:K=10*(I-1):Z(1,I)=S(D,K):NEXT
820  FOR I=51 TO 99:K=10*I:Z(1,I)=S(D,K):NEXT
830  ON D GOTO 840, 850, 860
840  FOR I=1 TO 100:P(1,I)=Z(1,I):NEXT:GOTO 870
850  FOR I=1 TO 100:P(5,I)=Z(1,I):P(6,I)=Z(1,I):NEXT:GOTO 870
860  FOR I=1 TO 100:P(10,I)=Z(1,I):NEXT
870  NEXT
880  FOR I=1 TO 100
890  K=(P(10,I)-P(6,I))/4
900  FOR J=1 TO 3:P(6+J,I)=P(6+J-1,I)+K:NEXT
910  K=(P(5,I)-P(1,I))/4
920  FOR J=1 TO 3:P(1+J,I)=P(1+J-1,I)+K:NEXT:NEXT
930  OPEN "O",#1,F$:FOR I=1 TO 100
940  WRITE#1,P(1,I),P(2,I),P(3,I),P(4,I),P(5,I),P(6,I),P(7,I),
     P(8,I),P(9,I),P(10,I):NEXT:CLOSE#1:END
```

BUSACT

The BUSACT program creates a multiyear projection of business activity. The business activity index itself, with values between 1 and 100, can be used as a substitute for a random number generator to further reduce the probability of extremely good and bad times. In addition, a year-to-year bias factor introduces multiyear periods of good and bad times.

The SIMONE program is first run with 1, 50, and 100 as the respective minimum, median, and maximum assessments with a scaling factor of 0.3 to create a file renamed BUS. The BUS file is fed into the program in statements 30 to 50. A one-hundred-year simulation is run for three situations (statements 60–100). For the first, business activity in one year is not affected by the level of business activity in the prior year. In other words, there is a 50–50 chance that any particular year would be a good or bad year, designated as such by business activity index values of above, or below, 50. The results are stored in a file named BUS5. For the second situation, there is only a 20 percent chance that times could change from bad to good, or good to bad. A bias of 80 percent is thus introduced to increase the chance of having succeeding years remain the same as the first year of good or bad times. The result is stored as BUS8. For the third situation, bias is increased to 90 percent and the results are stored as BUS9. Statements 80 to 100 introduce the degree of bias; statements 110 to 260 generate the one-hundred-year simulation of business activity; and statements 270 to 280 store the results.

```
10 REM NAME OF PROGRAM IS BUSACT
20 DIM A(100):DIM B(100)
30 OPEN "I",#1,"BUS"
40 FOR I=1 TO 100:INPUT #1,Z:A(I)=INT(Z+.5):NEXT
50 CLOSE #1
60 FOR I=1 TO 3
70 ON I GOTO 80,90,100
80 Z1=.5:OPEN "O",#1,"BUS5":GOTO 130
90 Z1=.8:OPEN "O",#1,"BUS8":GOTO 130
100 Z1=.9:OPEN "O",#1,"BUS9"
110 X=RND(X):IF X<.5 THEN 120 ELSE 130
120 Z=1:GOTO 140
130 Z=2
140 FOR J=1 TO 100
150 X=RND(X)
160 IF X>Z1 THEN 170 ELSE 200
170 ON Z GOTO 180, 190
180 Z=2:GOTO 200
190 Z=1:GOTO 200
200 X=RND(X):T=INT(100*X+.5)
210 IF T=0 THEN 220 ELSE 230
220 T=100
230 ON Z GOTO 240,250
240 IF T<=50 THEN 260 ELSE 200
250 IF T>=50 THEN 260 ELSE 200
260 B(J)=A(T):NEXT
270 FOR J=1 TO 100:WRITE #1,B(J):NEXT
280 CLOSE#1:NEXT:END
```

VOLSIM

The VOLSIM program generates the sales volume probability distribution using both a biased and unbiased set of random numbers. The biased set of random numbers is introduced in the program by entering the BUS file in statements 30 to 40. The BUS file is previously created using the SIMONE program with minimum, median, and maximum assessments of 1, 50, and 100, and with a scaling factor of 0.3. The ten possible volume values for each of one hundred business activity levels are entered into the program in statements 50 to 60. This file, named VOLUME, has been previously created using the SIMTWO program with the nine volume assessments as listed in the chapter. In a process to be repeated one hundred thousand times (statement 80), a random number between 1 and 100 is selected (statements 90–110) and the corresponding value for the BUS simulator is obtained (statement 120). This biases the random number to have values more frequently around 50 and less frequently around 1 and 100.

Another draw is made from the random number generator to obtain a random number between 1 and 10 (statements 130–150). The efficacy of statements 130 to 150 in selecting random numbers between 1 and 10 can be tested as follows.

```
10 REM NAME OF PROGRAM IS TEST
20 FOR S=1 TO 10000
30 X=RND(X):K=INT(10*X+.5)
40 IF K=0 THEN 50 ELSE 60
```

```
50 K=10
60 R(K)=R(K)+1:NEXT
70 FOR I=1 TO 10:PRINT I,R(I):NEXT
80 A=0:FOR I=1 TO 10:A=A+I*R(I):NEXT
90 S=S-1:PRINT "EXPECTED VALUE: "A/S:END
```

The resulting volume was determined and the results accumulated in statement 160; the process is repeated one hundred thousand times. The expected volume is calculated and printed on the screen in statements 170 to 180 and the results of the simulation stored in a file named RESULTS (statements 190–200).

The unbiased simulation was run by omitting statements 30 and 40, amending statement 120 to read K=T, and changing the name of the file for storing the results.

```
10 REM NAME OF PROGRAM VOLSIM
20 DIM V(10,100):DIM A(100):DIM S(1000)
30 OPEN "I",#1,"BUS"
40 FOR I=1 TO 100:INPUT #1,Z:A(I)=INT(Z+.5):NEXT:CLOSE #1
50 OPEN "I",#1,"VOLUME"
60 FOR I=1 TO 100:INPUT #1,V(1,I),V(2,I),V(3,I),V(4,I),V(5,I),
   V(6,I),V(7,I),V(8,I),V(9,I),V(10,I):NEXT:CLOSE #1
70 FOR I=1 TO 1000:S(I)=0:NEXT
80 FOR I=1 TO 100000!
90 X=RND(X):T=INT(100*X+.5)
100 IF T=0 THEN 110 ELSE 120
110 T=100
120 K=A(T)
130 X=RND(X):S=INT(10*X+.5)
140 IF S=0 THEN 150 ELSE 160
150 S=10
160 V=V(S,K):V=INT(V+.5):S(V)=S(V)+1:NEXT
170 A=0:FOR I=1 TO 1000:A=A+I*S(I):NEXT
180 PRINT "EXPECTED VOLUME IS: ";A/100000!
190 OPEN "O",#1,"RESULTS"
200 FOR I=1 TO 1000:WRITE #1,I,S(I):NEXT:CLOSE #1:END
```

3

The Equity Decision

The risk and reward of a proposed investment are measured by projecting the financial performance of the investment in an assumed business environment. Although there are various means of measuring risk and reward, the assessment of performance is only as valid as the appropriateness of the modeling of the business environment and the performance of the investment in such an environment. No model, no matter what its degree of complexity, can be validated as the right model to be used under the particular circumstances surrounding the investment because all models are approximations and simplifications of reality. No model can incorporate the infinite number of threads that make up the web of economic reality. The use of models is a testament that reality is too complex to be dealt with directly. We resort to models because we cannot deal with reality on reality's terms.

Nor, for that matter, can assessments of future business conditions and the financial performance of an investment be validated. Assessments are judgments of events before the fact. Validation of assessments would involve a comparative analysis of what is assumed to occur with what actually occurs. Such a comparison can only be made some time after the making of the decision. By then, it is too late to change the decision. Assessments cannot be validated before the fact. If assessments could be validated, then the assessments are no longer assessments, but facts. When dealing with facts, there is no such thing as risk analysis because risk analysis deals with uncertainty.

The future is fraught with uncertainty. Nevertheless, the decision whether to invest in a project demands that some assessment be made of the general business climate and how the project may fare within the prevailing pattern of business activity. Even if such assessments are pure conjecture, these assessments are necessary as a prop in the drama of the making of a business decision. The financial risk faced by all businessmen is that the assessments of the future, and the revealing of reality with the passage of time, are never quite the same.

The simulation to be proposed in this chapter is an attempt to mimic the ebb and flow of business activity. The proposed simulation is different from conventional "What If" analysis in that it recognizes that good times follow bad, bad times follow good, and good and bad times are multiyear phenomena. The incorporation of good and bad years lasting for a duration of time is an attempt to copy, or mimic, the cyclical nature of business activity. The other difference in the proposed simulation from conventional "What If" analysis is that the latter usually measures risk in terms of an undesirable rate of return on investment that is below the hurdle rate of the company. This is not a relevant measure of risk.

The conventional measure of risk as an undesirable or unacceptable rate of return on investment is not the actual risk faced by businessmen. The fact is that a firm can survive a low return on investment as long as there is sufficient cash reserves to fund shortfalls in revenue generation. The reality of business life is that a firm flush with cash can easily endure bad times when there is a low rate of return. Survival is threatened when there is insufficient cash generation or reserves to pay the bills. If bankruptcy is the true risk of conducting business, then the threat of bankruptcy should be the measure of risk.

Although the risk of a less than desirable return on investment is concomitant with an inability to pay bills, the two do not necessarily go hand-in-hand. One can have an unsatisfactory level of profits and still have enough money in the bank to keep creditors at bay. To a manager, and to the shareholders of a corporation, low returns may be disappointing, but are not necessarily fatal.

There is a major difference in the obligatory nature and ramifications of not being able to meet the payroll and not being in a position to pay a dividend on common stock. Not being able to meet the payroll, or pay suppliers, or pay a finance charge can lead to the creditors taking action against a company that can force it into bankruptcy. A poor return on the company's investments means that there is little money left after paying employees, suppliers, and bankers to pass on to shareholders in the company in the form of a dividend payment on the common stock. The inability to pay a dividend does not force a company into bankruptcy. Dividends on common stock are not obligatory and shareholders have no legal basis for pursuing the payment of dividends in court. Monies due to employees, suppliers, and bankers are obligatory in nature and these parties do have access to the judicial system to protect their rights. A low return on investment means a meager or nonexistent dividend. A shortage of cash and the exhaustion of borrowing capacity means impending insolvency and possible liquidation of the company. Since bankruptcy is not associated with poor returns as such, but with insufficient liquidity, then risk should be measured in terms of insolvency and its impact on corporate survival, and not solely in terms of an undesirable return on investment.

THE MEASURE OF REWARD

Unfortunately, using a shortfall in cash generation as a criterion for measuring risk entails modification of the conventional measure of reward. Cash thrown off from a venture during good times can be held in reserve to meet the contingency of not having sufficient funds during bad times. The conventional measure of reward, as will be seen, assumes that cash in excess of expenses is reinvested in projects with the same rate of return as the investment itself. Cash generated by a project is not held as cash in a tin box, but is continually reinvested in long-term projects which, presumably, provide little in the way of liquidity. A modification of the conventional methodology for calculating returns on investment is to hold some of the excess cash generation during the good times in reserve to satisfy potential cash shortfalls during the bad times. Risk is to be measured in terms of not generating, and of not having accumulated, sufficient cash to pay the bills. This, of course, is the "condition precedent" for insolvency, which, if not resolved to the satisfaction of creditors, is the prelude for declaring or being forced into bankruptcy. Risk will also be measured in conventional terms of having a return on investment that is below the minimum objective of the firm because that information is provided in the process of measuring reward.

Before making such a modification, it may be beneficial to first appreciate the conventional measure of reward, particularly with regard to the necessity of reinvesting cash inflows in some sort of an investment vehicle or medium bearing the same rate of return as the project itself.

Let us suppose that top management is discussing what to do about a proposal from a subsidiary to build a factory to cater to fads in the plastic goods business. Profits can be, as some have maintained, disgustingly obscene, in this facet of the plastic goods business. Management estimates that revenue less the variable cost of production—which includes the costs of raw materials, energy, packaging and shipping, and unskilled labor—ranges between $100,000 and $400,000 per week with a most likely value of $300,000. Thus a year's operation (fifty weeks) at the most likely assessment generates $15 million in annual gross margin. With fixed operating costs of no more than $4 million, a plant costing $10 million can be paid off in about a year's time on a before tax basis. In a manufacturing environment, this is a highly profitable business, to say the least.

Yet plastic fad items are not always in vogue. When there are no hula hoops tickling the fancy of the fickle public, the plant must compete in the ordinary nonfad plastic goods business where gross margins leave much to be desired. The plant is expensive to build because its machinery and equipment represent the latest in plastic goods manufacturing technology. The plant is capable of producing enormous quantities of plastic goods to satisfy the burgeoning demand for fad items while the demand is still burgeoning. There is far too much sophistication in the plant, however, for the nonfad plastic goods business. In addition, there is a top-heavy marketing and engineering organization geared to satisfying market demand for fad items. The plant is highly automated and requires a

minimal number of unskilled workers. Most of the workers are machine operators skilled in turning out an incredible variety of plastic goods. The skilled
workers, the engineers, and the marketers are necessary if the plant is to respond
rapidly to unexpected demand. This drives up fixed operating costs. Since these
specialists cannot be laid off without affecting the operational capacity of the
plant, fixed costs remain high when revenue falls. The plant is a very poor
competitor in the nonfad plastics side of the business where Far Eastern imports
have largely decimated domestic production of plastic goods. In the nonfad
plastic goods business, the plant is unable to satisfy the fixed operating costs, let
alone provide a return on investment.

Therefore, top management is very concerned about investing in a plant that in
some respects cannot be considered an ongoing concern. There is a very real
possibility of extended periods of time when the operation of the plant cannot
satisfy the fixed costs of operation. Those proposing the plant point to their
expertise in marketing fad plastic items and in being able to bring a new plastic
item to market faster than a competitor can place a telephone call to Taiwan.
They also point out that fixed costs can be reduced somewhat when the plant has
to operate in the nonfad plastic goods market. This is achieved by eliminating
bonuses, deferring maintenance, and not purchasing replacement equipment.
Layoffs are not a significant means of reducing costs because relatively few
unskilled workers are required—even at full production. Eliminating bonuses
and deferring maintenance can hold fixed costs between $2 and $3 million when
the plant must operate in the highly competitive market of nonfad plastic goods.
During better times, when gross margin exceeds $5 million per year, fixed costs
expand to about $3 to $4 million as bonuses are given out, replacement equipment is purchased, and maintenance routines are performed.

Of much greater importance than costs in determining the feasibility of investing in the new plant is gross margin—revenue less all variable costs of production
(raw material, energy, packaging and shipping, unskilled labor). What is particularly critical is the number of weeks per year of production for fad items.
Management has observed that business can be either brisk (good times) or in the
doldrums (bad times) without rhyme or reason. Looking back in time, management has noted that good and bad times usually last anywhere from two to five
years. The management of the subsidiary proposing this project has made the
following assessments as to gross margins for fad and nonfad plastic goods and the
length of time in weeks for fad items to be in demand for both good and bad times.

GOOD TIMES IN THE PLASTIC GOODS BUSINESS

	WEEKS OF PRODUCING FAD ITEMS	WEEKLY GROSS MARGIN FAD	NON-FAD
MINIMUM	0	$100,000	$10,000
MOST LIKELY	20	300,000	30,000
MAXIMUM	40	400,000	50,000

BAD TIMES IN THE PLASTIC GOODS BUSINESS

	WEEKS OF PRODUCING FAD ITEMS	WEEKLY GROSS MARGIN FAD	NON-FAD
MINIMUM	0	$100,000	$ 5,000
MOST LIKELY	10	200,000	20,000
MAXIMUM	15	300,000	30,000

Suppose that top management of the parent corporation has come to the conclusion that these estimates are reasonable. Their conclusion can be made on the basis of obtaining an outside opinion from an unbiased source, or from direct experience in the fad and nonfad plastic goods business, or from a review of the operation of the subsidiary in both facets of the plastic goods market. Top management is interested in evaluating the profit potential of the proposal. How would this project be analyzed in a conventional manner?

Usually everything is reduced to a single discrete value. The good times gross margin, for instance, would be calculated by assuming that the most likely estimates prevail each year of good times. The most likely gross margin for good times is 20 weeks of production of fad items that generate $6 million (20 weeks × $300,000 per week) plus 30 weeks of production of nonfad items that generate $0.9 million (30 weeks × $30,000) for a total of $6.9 million. Fifty weeks per year of operation are assumed to permit two weeks for vacation and performance of annual maintenance routines. Once the number of weeks for producing fad items has been determined, nonfad plastic production is simply fifty weeks less the number of weeks of fad plastics production.

The most likely gross margin for bad times is 10 weeks of fad item production at $200,000 per week plus 40 weeks of nonfad item production at $20,000 per week for a total of $2.8 million in gross margin. Since good and bad times are evenly split, the single value for gross margin over the twenty-year life of the investment is the average of the two, or $4.85 million. Suppose that for this level of gross margin, fixed operating costs—another figure that remains unchanged for twenty years—is assumed to be $2.8 million per year.

Furthermore, suppose that the plant is estimated to cost $8 million to build and equip. Management of the subsidiary pushing the project admits, under pressure, that there may be a likely cost overrun of 10 percent with the remote possibility that the cost overrun, primarily in the form of unanticipated startup costs, may be as high as 50 percent. Working capital requirements are estimated at $500,000, and $200,000 is required for the purchase of the land. For calculating residual value at the end of a twenty-year projection period, management estimates that working capital, land, plant, and equipment can be liquidated for an after tax value of between $1 and $3 million.

For measuring reward in the conventional sense, that is, calculating the rate of return on a single-value basis, the capital commitment would most probably be

$9.5 million. This includes the anticipated 10 percent cost overrun on constructing the plant for $8.8 million plus $0.7 million for purchasing the land and providing working capital. Taxes would be calculated at a tax rate of 35 percent after providing for an allowance for depreciation of plant and equipment. At the end of the twenty-year projection, the investment would be liquidated for a single discrete value between $1 and $3 million—the logical choice being $2 million. The residual value assumes the sale of all assets, including the land, the recoupment of working capital, and payment of all expenses associated therewith, including any potential taxation on capital gains.

The calculation of reward in terms of the internal rate of return with all figures reduced to discrete single values would be presented to top management in the following format.

New Plastics Plant Proposal

INVESTMENT: $9.5 million of which $8.8 million is depreciable
DEPRECIATION: Twenty-year straight line, 5 percent residual
DEBT LOAD: None
TAX RATE: 35 percent
RESIDUAL
   CASH VALUE: $2 million

In year 0, there is a cash outflow of $9.5 million to purchase the land, build and equip the plant, and provide the working capital requirements. The following is the calculation of cash flow for the next nineteen years.

GROSS MARGIN (REVENUE LESS VARIABLE COSTS):	$4,850,000
FIXED OPERATING COSTS:	2,800,000
NET INCOME BEFORE TAXES:	2,050,000
DEPRECIATION (95 PERCENT OF $8,800,000/TWENTY YEARS):	418,000
TAXABLE INCOME (NET INCOME LESS DEPRECIATION):	1,632,000
TAXES PAYABLE (35 PERCENT OF TAXABLE INCOME):	571,200
NET CASH FLOW (NET INCOME LESS TAXES):	1,478,800

In year 20, the net cash flow is $1,478,800 for one year's operation plus the liquidation of the investment for $2,000,000, or $3,478,800. The internal rate of return is 14.7748 percent. This is the discount factor that reduces the net present value of the total annual cash flow of the investment to zero. Table 3.1 is the discounted cash flow stream for this investment.

Year 0 is the start of the investment analysis with an outflow of $9.5 million representing the capital commitment in the new factory. Its present worth is $9.5 million as it is the zero reference point for a time-sensitive analysis of a rate of return. One year after the outflow of $9.5 million, there is an inflow from operations of $1,478,800. What is it worth? For a discount factor of 14.7748 percent, the present value of $1,478,800 to be realized one year in the future is

Table 3.1
Discounted Cash Flow Stream

YEAR	NET CASH FLOW	DISCOUNT FACTOR	DISCOUNTED CASH FLOW
0	-$9,500,000	1.000000	-$9,500,000
1	1,478,800	1.147748	1,288,436
2	1,478,800	1.317326	1,122,577
3	1,478,800	1.511959	978,069
4	1,478,800	1.735348	852,163
5	1,478,800	1.991743	742,465
6	1,478,800	2.286020	646,888
7	1,478,800	2.623776	563,615
8	1,478,800	3.011435	491,061
9	1,478,800	3.456369	427,848
10	1,478,800	3.967042	372,771
11	1,478,800	4.553166	324,785
12	1,478,800	5.225890	282,976
13	1,478,800	5.998006	246,549
14	1,478,800	6.884202	214,811
15	1,478,800	7.901332	187,158
16	1,478,800	9.068741	163,066
17	1,478,800	10.40863	142,074
18	1,478,800	11.94649	123,785
19	1,478,800	13.71156	107,850
20	3,478,800	15.73742	221,053

$1,288,436. In essence, it is immaterial whether we receive $1,288,436 today, or $1,478,800 one year from now as long as the $1,288,436 can be invested in an investment vehicle of some sort bearing a return of 14.7748 percent. Therefore, the discounted value of $1,478,800 to be received one year from now, that is, its present worth, is $1,288,436.

The discounted value of $1,478,800 to be received two years from now is $1,122,577. This is because $1,122,577 deposited today in an investment vehicle that earns 14.7748 percent will be worth $1,478,800 in two years' time. Therefore, it does not matter if someone receives $1,122,577 today or waits two years to receive $1,478,800 as long as the proceeds can be invested in something earning 14.7748 percent. The factor 1.317326 is the sum of 1 plus the discount factor of 0.147748 raised to the second power to account for the two-year waiting period before the cash is generated from the operation of the plant. This process of discounting the future value of cash flow to obtain its present value continues throughout the projection period. The present or discounted value of $3,478,800 to be received twenty years from now is only $221,053 because this amount, when deposited in something earning 14.7748 percent, will grow to $3,478,800 in twenty years—the miracle of compound interest and the meaning of present value.

The sum of the discounted inflows for years 1 through 20 is $9.5 million. This just balances the outflow of $9.5 million made in year 0. Therefore, the net present value of the entire discounted cash flow stream from beginning to end (years 0 through 20) is zero. This can only happen for one discount factor (in this case, 14.7748 percent). The definition of the internal rate of return (IRR) is the discount rate that reduces the net present value of a cash flow stream to zero. Therefore, the internal rate of return of the investment is 14.7748 percent.

There are two difficulties that have to be faced with the IRR methodology of evaluating projects. One is the presumption that the return on all cash inflows is earning the same rate of return as the IRR. This might be very difficult to achieve for projects that happen to have a high IRR. A more serious difficulty is the possibility of negative cash flows in the latter part of the life of the project. Discount factors in the latter years are much larger than discount factors in the early years of a projection. A small positive cash flow in the early years can easily mask a huge negative cash flow in the latter years of a twenty-year projection. The consequences of discounting negative cash flows in the real world of business are very serious. There is also a difficulty in the interpretation of the meaning of discounting future negative cash flows in the hypothetical world of financial analysis. Both of the issues of having to earn the same rate of return on cash inflows during the projection period and the implications, if not the meaning, of discounting future negative cash flows deserve attention. The latter issue can be avoided by modifying the measure of reward.

Suppose that the cash flow remains the same except that the proceeds are deposited in a conservative fund made up of high grade short-term municipal bonds bearing an after tax return of, say, 6 percent. The fund can be called the project investment fund because it is the repository of all excess cash generated by the project throughout its life. There is no need for the funds to remain uninvested. The proceeds can be invested in anything that possesses a reasonable degree of liquidity. The money in the project investment fund accumulates with the compounding of interest until the end of the twentieth year when there is a full payout of proceeds to the company including the cash residual value of the plastics plant. The measure of reward is modified from measuring the internal rate of return of annual cash flows over a period of twenty years to the internal rate of return for two cash flows separated by twenty years. One is the payment of $9.5 million in making the investment. The other is the liquidation of the project investment fund at the end of the twentieth year. The liquidating value of the project investment fund is calculated in Table 3.2.

The methodology for determining the end-of-year status for the project investment fund is to take the previous year's end-of-year status, increase it by 6 percent, and then add in the present year's cash flow. For instance, the status of the investment fund at the end of year 13 is $27,921,300. Adjusting this by an after tax 6 percent gain in value increases the balance to $29,596,600 (1.06 ×

Table 3.2
Project Investment Fund

YEAR	PROJECT CASH FLOW	INVESTMENT FUND STATUS END OF YEAR	INVESTMENT CASH FLOW
0	-$9,500,000		-$9,500,000
1	$1,478,800	$1,478,800	$0
2	1,478,800	3,045,500	0
3	1,478,800	4,707,000	0
4	1,478,800	6,468,200	0
5	1,478,800	8,335,100	0
6	1,478,800	10,314,000	0
7	1,478,800	12,411,700	0
8	1,478,800	14,635,200	0
9	1,478,800	16,992,100	0
10	1,478,800	19,490,400	0
11	1,478,800	22,138,600	0
12	1,478,800	24,945,800	0
13	1,478,800	27,921,300	0
14	1,478,800	31,075,400	0
15	1,478,800	34,418,700	0
16	1,478,800	37,962,600	0
17	1,478,800	41,719,200	0
18	1,478,800	45,701,100	0
19	1,478,800	49,922,000	0
20	3,478,800	0	$56,396,100

$27,921,300). After adding in year 14 cash flow of $1,478,800, the end-of-year status for year 14 becomes $31,075,400.

The end-of-project payout to the investors or equity owners in year 20 is $56,396,100. This represents the liquidation of the investment fund (end-of-year-19 balance of $49,922,000 × 1.06, or $52,917,300), plus the cash flow from operations in the twentieth year of $1,478,800, plus the liquidation of the business for $2,000,000, for a grand total of $56,396,100. The discount factor that reduces the final value of the project investment fund from $56,396,100 to its initial value of $9,500,000 with a twenty-year interim period between making and liquidating the investment is 9.31 percent. This is the internal rate of return for the single outflow and the single inflow of the investment cash flow projection.

This is considerably less than the original IRR of 14.7748 percent. The difference resides solely in the fact that the cash flow stream is not being reinvested in an investment vehicle earning the same exact internal rate of return of 14.7748 percent. Were each of the individual cash flows reinvested in something that earned 14.7748 percent, then the ending balance would have been $149,493,900, not the indicated $56,396,100. Then the IRR of the investment represented by a single outflow in year 0 of $9.5 million and a single inflow in year 20 of $149.5 million would have been 14.7748 percent, not the 9.31 percent obtained in the modified approach to measuring reward. This is what is meant by the statement that the IRR method of calculating a return on an investment implies, or rather requires, that the individual cash flows be reinvested in an investment medium bearing the same rate of return as the investment itself. For projects with high rates of return as measured by the IRR method, reinvesting at the same rate of return may well be impossible. Even if such could be achieved, such high returns are associated with projects that absorb liquidity, not provide liquidity.

Taking the excess cash flow and depositing it in a project investment fund that can be fairly easily liquidated has an important and vital feature. Negative cash flows can now be accommodated to the degree allowable by the magnitude of the deposits made in the project investment fund. If the volume and price combination for the goods sold, when compared to costs, generates a negative cash flow, then the investment fund can be tapped to the extent necessary to keep the project solvent. This assumes, naturally, that the investment fund possesses sufficient funds to satisfy the negative cash flow. If this is so, then this takes care of the situation for handling negative cash flows. The modified IRR approach provides a mechanism for avoiding the discounting of negative cash flows that is not present in the conventional IRR method of evaluating financial performance. Attention does have to be paid to the situation where negative cash flows during the projection period exceed the amount in the investment fund.

Summing up, the measure of reward to be incorporated in the simulations is a modified IRR approach containing the essential features of the IRR methodology. The difference is that excess funds generated by the project are not assumed to be reinvested at the same rate of return. In reality, this is a rather dubious assumption that cannot always be easily accomplished, particularly for investments with a high IRR. In the modified approach, funds generated by the project are assumed to be deposited in an investment fund that can be used as a source of funds when there is a cash deficit in operations.

As will be seen, it is not necessary for all funds to be deposited in the project investment fund if the fund is of sufficient size to meet a contingency of a shortfall in cash. A fund of a stipulated size established with the intent of providing a source of funds to meet unforeseen contingencies is called an escrow account. It would be better to describe the project investment fund as an escrow account if cash generated by the project in excess of a stipulated amount can be paid out to the equity owners. The exact nature of the investments in the escrow account will be left undefined other than there being a sufficient degree of liquidity to allow for a partial or total liquidation to fund negative cash flows. Assuming that the size of the escrow account is sufficient to cover any negative cash flow, then there is no need to consider the meaning of discounting future negative cash flows. This makes the method of evaluating projects more realistic. Theorists may cringe at this arbitrary decision to modify the IRR method of evaluating projects, but the practical considerations on how to handle times when there are negative cash flows dictate that some action of this sort be taken.

THE MEASURE OF RISK

Every company has a minimum objective with regards to the return on investment because every company is a capital sink. A company consisting of real assets begins life by issuing stock to garner the funds to purchase the assets. The source of cash to finance a new company is the savings of investors or monies paid to, or deposited in, financial institutions such as mutual funds, insurance companies, pension funds, and banks.

A company is a capital sink in the sense that it absorbs capital when it issues stock. The same is true when it issues bonds. A person, or institution, that buys the bonds of an issuing company expects a return on investment in the form of interest and a return of the investment in the form of amortization, or repayment of principal. The same is true for investing in the stock of a company. There must be a return both on and of the investment. The return on and of the investment can be in the form of dividends, repurchase of the stock by the company, or a buyout by another company.

Thus a company owes, so to speak, a rate of return to those who buy its stock. Part of that rate of return is yield—dividend payments divided by the price of the stock—and the potential for price appreciation. But price appreciation, or buyout of a company, presumes a flow of dividends to justify the price of a share of stock or the purchase value of a company. Therefore, the price of a share of stock, in theory—and perhaps strictly in theory—is the investment community's perception of the aggregate discounted value of future dividend payouts.

Every company has a minimum hurdle rate that an investment must exceed in order for a firm to remain in business. This hurdle rate varies from one company to another depending on the respective roles of equity and debt in its capital structure and the cost of capital associated with equity and debt. The hurdle rate can be calculated on a before or after tax basis, which is not as simple as it may seem because a dividend on a common share of stock is paid with after tax dollars while interest on debt is paid with before tax dollars. This is a consequence of interest on debt being a tax deductible expense whereas dividends are not.

The hurdle rate can be illustrated as follows. Suppose that an individual's only source of capital is borrowing on a line of credit from a bank that charges 15 percent in annual interest. What is the minimum hurdle rate for this individual if he desires to lend money to other individuals? If he lends $1,000 to someone at 10 percent interest, he will receive $100 in interest income while making $150 in interest payments to the bank—not really a smart move. His minimum hurdle rate has to be 15 percent, which is his cost of capital. If he charges 15 percent when he lends money out to another individual, the return on his investment—

the interest income from a loan to another person—is equal to his cost of capital—the interest payable on his line of credit. Therefore, to operate this business profitably, he must beat the hurdle rate of 15 percent. This same principle holds for a corporation except that it is more of a challenge to establish the minimum hurdle rate given the relative complexity of selecting an appropriate rate of return on equity.

Whenever an investment does not exceed the minimum hurdle rate, the company is in the same position as an individual who lends out money at 10 percent while paying 15 percent to a bank as the source of funds. Although not something to be eagerly sought, earning an undesirable rate of return does not have to be fatal. A person who lends out $1,000 at 10 percent interest while paying 15 percent interest for the funds may feel foolish about the transaction, but it is not going to send him to the poor house. A company that invests $100 million in a project that falls short of the hurdle rate may not be so lucky.

Therefore, there should be two measures of risk. One is the conventional view of a less than desired rate of return on investment. The other is negative cash flows that overwhelm the escrow account—negative cash flow drains of such a magnitude that the escrow account is emptied of all assets and there is still a shortfall in cash to meet expenses. This is called insolvency. This is a real problem for a corporation, or an individual for that matter, which, if not resolved, could lead to liquidation. Naturally, small shortages of funds are manageable while large shortages may not be manageable. Whether these deficits are manageable is a judgment call. The computer is excellent in performing calculations and poor in making judgment calls. Therefore, the objective in measuring risk is to identify the existence, magnitude, and frequency of times when the escrow account is exhausted of funds. The evaluation of the potential consequences of this measure of risk will be left to humans.

A SIMULATION MODEL

The purpose of running a simulation of the proposal for a new plastic goods factory is to obtain a measure of risk and reward. The simulation will, in effect, be pulling numbers out of a hat to determine the number of weeks of fad plastic production, the level of gross margin during this period of time, and the level of gross margin during the rest of the year when nonfad production keeps the factory busy. The risk inherent in this particular project is the wide variance in the annual gross margin in relation to fixed operating costs. The risk can be better appreciated by bracketing the extremes in annual gross margin for both good and bad times.

The best annual gross margin during the good times is 40 weeks with a weekly gross margin of $400,000, plus ten weeks with a weekly gross margin of $50,000, for an incredible total of $16,500,000. The worst during the good times is no weeks of fad production, which means that there are fifty weeks of nonfad plastic goods production. The annual gross revenue for the lowest weekly gross margin for nonfad plastic goods production is $10,000 per week for fifty weeks, or $500,000. This is far less than what is needed to satisfy fixed operating costs.

During the bad times in the business, the best that can be achieved is fifteen weeks of fad production at $300,000 per week, or $4,500,000, plus thirty-five weeks at $30,000 per week, or $1,050,000, for a total of $5,550,000. At rock bottom is no fad production, and, therefore, fifty weeks at $5,000 per week of nonfad production, or $250,000. The following table brackets the extremes of gross margin for any single year in a simulation. There is a relatively large degree of variance in gross margin between the best and the worst of the good and bad times in the plastic goods business.

Gross Annual Margin

	GOOD TIMES	BAD TIMES
Best performance	$16,500,000	$5,550,000
Worst performance	500,000	250,000

The financial risk of this project is not so much the variance of gross margin, but the relationship between the variance of gross margin and fixed costs. Management has given the following assessment of fixed costs:

ANNUAL RANGE, GROSS MARGIN	ANNUAL RANGE, FIXED COSTS
< $5 MM	$2−3 MM
> $5 MM	$3−4 MM

In considering the nature of fixed costs in relation to the gross margin when there is little in the fad side of the plastic goods business to keep the factory busy, we must conclude that there is a good chance that this project will experience negative cash flows.

What can be said about the probability that the factory will experience any single gross margin for twenty consecutive years? To answer this, we must first realize that the probability of the most likely figure occurring in a single year is actually quite small given the possible range, or variance, of gross margin. Therefore, twenty consecutive years with the same gross margin, no matter how likely for one particular year, is an extremely remote event. We would have a much better chance betting on a lottery ticket and winning than to see twenty years of the most likely gross margin, and this is assuming that there is virtually no chance of winning with the lottery ticket. To perform a "What If" scenario with a gross margin estimate remaining unchanged throughout the life of the project misses the point of the extreme unlikeliness of having twenty consecutive years with the same gross margin.

The cost of the plant is $8 million. There is a likely cost overrun of 10 percent with an outside chance of being as high as 50 percent. Suppose that in a simulation run, we reach into a bag of ping-pong balls containing one hundred balls numbered from 0 to 50 with a tendency for the ping-pong balls to have a number around 10. Suppose that the selected number is 25. The cost of the plant is then $10 million (125 percent of $8 million). Annual depreciation is 95 percent of $10 million divided by 20 years, or $475,000 per year. Working capital of $500,000 and land cost of $200,000 will remain unchanged for all simulations. Therefore, the capital commitment, under these circumstances, is $10,700,000.

Good and bad times in the plastic goods business seem to run in spurts of two to five years. The simulation, contained in the appendix, starts, figuratively, by throwing one of a pair of dice. If an odd number appears, that signifies the start of good times; if even, the start of bad times. How long does either last? Management has already given its assessment of two to five years. That is a total of four possibilities. One die can still do the trick. Throw it again. If the number 1 or 6 appears, throw the die again. If the numbers 2 through 5 appear, that is how long the good or bad times last.

In addition for a simulator on cost overruns, six simulators are constructed that are merely computer renditions of six bags of ping-pong balls or six roulette wheels where the balls or the slots are numbered according to the least and most likely assessments provided by management. One simulator will be set up for the spread on the number of weeks of fad production, one for the spread on the weekly gross margin during fad plastic goods production, and one for the spread on the gross margin during nonfad plastic goods production. A simulator does not have to be constructed for the number of weeks for nonfad plastic goods production because nonfad production is 50 weeks less the weeks of production of fad plastic goods. Three of these simulators are constructed for good times and three for bad times for a total of six simulators.

All of these simulators are computer renditions of numbering one hundred ping-pong balls and placing them in a bag, or numbering one hundred slots on a roulette wheel, to simulate management's assessments of the key variables. The simulation program is instructed to reach into the bag, pull out a ping-pong ball, note the number on it, and place the ball back in the bag. Or equivalently, to give the roulette wheel a spin and announce the winning number.

The annual gross margin is calculated by taking the number of weeks of fad plastic goods production and multiplying it by the weekly gross margin that applies to fad plastic goods production. The remaining weeks of the year are then multiplied by the weekly gross margin applicable for the nonfad plastic goods. Then the two are added to obtain the annual gross margin, the extremes of which have already been calculated. The next step is to obtain the fixed operating costs by examining whether the gross margin is above or below $5 million. If the gross margin is below $5 million, the fixed operating costs are obtained by selecting any figure between $2 and $3 million. If the gross margin is above $5 million, the simulation program is instructed to pick any number between $3 and $4 million. This process can be repeated twenty times for the twenty-year life of the project. In the twentieth year, a random number between $1 and $3 million is selected to represent the after-tax liquidation value of the investment and is added to the cash flow from operations.

It should be noted that financial analysis can be done on a before or after tax basis. Some have maintained that before tax analysis is appropriate, particularly during times when it is possible to enter into leveraged transactions with accelerated depreciation that could postpone tax liabilities for long periods of time, if not indefinitely.

Recent tax legislation, however, encourages the current payment of taxes by wiping off the books such tax saving and deferring tactics as the investment tax credit and accelerated depreciation. This favors those who contend that taxes represent a cost of doing business and should be treated as a current expense. The methodology illustrated here pays taxes on a current basis, assuming no tax loss carryforwards from previous years, because the payment of taxes during the good times reduces the cushion of cash for getting through the bad times. This increases the risk of the project becoming insolvent through excessive cash deficits in the operation of the company. There are a number of ways to treat taxes, any one of which can be modeled to satisfy the desires of the decision makers.

Table 3.3 is a computer-generated simulation following the previously described procedure. For this particular run, the total investment was $9,511,203,

Table 3.3
Derivation of Tax Liabilities

YEAR	ANNUAL GROSS MARGIN	ANNUAL FIXED OPERATING COSTS	TAX DEPREC	TAXABLE INCOME	TAX LOSS CARRY FORWARD	TAX PAYABLE
1	$7,988	$3,035	$419	$4,535	$ 0	$1,587
2	3,941	2,794	419	728	0	255
3	2,572	2,716	419	-562	562	0
4	1,660	2,339	419	-1,097	1,659	0
5	1,043	2,182	419	-1,557	3,216	0
6	1,330	2,769	419	-1,857	5,074	0
7	2,425	2,794	419	-787	5,861	0
8	6,572	3,641	419	2,512	3,349	0
9	5,592	3,464	419	1,709	1,640	0
10	5,935	3,062	419	814	0	285
11	7,508	3,921	419	3,169	0	1,109
12	3,356	2,787	419	150	0	53
13	8,355	3,370	419	4,566	0	1,598
14	2,941	2,511	419	12	0	4
15	1,618	2,152	419	-952	952	0
16	2,711	2,742	419	-449	1,401	0
17	2,649	2,828	419	-598	1,999	0
18	8,696	3,102	419	3,176	0	1,112
19	6,168	3,037	419	2,713	0	949
20	7,984	3,233	419	4,333	0	1,517

including $700,000 in working capital and land. Netting out $700,000 leaves $8,811,203 as the depreciable asset. At the start of the simulation, a cost overrun factor of slightly over 10 percent was randomly selected from a bag of cost overrun ping-pong balls. This was then applied against the base cost of $8 million. The cost of the factory, when depreciated over twenty years with a 5 percent depreciable residual value, has an annual depreciation charge of $418,532 (95% × $8,811,203/20 years).

If gross margin is less than fixed costs and depreciation, the before tax income will have a negative value. A negative taxable income is not considered a tax credit. Any negative taxable income is accumulated as a tax loss carryforward to shield future tax liabilities. Once the tax loss carryforward is exhausted, any further tax liabilities are paid as a current expense. Some rounding errors are present as all figures are expressed to the nearest thousand of dollars.

In the first two years, taxes are payable on 35 percent of before tax income, which is gross margin less fixed costs less depreciation. In the third year, there is a negative before tax income that accrues to a tax loss carryforward account with no resulting tax liabilities. In the fourth year, the negative before tax is added, or accrued, to the tax loss carryforward account. This continues until year 8, when the before tax income of $2,512,000 is applied against the tax loss carryforward account of $5,861,000, reducing the tax loss carryforward to $3,349,000 with no resulting tax liabilities. In the ninth year, the before tax income of $1,709,000 is applied against the tax loss carryforward account reducing it further to $1,640,000. In the tenth year, the gross margin less fixed costs and depreciation is $2,454,000. The balance in the tax loss carryforward account reduces the before tax income to $814,000, resulting in a tax liability of $285,000 (35% × $814,000).

Table 3.4 shows the net cash flow and the disposition of the cash flow to the escrow account and to the equity owners. The net cash flow is gross margin less fixed operating costs and taxes. In the twentieth year, the after tax residual value of $1,135,543 is added to the cash flow representing the liquidation of the investment. The annual cash flow accrues in an escrow account. If the accumulated cash in the escrow account is more than the indicated maximum balance, the excess proceeds are paid out to the equity owners. Funds in the escrow account earn an after tax rate of return of 6 percent.

The description of the mechanics of Table 3.4 is appropriate before we discuss its implications. Equity owners receive a payout only when the escrow account is fully funded. Any monies in excess of the maximum balance in the escrow account are paid to the equity owners. For the case where the maximum balance in the escrow account is zero, representing, in essence, no escrow account, all positive cash flows are paid directly to investors. A negative cash flow cannot flow to the investors; a negative cash flow means that there is an inability to pay the bills. This negative amount accrues in the escrow account where it is presumed that someone, somewhere, somehow is funding the cash shortfall.

In the third year, there is a shortfall of $144,000 that accrues in the escrow

Table 3.4
Disposition of Cash Flow

YEAR	NET CASH FLOW	MAXIMUM BALANCE IN ESCROW ACCOUNT			
		$0 MILLION		$3 MILLION	
		ESCROW ACCOUNT BALANCE	PAYOUT TO EQUITY OWNERS	ESCROW ACCOUNT BALANCE	PAYOUT TO EQUITY OWNERS
1	$3,366	$ 0	$3,366	$3,000	$ 366
2	892	0	892	3,000	1,072
3	-144	-144	0	3,000	36
4	-678	-830	0	2,502	0
5	-1,139	-2,019	0	1,513	0
6	-1,439	-3,580	0	165	0
7	-368	-4,163	0	-194	0
8	2,930	-1,482	0	2,725	0
9	2,127	0	556	3,000	2,015
10	2,588	0	2,588	3,000	2,768
11	2,478	0	2,478	3,000	2,658
12	516	0	516	3,000	696
13	3,387	0	3,387	3,000	3,567
14	426	0	426	3,000	606
15	-534	-534	0	2,646	0
16	-31	-564	0	2,774	0
17	-179	-744	0	2,762	0
18	4,482	0	3,622	3,000	4,410
19	2,182	0	2,182	3,000	2,362
20	4,370	0	4,370	0	7,550

account. It is assumed that a "rich uncle" is funding the shortfall and desires to be repaid only when there is a net inflow of cash. The next year is another shortfall of $678,000. Although the "rich uncle" is generous in providing the funds, he does demand a return on the money he advances to keep the firm from becoming insolvent. The program is set up for his charge to be an after tax return of 6 percent. Hence, the $144,000 from the previous year becomes $152,000, which, with the additional shortfall of $678,000, increases the deficit in the escrow account to $830,000. Negative cash flows continue until the seventh year when the accumulated shortfall in funds, plus accrued interest, is $4,163,000.

There is an inflow of funds in the eighth year of $2,930,000. The deficit in the escrow account has increased by 6 percent to $4,413,000, which net of the inflow, becomes $1,482,000 (rounding error). This deficit grows to $1,571,000 in the ninth year when there is a cash inflow to $2,127,000. This wipes out the deficit in the escrow account; the "rich uncle" is repaid in full, leaving $556,000 for the equity owners.

For the case where a maximum balance of $3 million is maintained in the escrow account, money flows into the escrow account until the balance reaches $3 million, and any excess is paid out to the equity owners. Of the initial cash generation of $3,366,000, $3,000,000 is distributed to the escrow account and the remainder is paid out to the equity owners. In the second year, the escrow account earns an after tax return of 6 percent, or $180,000, which is paid out to the investors along with the cash generation of $892,000 for a total of $1,072,000. In the third year, the escrow account earns $180,000 and the cash flow is a negative $144,000, so the investors receive the difference of $36,000 after paying the outstanding bills.

In the fourth year, the deficit in operations of $678,000 is funded from the escrow account. The escrow account earned $180,000 on the previous year's balance, paid $678,000 to the company to keep it solvent, and ended up with an end-of-year balance of $2,502,000. Nothing was paid to the equity owners because the escrow account is below the maximum limit of $3 million. The next year's earnings of the escrow account is 6 percent of $2,502,000, or $150,000. This increases the escrow account to $2,652,000; $1,139,000 is then drawn down to fund the cash deficit. This leaves $1,513,000 in the escrow account at the end of the fifth year.

By the end of the sixth year, there is only $165,000 in the escrow account. This increases to $175,000 in the seventh year when there is a net deficit in operational cash flow of $368,000. This reduces the escrow account to a negative $194,000, (neglecting the rounding error), which is funded by a "rich uncle," who charges 6 percent for his services. The money owed to the "rich uncle" is $206,000 by the end of the eighth year when there is a cash inflow of $2,930,000. $206,000 is paid to the "rich uncle" and $2,725,000 (again, rounding) is placed into the escrow account. The equity owners receive nothing because the escrow account has not yet been replenished to its maximum extent. This is accomplished in the ninth year when the escrow account earns 6 percent, growing to $2,889,000. The after tax cash flow of the company is $2,127,000, of which $111,000 is placed into the escrow account to bring it up to $3 million and the remainder, $2,016,000 (again, rounding), is paid out to the equity owners. In the twentieth year, the equity owners receive any positive balance in the escrow account.

A negative balance in the escrow account means that it is necessary for an unknown source of funds to be advanced to avert a liquidity crisis. A negative balance occurs when the escrow account has been exhausted of funds and there still remains a cash shortfall to pay the bills. Insolvency may, or may not, lead to bankruptcy, but that is a judgment call, not the result of a quantitative calculation.

The appropriate capital charge associated with a negative balance in the escrow account and the earnings rate when there is a positive balance in the escrow account can be whatever is desired by the decision makers. The 6 percent charge and earnings rate were arbitrarily selected to describe the nature of the system. In reality, the charge should be higher than the earnings rate. Regardless of the rates selected, the importance of the escrow account is the presence of a negative balance. A negative balance indicates the amount of money that has to be injected into the project to keep it financially afloat. Its function is to measure how far the project can sink into the quagmire of insolvency. The magnitude of the accumulated cash deficits and their frequency over the life of the project are certainly measures of risk.

The risk of bankruptcy is always present when there is a negative balance in the escrow account. The risk of bankruptcy is greater, however, when there is a negative balance in the escrow account and a negative cash flow from operations. These are the two conditions that can exhaust the patience of the most patient creditor. This is when the creditors are most apt to pull the plug on a company. The risk of bankruptcy is considerably lessened when a company is generating a positive cash flow, even though the company is still buried upside down in a fiscal hole. Under these conditions, the company is making financial progress to upright itself and creditors are much more patient when it appears that it is only a matter of time before they receive one hundred cents on every dollar owed plus accrued interest.

For the particular simulation run under scrutiny, the existence of the escrow account with a maximum balance of $3 million considerably lessened the risk of the company being insolvent.

	Maximum Balance in Escrow Account	
	$0 MILLION	$3 MILLION
Number of years of a negative cash flow and a negative balance in escrow account	8	1
Maximum shortfall	$4,163,000	$194,000
Internal rate of return (IRR)	9.0%	8.2%

There was both a negative cash flow and a negative balance in the escrow account in eight years (years 3, 4, 5, 6, 7, 15, 16, 17) of the twenty-year simulation for the situation where there was, in effect, no escrow account. With an escrow account of $3 million whereby only proceeds above $3 million are paid out to the equity owners, such a condition occurred only once (year 7). Moreover, the magnitude of the maximum degree of insolvency fell from $4.1 million to $0.2 million with the presence of an escrow account. A decision by management to maintain an escrow account of $3 million was, for this simulation, more than adequate to meet shortfalls in revenues with respect to costs. The earnings of the escrow account also contributed to covering shortfalls. The internal rate of return, which is calculated on monies actually paid out to the investors, is less with an escrow account with a maximum limit of $3 million because monies deposited in the account earn only 6 percent, which is less than the presumed higher IRR rate on the monies paid out to the equity owners.

We should not be fooled by the higher IRR rate associated with full payout to the equity owners (zero maximum balance in the escrow account). The sacrifice in IRR in having an escrow account with a maximum limit of $3 million kept the firm solvent for all but one year and here the magnitude of the insolvency was relatively small. Without an escrow account, an insolvency of the order of $4 million would most probably have induced a creditor to pull the plug on this company. Once this happens, the higher IRR rate becomes something less than what is indicated.

Summing up, the conventional IRR method does not handle negative cash flows other than in discounting them along with positive cash flows. Nor is there any measure of insolvency. A hemorrhaging of cash deserves more attention than simply being discounted.

The aforementioned description of the simulation is incorporated in the program contained in the appendix to this chapter. The simulation was run with two maximum amounts in the escrow account. One was a maximum amount of zero, which meant that there was no escrow account. All monies in excess of $0 were paid to the equity owners. The other maximum amount in the escrow account was $3 million. No monies could be passed on to the equity owners unless the escrow account was first fully funded at $3 million. Any cash flow in excess of the fully funded escrow account, including the earnings of the escrow account, was passed on to the equity owners.

The simulation in the appendix performed the previously described simulation two thousand times with no escrow account (maximum zero balance) and two thousand times with a maximum of a $3 million balance in the escrow account. Each of these two thousand runs represented a single twenty-year projection of the financial performance of the plastics factory.

	Maximum Balance in Escrow Account	
	$0 MILLION	**$3 MILLION**
Number simulations with at least one year of a negative cash flow and a negative balance in escrow account	1,996	728
Percent of 2,000 simulations	99.8%	36.4%

With no escrow account, the plastics factory is virtually certain to experience at least one year of insolvency. By establishing an escrow account of $3 million from the earnings of the company, the chance of experiencing insolvency at any time during the twenty-year life of the project falls from 99.8 percent to 36.4 percent. Table 3.5 indicates the number of years in each twenty-year simulation when there is both a negative cash flow and a negative balance in the escrow account. Insolvent years are years of both a negative cash flow and a negative balance in the escrow account. The associated cumulative probability provides an indication of how many insolvent years are being experienced over the twenty-year simulated life of the project. The cumulative probability applies only for those simulations

Table 3.5
Probability Distribution of Number of Insolvent Years

NUMBER INSOLVENT YEARS	MAXIMUM BALANCE IN ESCROW ACCOUNT			
	$0 MILLION		$3 MILLION	
	NUMBER OCCURRENCES	CUMULATIVE PROBABILITY	NUMBER OCCURRENCES	CUMULATIVE PROBABILITY
1	44	2.2%	397	54.5%
2	156	10.0	202	82.3
3	320	26.0	86	94.1
4	441	48.1	31	98.4
5	432	69.8	8	99.5
6	306	85.1	2	99.7
7	190	94.6	1	99.9
8	75	98.4	1	100.0
9	24	99.6		
10	6	99.9		
11	2	100.0		
TOTAL	1996		728	
EXPECTED NUMBER INSOLVENT YEARS	4.7		1.7	

that experienced an instance of insolvency as measured by both a negative cash flow and a negative balance in the escrow account (see Table 3.5).

For the case of a $3 million maximum balance in the escrow account, there were 728 occurrences of both a negative cash flow and a negative balance in the escrow account in two thousand simulations. That meant that there was a 36.4 percent chance of being insolvent at least one time during the twenty-year life of the project. For those times when insolvency actually occurred, the expected number of insolvent years was 1.7 years over the twenty-year life of the project.

The cumulative probability distribution provides a little more detail. There is a 55 percent chance that there will be just one insolvent year in the twenty-year life of the project. There is an 82 percent chance that the number of years of insolvency will be two or less; a 94 percent chance that it will be three or less; and a 98 percent chance that the number of insolvent years will be four or less. The summation of the multiplication of the discrete probability (not shown) for each associated number of insolvent years provides the expected value of 1.7 insolvent years.

The reason for the preponderance of single and double year occurrences of insolvency is that there is no escrow fund at the time of startup of the plastics plant. The escrow account accrues funds from the earnings of the firm. If the first years are years of negative cash flows, then these would be instances of insolvency. Funding the escrow account as part of the capital commitment in the plant will be examined shortly.

For the case of no escrow account, there is a 99.8 percent chance that there will be at least one year of negative cash flow and a negative balance in the escrow account. During these instances where such a condition exists, there is only a 2 percent chance that it will occur only once in twenty years. There is only a 10 percent chance that it will occur twice or less in twenty years; a 26 percent chance that it will occur thrice or less; and so forth. The expected number of years of insolvency where the risk of bankruptcy is real is 4.7 years out of a twenty-year project. How real the risk of bankruptcy is depends on the magnitude of the insolvency. The following is the maximum magnitude of insolvency for each simulation where there was an instance of insolvency.

	Maximum Balance in Escrow Account	
	$0 MILLION	**$3 MILLION**
Maximum Degree of Insolvency in Millions	**Cumulative Probability**	**Cumulative Probability**
$0.0	0.0%	0.0%
0.5	5.0	34.0
1.0	20.3	59.1
1.5	44.7	78.0
2.0	65.5	89.1
2.5	79.4	94.3
3.0	87.9	96.9
3.5	93.0	98.1
4.0	96.9	99.1
4.5	98.5	99.6
5.0	99.3	99.9
5.5	99.7	99.9
6.0	99.9	100.0
6.5	100.0	

Suppose that management, in considering this proposal, feels that a $1 million deficit in the escrow account is probably sufficient for someone to pull the plug on the company by insisting on payment for an outstanding bill that cannot be paid. If there is no escrow account, then the chance of the maximum degree of insolvency being less than $1 million is only 20 percent. Alternatively, there is an 80 percent chance that the maximum degree of insolvency will be above $1 million. Since the risk of insolvency to some degree is 99.8 percent, and with an 80 percent chance of the maximum magnitude of that insolvency being in excess of $1 million, then risk of bankruptcy is 99.8% × 80%, or 80 percent. Proceeding with this project has a risk of bankruptcy of four chances out of five if there is no provision for an escrow account.

If an escrow account of a maximum amount of $3 million to be funded from the earnings of the company is added to the picture, there is a 60 percent chance that the maximum magnitude of insolvency will be less than $1 million. Alternatively, that means that there is a 40 percent chance that it will exceed $1 million. With an escrow account of $3 million, however, there is a 36.2 percent chance of insolvency. Now the risk of bankruptcy is 36.2% × 40%, or about 14 percent, or one chance in seven.

The remaining distribution to be examined is the internal rate of return.

| | Maximum Balance in Escrow Account | |
| | $0 MILLION | $3 MILLION |
Internal Rate of Return	Cumulative Probability	Cumulative Probability
0%	0.1%	0.0%
5	3.1	2.4
10	32.5	42.0
15	75.1	86.6
20	92.5	98.0
25	98.4	99.9
30	99.5	100.0
35	99.9	
Expected return	12.0%	10.6%

The calculated IRR is on an after tax basis. Suppose that the company has a minimum after tax hurdle rate of 10 percent. The chance that the IRR of the project may not satisfy a minimum hurdle rate of 10 percent is about 33 percent for the case of no escrow account and 42 percent for the case of a $3 million escrow account. The lower rates of return in general compared to the initial single-value assessment of nearly 15 percent are caused by a higher capital commitment. The simulation permits cost overruns up to 50 percent whereas the single-value assessment of IRR was performed with the most likely cost overrun of 10 percent. The lower expected IRR associated with the $3 million escrow account is a result of limiting the earnings of money in the escrow account to ensure proper liquidity for meeting operating cash deficits.

One problem with having the escrow account funded by earnings is that negative cash flows at the start of the project cause immediate instances of insolvency. Positive cash flows are necessary during the startup years to fund the escrow account from earnings before the escrow account can compensate for deficits in operations. A solution to this is to fund the escrow account as part of the capital expenditure of the new plant. The initial funding of the escrow account with $3 million can be considered part of the nondepreciable portion of the capital commitment. The program in the appendix was amended to evaluate this course of action.

There was a significant reduction in the total number of instances of insolvency from 728 to 96 in the 2,000 simulations run on the basis of the upfront funding of the escrow account. The risk of insolvency fell from 36.2 to 4.8 percent (96/2,000) with an upfront funded escrow account. The expected number of insolvent years for those times when there were instances of insolvency fell from 1.7 to 1.3.

NUMBER OF INSOLVENT YEARS	NUMBER OF OCCURRENCES	CUMULATIVE PROBABILITY
1	72	75.0%
2	20	95.8
3	4	100.0
Total	96	

The maximum amount of insolvency was also reduced by funding the escrow account upfront rather than through accumulated earnings.

MAXIMUM DEGREE OF INSOLVENCY (IN MILLIONS)	CUMULATIVE PROBABILITY
$0.0	0.0%
0.5	61.3
1.0	81.7
1.5	93.5
2.0	93.5
2.5	100.0

The expected maximum degree of insolvency is $529,000. The chance that it will be below $1 million is 81.7 percent. Therefore, the risk of the maximum degree of insolvency being above $1 million, the demarcation point for the creditors possibly taking adverse action such as pulling the plug, is 18.3 percent. Hence, the real risk of bankruptcy is 4.8 percent that an instance of insolvency occurs multiplied by the 18.3 percent chance that the degree of insolvency is above $1 million, or about 0.9 percent (4.8% × 18.3%). Hence funding the escrow account from capital funds rather than from earnings reduces the risk of bankruptcy from one chance in seven to one chance in a hundred.

Finally, another diminution in the IRR is caused by increasing the capital investment by $3 million to fund the escrow account.

INTERNAL RATE OF RETURN	CUMULATIVE PROBABILITY
0%	0.0
5	5.2
10	58.7
15	92.7
20	99.1
25	99.9

The expected internal rate of return is 10.3 percent for upfront funding of the escrow account versus 10.6 percent for funding the escrow account from earnings. The diminution is not that significant because positive earnings in the first year flow right back to the investors since the escrow account begins life, so to speak, fully funded. However, there is now nearly a 60 percent chance that the internal rate of return of the project will not satisfy the corporate goal of 10 percent.

ALTERNATIVES

Four alternatives have been examined. The conventional view has no allowance for risk. Everything is on a most likely schedule. There is no appreciation for risk other than attempting a few "What If" scenarios to examine cases where production is something other than the most likely case. Even here, one wonders what to do about the results of "What If" scenario analysis besides noting each one individually and finding out that all may not go well with this project if the scenario deviates somewhat from the most likely course.

The second alternative is simulating the range of possibilities as provided from management assessments with a payout of all positive cash proceeds to the equity owners (zero maximum balance in the escrow account). Presumably this money is to be invested in other long-term projects bearing the same rate of return. Under these circumstances, the risk of insolvency of some degree is virtually certain, with an 80 percent probability of insolvency being in excess of $1 million, the demarcation line for a real possibility of bankruptcy. The IRR is lower primarily because the former IRR of 14.77 percent is calculated on the basis of a 10 percent cost overrun. In the simulation, the most likely cost overrun was 10 percent, with a possibility of being as high as 50 percent. This, in effect, increased the capital investment and lowered the rate of return. In addition, positive cash flows were used to repay the accumulated deficits in the escrow account before being passed on to the equity owners. Nevertheless, there was over a 30 percent chance that the corporate hurdle rate of 10 percent would not be satisfied.

The third alternative is an escrow account where the equity owners are restricted to receiving payouts from operations to those times when there is at least $3 million in the escrow account. The indicated IRR is less because funds in the escrow account earn less than the presumed rate of return for money handed over to the equity owners. Yet the diminution in return is miniscule compared to the diminution in the risk of bankruptcy which falls from four chances in five to one chance in seven.

Higher escrow accounts could be evaluated, but considering the probability of a negative cash flow occurring during the startup years, a wiser course of action is the initial funding of the escrow account as part of the capital commitment to the project. If there are no deficits during the startup years of a project, then all funds generated by the project, plus the earnings of the escrow account, pass on to the equity owners. The reduced IRR of upfront funding of the escrow account is caused primarily by the larger capital commitment. Its diminution from the IRR associated with the escrow account being funded by earnings is relatively minor because the upfront funding of the escrow account can be quickly refunded, so to speak, to the equity owners when there are positive cash flows during the startup phase of the project.

Upfront funding of the escrow account reduces the risk of bankruptcy to something on the order of one chance in a hundred. With upfront funding of the escrow account, deficits generated in the early years of the project's life can be funded. This significantly diminishes the risk of insolvency, but the cost is an increase from 40 to 60 percent in the probability that the minimum hurdle rate of the company will not be satisfied.

Whether management will find any of these alternatives helpful in deciding whether to proceed with a project can only be answered by management. Management might be upset with the fact that risks are expressed in terms of probabilities. Someone is bound to ask: "But what will the project actually earn?" Or "What will actually happen?"

That is the entire problem. If we know what is going to happen, there is no point in going through this exercise because there is no risk. Risk is possible only when the outcome is uncertain. If we know what will happen, then the outcome is certain and there is no need to get involved in financial risk management. The point is that anything can happen in investing in the proposed plastics goods plant. And if that "anything" happens to lie within the assessments that management has settled on as reasonable, then the return on investment can vary from 0 to 30 percent or more. The chances of bankruptcy depend on the selected maximum balance in the escrow account and its source of funding.

At this point, we have a tool for measuring risk that can be easily adapted to evaluate alternatives such as various sized escrow accounts and ways of funding such accounts. We have the results of such simulations and ways to evaluate the results. However, management has something even more valuable. Through the use of the escrow account, management can control the degree of risk. Adding to the escrow account reduces both the degree of risk and reward. Suppose that management is considering two projects and there are capital funds for only one project. Both can be evaluated for risk and reward, but they cannot be compared to reach a decision on which to select because the nature of the risk is different for each project. By adjusting the initial funding of an escrow account, however, the risk of bankruptcy can be equated with some corporate objective. Suppose the corporate objective in accepting a degree of risk of bankruptcy is 1 percent. The corporate objective should not be 0 percent because the risk of bankruptcy can never be totally eliminated. Once the risk of both projects have been equated with some corporate objective, such as 1 percent, then the reward of the two can be compared to see which is higher. All other things being equal, the project with the higher expected reward should be selected as the one to be funded since the risk of both projects is the same.

The ranking of projects is usually in terms of reward with little regard to risk. The use of simulation and the adjustment of the escrow account permit projects to be ranked by reward for a given level of risk. This should place managers in a better position to select those projects that should be funded and those that should be shelved. A general purpose simulation program could be written containing the principles described here. Management would enter assessments of the most likely values, and the limits on the range of values, for the key variables along with a maximum negative balance in the escrow account to separate insolvency from bankruptcy. The program would determine an initially funded escrow account that satisfies the corporate objective on risk. The funding of the escrow account becomes part of the capital commitment of the project. Projects can then be ranked by reward for the given specification of risk.

Is management better off having this additional information when making decisions on which projects to fund? Only management can answer this.

APPENDIX

The program in this appendix was used to derive the financial risk profile for the proposed plastics goods factory. It is a special purpose program designed for this application. A general purpose program would contain the essential elements of this program.

SIMONE was run to generate the cost overrun distribution and was renamed OVER. SIMONE was then run six times to generate the various distributions associated with good and bad times in the plastics business as described in the chapter. These simulators are fed into the program in statements 40 to 170. The arrays for weeks of fad plastic production and weekly gross income for fad and nonfad plastic production are two row arrays, where the first row is applicable to the good times and the second row is applicable to the bad times. Statements 180 to 200 provide a 50–50 opportunity for the plastics plant to start off with good times or bad. This is indicated by assigning a value of 1 or 2 to the Z variable. This determines which row of the aforementioned arrays is to be referenced. Statement 210 assigns a value between 2 and 5 to the variable H that determines how long the good or bad times will last. Variable H1 is the counter keeping track of the length of good and bad times during the simulation run.

The two thousand simulations start in statement 220 with the selection in statement 230 of the cost overrun, the determination of annual depreciation, and the capitalized cost for each individual simulation. The variable U in statement 240 is the maximum balance in the escrow account. The twenty-year cash flow projection for each simulation starts in statement 250, with the duration of the successive good and bad times being determined in statements 260 to 300. Annual gross margin is determined in statements 310 to 320 by multiplying the weeks of fad and nonfad plastic production by the respective weekly gross margins and summing the two. Fixed operating costs are established in statements 330 to 350. Before tax income is calculated in statement 360, and statements 370 to 430 handle whether taxes are payable or not and the accruing of tax losses.

The net cash flow is calculated in statement 440 with provision for adjustment during the twentieth year for the project's residual value (statement 450) and the liquidation of the escrow account (statements 520–540). The interplay between the escrow account and the payout to equity investors is performed in statements 460 to 540. Statements 470 and 480 permit different rates to be applied against the escrow account, depending if its balance is positive or negative. Statements 570 to 620 permit screen printout of the twenty-year projection by eliminating GOTO 630 in statement 560.

The number of years of insolvency in each simulation run and the maximum extent of the insolvency are calculated and stored internally in statements 630 to 690. The internal rate of return is derived in statements 700 to 890 to the nearest whole percent and stored internally in statement 910. Results of single simulations are printed on the screen in statement 900, whereas the aggregate results of all the simulations are stored externally in the indicated files in statements 920 to 1100.

The files were fed into a LOTUS spreadsheet from which the data was summarized as indicated in the chapter. The upfront funding of the escrow account was accomplished by amending statement 240 to read:

$$240 \ A=0:P=3000:U=3000:C=C+P$$

Note that the initial funding of the escrow account can be varied by changing the value of P. If P is assigned a value of 1000 ($1 million), for instance, then the escrow account would be initially funded with $1 million from capital funds and would then increase to $3 million as allowed by company generated earnings before there would be any payout to equity owners.

```
10 REM NAME OF PROGRAM IS PLASTIC
20 DIM O(100):DIM W(2,100):DIM F(2,100):DIM N(2,100)
30 DIM A(9,20):DIM Y(20):DIM M(1000):DIM R(200)
40 OPEN "I",#1,"OVER"
50 FOR I=1 TO 100:INPUT #1,O(I):NEXT:CLOSE #1
60 OPEN "I",#1,"SIM1"
70 FOR I=1 TO 100:INPUT #1,W(1,I):NEXT:CLOSE #1
80 OPEN "I",#1,"SIM2"
90 FOR I=1 TO 100:INPUT #1,W(2,I):NEXT:CLOSE #1
100 OPEN "I",#1,"SIM3"
110 FOR I=1 TO 100:INPUT #1,F(1,I):NEXT:CLOSE #1
120 OPEN "I",#1,"SIM4"
130 FOR I=1 TO 100:INPUT #1,F(2,I):NEXT:CLOSE #1
140 OPEN "I",#1,"SIM5"
150 FOR I=1 TO 100:INPUT #1,N(1,I):NEXT:CLOSE #1
160 OPEN "I",#1,"SIM6"
170 FOR I=1 TO 100:INPUT #1,N(2,I):NEXT:CLOSE #1
180 X=RND(X):IF X<.5 THEN 190 ELSE 200
190 Z=1:GOTO 210
200 Z=2
210 X=RND(X):H=INT(2+X*3+.5):H1=0
220 FOR S=1 TO 2000
230 GOSUB 1110:C=8000!*(1+O(T)/100):D=.95*C/20:C=C+700
240 A=0:P=0:U=3000
250 FOR I=1 TO 20
260 H1=H1+1:IF H1>H THEN 270 ELSE 310
270 IF Z=1 THEN 280 ELSE 290
280 Z=2:GOTO 300
290 Z=1
300 H1=0:X=RND(X):H=INT(2+X*3+.5)
310 GOSUB 1110:W1=W(Z,T):W2=50-W1
320 GOSUB 1110:R1=F(Z,T):GOSUB 1110:R2=N(Z,T):R=(W1*R1+W2*R2)/1000
330 X=RND(X):IF R<5000! THEN 340 ELSE 350
340 O=2000!+X*1000!:GOTO 360
```

```
350 O=3000!+X*1000!
360 T1=R-O-D
370 IF T1<0 THEN 380 ELSE 390
380 A=A-T1:T=0:GOTO 440
390 IF A=0 THEN 400 ELSE 410
400 T=.35*T1:GOTO 440
410 IF A>T1 THEN 420 ELSE 430
420 A=A-T1:T=0:GOTO 440
430 T1=T1-A:A=0:T=.35*T1
440 F=R-O-T:IF I=20 THEN 450 ELSE 460
450 X=RND(X):R1=1000+X*2000:F=F+R1
460 IF P>0 THEN 470 ELSE 480
470 P=1.06*P+F:GOTO 490
480 P=1.06*P+F
490 IF P>U THEN 500 ELSE 510
500 V=P-U:P=P-V:GOTO 520
510 V=0
520 IF I=20 THEN 530 ELSE 550
530 IF P<0 THEN 550
540 V=V+P:P=0
550 A(1,I)=R:A(2,I)=0:A(3,I)=D:A(4,I)=T1:A(5,I)=A
560 A(6,I)=T:A(7,I)=F:A(8,I)=P:A(9,I)=V:NEXT:GOTO 630
570 PRINT "TOT COST: ";C,"RES VALUE: ";R1
580 PRINT "GROSS M","FCOST","DEPREC","BEFTAX"
590 FOR I=1 TO 20:PRINT A(1,I),A(2,I),A(3,I),A(4,I):NEXT:INPUT Z$
600 PRINT "TAXCARFOR","TAXES","CASHFLOW","ESC ACCT","PAYOUT"
610 FOR I=1 TO 20:PRINT A(5,I),A(6,I),A(7,I),A(8,I),A(9,I)
620 NEXT:INPUT Z$
630 Y=0:M=0:FOR I=1 TO 20
640 IF A(7,I)<0 THEN 650 ELSE 680
650 IF A(8,I)<0 THEN 660 ELSE 680
660 Y=Y+1:IF A(8,I)<M THEN 670 ELSE 680
670 M=A(8,I)
680 NEXT
690 Y(Y)=Y(Y)+1:M=INT(-M/10+.5):M(M)=M(M)+1
700 A=0:FOR I=1 TO 20:A=A+A(9,I):NEXT:D=A-C
710 IF D=0 THEN 720 ELSE 730
720 R=0:GOTO 900
730 IF D>0 THEN 820 ELSE 740
740 FOR K=1 TO 100:R=-K/100
750 A=0:FOR I=1 TO 20:A=A+A(9,I)/((1+R)^I):NEXT
760 D=A-C:IF D<0 THEN 810
770 R1=R+.005:A=0:FOR I=1 TO 20:A=A+A(9,I)/((1+R1)^I):NEXT
780 D=A-C:IF D>0 THEN 790 ELSE 800
790 R=R+.01
800 K=500
810 NEXT:GOTO 900
820 FOR K=1 TO 100:R=K/100
830 A=0:FOR I=1 TO 20:A=A+A(9,I)/((1+R)^I):NEXT
840 D=A-C:IF D>0 THEN 890
850 R1=R-.005:A=0:FOR I=1 TO 20:A=A+A(9,I)/((1+R1)^I):NEXT
860 D=A-C:IF D<0 THEN 870 ELSE 880
870 R=R-.01
880 K=500
890 NEXT
900 PRINT S;" # YRS INSOLVENT: ";Y;"  MAX INSOLVENCY: ";10*M;" IRR: ";R
910 R=100*R+100:R(R)=R(R)+1:NEXT:S=S-1
920 A=0:B=0:FOR I=1 TO 20:A=A+Y(I):NEXT
930 PRINT 100*A/S;" PERCENT OF SIMULATIONS EXPERIENCED INSOLVENCY"
940 OPEN "O",#1,"YRINSOL"
950 IF A=0 THEN 1040
960 FOR I=1 TO 20:B=B+Y(I):IF Y(I)=0 THEN 980
```

```
970 WRITE #1,I,Y(I),100*Y(I)/A,100*B/A
980 NEXT:CLOSE #1
990 OPEN "O",#1,"AMTINSOL"
1000 A=0:B=0:FOR I=1 TO 1000:A=A+M(I):NEXT
1010 FOR I=1 TO 1000:B=B+M(I):IF M(I)=0 THEN 1030
1020 WRITE #1,I,M(I),100*M(I)/A,100*B/A
1030 NEXT:CLOSE #1
1040 A=0:B=0:FOR I=1 TO 200:A=A+I*R(I)/S:NEXT
1050 PRINT "EXPECTED IRR: ";A-100:A=0
1060 OPEN "O",#1,"IRR"
1070 FOR I=1 TO 200:A=A+R(I):NEXT
1080 FOR I=1 TO 200:B=B+R(I):IF R(I)=0 THEN 1100
1090 WRITE #1,I-100,R(I),100*R(I)/A,100*B/A
1100 NEXT:CLOSE #1:END
1110 X=RND(X):T=INT(100*X+.5)
1120 IF T=0 THEN 1130 ELSE 1140
1130 T=100
1140 RETURN
```

4

The Loan Decision

The three "Cs" of banking are credit, character, and collateral. There are also five "Ps": people, purpose, payment, protection, and perspective. People and character have to do with the reputation of the borrower. Loans made to basically honest and trustworthy people have a better chance of being repaid than loans to those who are not. In the nineteenth and early twentieth centuries, it was not unusual for debtors to work for the rest of their lives to pay off loans that they had earlier defaulted on because of an adverse turn of events. Banking folklore could provide many examples of individuals whose whole purpose in life was to fulfill promises they had earlier made to a bank. A man's word was golden, and if it took twenty years of sweat and anguish to keep that word untarnished, so be it.

Of course, in those days, there was debtor's prison, an ingeniously designed institution to preclude a debtor from ever making good on debts. Perhaps debtor's prison was set up to motivate people to honor their debt obligations rather than giving them an opportunity to make restitution to someone they had financially wronged. In some respects, it was a step up from today's loansharks' way of enforcing repayment. Maybe the idea of dedicating oneself to making good on a debt gone bad was also a step up from today's street-smart advice to live a life of instant gratification. Not too long ago, spending was controlled by income with some thought given to saving a portion of every paycheck. Income now determines how much credit we can accumulate in order to sustain a degree of spending that exceeds the limit set by income.

Protection and collateral deal with assets that may have to be called upon if the payment and credit aspects of the loan fail to perform their purpose. Protection and collateral provide the primary defense against a loan going sour. Payment and credit provide the primary means of ensuring a loan will be repaid as originally scheduled. Payment and credit are not a defense mechanism to protect the banker. They are the mechanism by which a loan is originated and approved. A loan application would not be approved without adequate provisions for payment and credit. Payment and credit are the foundation upon which the structure of a loan rests. That foundation can be built on a rock or on sand. Unfortunately, a foundation of rock can be shaken by events and transformed into sand. When the foundation of rock has crumbled into sand, protection and collateral can be looked upon as an external structural support to prop up the loan.

The most important aspect of payment and credit is the projected cash flow. Can the projected cash flow support the payment of interest and the repayment, or amortization, of the loan? Is there sufficient coverage in the projected cash flow to cover contingencies—particularly, adverse contingencies? And if the cash flow projection fails to materialize and the interest and amortization payments cannot be made, is there sufficient collateral to repay the loan?

Suppose that an individual borrows money to open a business using the business itself as collateral for the loan. Suppose that the business then fails. If the business cannot generate sufficient cash flow to repay the loan, the collateral value of the business itself will probably fail to make a bad loan good. It would be unusual for someone to pay a million dollars for an asset that cannot generate the funds to repay a million-dollar loan. Usually collateral and protection are assets lying outside the purpose of the loan to provide the external structural prop to support a loan. For instance, suppose that an individual borrows money to open a business using his home as collateral. If the business fails, the question then becomes whether there is sufficient value in his home to repay the balance of the loan. If the answer is "yes," the banker is happy and the borrower is homeless. If the answer is "no," the banker is unhappy and the borrower is homeless.

Bankers are concerned about the purpose of loans. If the purpose of a loan is to squander the money on a grand tour of gambling havens, perhaps the loan should not be made even though the other Ps and Cs are acceptable. Perspective has to do with taking a step back from the loan application and thinking in terms of whether the whole thing makes sense. A banker swings his chair around and looks out of the window. He sees a skyline cluttered with new office buildings under construction. He swings around again and looks at a prospective borrower who wants a loan so he can clutter the skyline with yet another office building. He is seeking 100 percent financing, has no prospective tenants, and his personal guarantee is not worth the paper it is written on. Does it make sense to proceed with this loan even though office rental rates are still skyrocketing?

THE FUNDAMENTAL PRINCIPLE OF BANKING

The first principle of sound banking is to lend money only to those who do not need the money. This may sound contradictory to the intent of banking, but it is not. Banking is a business where the banker takes the savings of a number of individuals and lends the money to others. Those whose savings are being redirected to others as loans do not know, or care, that this is happening. All they care about is the timely payment of interest and the right to withdraw money at one hundred cents on every dollar. Bankers are lenders not of personal or bank funds, but the funds of depositors. Bankers are, in effect, borrowers. Bankers borrow money from depositors and pay them interest. They take the money and lend it out to others at a higher rate of interest. What bankers expect from borrowers is what depositors expect from bankers. Depositors, borrowers, and bankers function in a system where repayment is in terms of one hundred cents for every dollar deposited or borrowed. Depositors expect one hundred cents on every dollar that bankers have borrowed from them. For bankers to honor their obligations to depositors, bankers must expect one hundred cents returned on every dollar that they have lent to borrowers. From the bankers' perspective, a deposit is a liability on the books because they "owe" this to depositors at the time when depositors desire to withdraw money. A loan to a borrower is an asset from the perspective of a banker because its interest represents income and its repayment represents cash flow into the bank. To maintain a balance between assets and liabilities, a dollar's worth of assets and a dollar's worth of liabilities must be in terms of one hundred cents on the dollar.

The profit bankers enjoy lies partly in the interest rate differential between what they charge borrowers and what they pay for borrowing from depositors. Suppose that the rate of interest on loans is 2 percentage points higher than what is being paid to depositors. How much leeway is there in not having the borrower repay the loan? An annual loss rate of 2 percent wipes out the entire profit margin in a portfolio of loans whose spread in interest rates is 2 percent. Put another way, a banker must be 98 percent confident of repayment before making a loan just to break even.

Keeping that in mind, making loans to those who do not need a loan makes sense. Repayment is certain. A prospective borrower who walks into a bank desiring a loan because he needs a loan will not receive the same reception as one who does not need a loan. A millionaire desiring a $60,000 car loan so that he does not have to disturb his investments will not have much trouble borrowing the money. A minimum wage earner with two children and a wife wanting a loan for $1,000 to purchase a used car to get him to work will have much more trouble. Why? Because he needs the money; hence, repayment is not as certain.

Is there a lesson in all this? Yes, borrow money when you do not need it. Obtain a line of credit when there is no question that you do not need it. Then if, and when, you do need it, it is already there. Good financial managers know that the time to float a new issue of stock or bonds is right after a string of three to five years of straight earnings increases—usually the very time a company does not need the money. The worst time to go hat in hand to institutions or the public for a sale of stock or bonds is when the company needs the money.

In viewing loan applications or proposals, bankers focus on the prospects of repayment. We may wonder why there are so many bad loans if bankers are so careful. This is because loans are made when it is perceived that the borrower does not need the money. In other words, loans are made when business conditions are such that the perception of repayment is certain. The use of the word "perception" points to a major difficulty in banking. Many loans are made on perceptions and qualitative judgments. Bankers were falling all over themselves to make loans to Mexico when the price of oil was $35 per barrel. The perception was that Mexico would be able to repay any amount of outstanding loans. No questions were asked about the purpose of the loans. Even if the questions were asked, it did not matter what the responses were. It did not matter if the Mexicans admitted that a large portion of the loan proceeds was being squandered. Bankers could not satisfy their insatiable appetite to book loans to the government of Mexico. The perception that Mexico did not need the money, and therefore was a riskless credit risk, did not survive a 50 percent fall in the price of oil. Only then was it discovered that a significant portion of the borrowings had been squandered in ways that ensured that the money could never be repaid.

Once an industry is perceived as being creditworthy, bankers tend to start acting as money salesmen. The reason for this change in behavior from credit consciousness to a salesman's desire to move the merchandise off the shelf as quickly as possible is that a bank does not make money turning down loans. The profit in a loan is the difference between what is being charged to the borrower and what is being paid to the depositor multiplied by the amount of the loan. The larger the loan, the greater the profit in making the loan. The larger the portfolio of loans, the greater is the profitability of the bank. The number and magnitude of loans are constrained by both the size of the deposit base of a bank and the demand for loans.

Depositors can be people or a varied selection of sources of capital, some of which may even be real. Naturally, the most important source of funds that can be lent out to borrowers is unreal. It is credit that can be generated as needed by fractional reserve banking. An individual bank is restricted in the amount of loans that are placed on its books with relation to its capital base and in its exposure to a single borrower. However, the banking system, in the aggregate, for all intents and purposes, is not restricted in its lending by the supply of capital or credit. In the zero fractional reserve system of international banking, it is theoretically possible for a sufficiently large number of banks to support any amount of bank credit through individuals and corporations borrowing from one bank and depositing the proceeds in another. If there is a shortage of credit in the international banking arena, the supply of credit can be increased simply by forming new banks. And these need not be substantial banks. There are "banks" in the Caribbean whose physical proof of existence consists solely of a delivery box in a post office.

The recognition that the depositor is fictitious and that a loan cannot be repaid should have some impact on the concept of every loan having to be repaid one hundred cents on every dollar. Why does a loan have to be repaid one hundred cents on every dollar when there really is not a depositor asking for one hundred cents for every dollar? This is not an impertinent question. The Mexican banking authorities ask it every time they sit down for another round of debt repayment talks. And they are not the only ones bringing up the subject. Be that as it may, it is not the availability of credit that restricts the profitability of the banking business, but the *availability of creditworthy loans*.

The profitability of a bank is the spread in the interest rates between buying and selling money multiplied by the size of the loan portfolio. There is no trouble finding sellers of money because credit can be created out of nothing. The problem is finding buyers. In the competition for creditworthy buyers, the spread between borrowing and lending, or the interest rate differential, becomes essentially the same for all banks. Then the thirst for profits can only be satisfied by the size of the loan portfolio. The larger the loan portfolio, the greater the profits.

If there is a shortage of office space in, say, Colorado Springs, and if the perception of bankers is that office building loans are safe because office rentals are soaring, then it becomes fairly likely that loan applications for building new office buildings will be approved. The ever-increasing rental rates reinforce the perception of bankers that the owners of new office buildings do not need to borrow from the bankers to construct a new office building. Profits from the sale of existing office buildings can do the job. The perception that the magnitude of the profitability in a business nullifies the need to borrow funds fuels the enthusiasm of bankers to lend money to those desiring to build office buildings. The inevitable overbuilding of office buildings is not accomplished by the excessive approval of loans by a single banker, but by the aggregate approval of many bankers—and not just bankers in Colorado Springs, but bankers across the nation and across the world. This causes 100 and 1 new office buildings to be built, when perhaps 11 new office buildings would have been sufficient to satisfy demand. One does not have to be a genius to predict the eventual outcome. The perception that the borrower does not need the money to build another office building because skyrocketing office rentals make it unnecessary to borrow the money is punctured the day the twelfth office building hits the market. Office rents cease to skyrocket when there are an insufficient number of tenants to fill the available space. Rents do not stay in the stratosphere when space goes unrented. Rents plummet and bankers and builders are at odds from that moment on.

Why do bankers fall over themselves when it is perceived that an industry is infallibly creditworthy? Why, in their euphoria, do they insist on lending to such a degree that they destroy the very industry or business they intend to help? The reason for this perverse behavior is that the ultimate advancement of an individual within the banking organization hinges on the size of his loan portfolio. The larger the portfolio, the greater the chances of promotion. Anyone who contributes more to the profitability of a company stands a better chance of moving ahead when the company judges its success by the amount of money it makes. It does not take a young go-getter long to learn that the way to the president's office is by being a successful lending officer, not by being a successful credit analyst.

THE REALITY OF BANKING

Conservative banking practices are not the panacea for preventing bank failures. The following quote from the financial section of the *New York Times* of January 16, 1990, of the last portion of a feature article entitled "Where the Savings Crisis Hits Hard" illustrates that excesses in lending practices during the good times can take down banks that do follow conservative banking practices. The article also illustrates the limitations of management in avoiding losses.

Just a few years ago it would have been inconceivable to almost anyone in Colorado Springs that the city would become a symbol of a huge real estate debacle. After growing steadily for several decades, the local economy in the early 1980's seemed on the verge of a boom. The city was successful in persuading major electronics companies to put big operations here.

Home to the Air Force Academy and Fort Carson, a large army base, the city had long relied heavily on military spending. Colorado Springs became the home of a major testing center for the "Star Wars" anti-missile program and was designated as the site of a new military space command. Suddenly, the city was one of the fastest-growing in the nation and one of the most attractive markets for developers.

Housing developments, office buildings, retail space and other projects were built with abandon, anticipating consistently strong growth.

The three biggest local savings institutions . . . financed most of the building, often lending 100 percent of the cost of a project in return for a share of the profits. The institutions all grew rapidly. . . .

But then the city was struck by layoffs in the electronics business, cuts in military spending plans and the fallout from the depressed oil prices. . . . Suddenly there was no demand for new office space, buyers for houses became scarce, defaults started mounting and the financial health of the savings institutions deteriorated rapidly.

The reality of the situation is that banks that gamble rather than lend can harm banks that conduct their affairs in a conservative fashion. Office buildings constructed with no tenants signed up to lease a sizable portion of the fifty new floors of space affect the collateral value of office buildings that do have tenants. The collateral value of office buildings depends on their market, or resale, value. With a glut of office space, the market value of office buildings declines and that adversely affects the collateral value of a loan. Furthermore, excess office space capacity acts as a lure for tenants to leave "high-rental" buildings, whose mortgage payments are being made, for "low-rental" buildings, whose mortgages are in default. Thus an office building that started its commercial life with a sufficient number of leases may, in succeeding years, have an insufficient number of leases because of an excess of office space drawing away prospective and existing tenants.

An overbuilding of homes affects the underlying collateral value of mortgages. Mortgages made on homes whose resale values are soaring do not look so good after a glut of new homes knocks the props out of the market. Looking back with all the benefit of hindsight, the best course of action for a savings institution to take in Colorado Springs was to liquidate its entire portfolio of real estate loans when it was the perception of all that it was inconceivable that the real estate market could collapse. Not only is this too much to expect from a human organization, but it is the very purpose of banking to support the economic development of its constituency—the depositors whose savings support the bank. A conservatively run bank would have been hit hard by both the excesses of the not so conservatively run banks and by the turn of events that tore the underpinnings out from under the local economy.

Bankers cannot say "no" to everything and everybody. They would have no excuse for existence if they did. Bankers must lend money just as automobile manufacturers must make cars. Any loan, no matter how carefully structured, carries with it the risk of default just as living carries with it the risk of dying. No portfolio of commercial loans is 100 percent safe. For that matter, no portfolio of any type of loan is entirely safe. Governments have been known to walk away from their obligations when the cost of honoring those obligations became too much to bear. Within the spread between borrowing money from depositors and lending it to borrowers, there must be a little differential set aside to cover loan losses. In essence, a bank must self-insure itself not against the probability of a loan loss, but its certainty. It is a certainty that some loans will go bad; it is a probability as to which loans will go bellyup. Conservative banking practices can reduce the probability, but not eliminate it. Yet it must not be forgotten that while conservative banking practices are necessary to reduce the potential for loan losses, conservative banking practices may not be sufficient to avoid the consequences of unforeseen, and unforeseeable, economic calamities.

THE BACKGROUND OF A LOAN REQUEST

A subsidiary of a large conglomerate is a manufacturer of parts that are commonly consumed in large numbers by major companies in their production of such items as automobiles, home appliances, and air-conditioning units. There is a long-standing tradition on the way the customers, the industrial buyers of the output of the suppliers, obtain the requisite parts needed in the assembly or production of the finished products. The first step in the process of obtaining needed parts is to issue an invitation to bid on the manufacture of the part, component, or subassembly. This invitation is sent to as many suppliers as possible. The winning supplier, or suppliers, are granted a short-term contract that lasts a few months before the process repeats itself. Losing suppliers canvass the market of other manufacturers and bid on their needs. Occasionally, they are lucky.

Suppliers never have any certainty of ongoing work. Short-term contracts ensure that prices will be driven down to the absolute lowest level as long as the condition of few customers and many suppliers exists. To ensure a large number of suppliers, it is not unusual for customers to award a contract to a newcomer to increase, or maintain, the number of suppliers to be stirred in the pot. Similarly, customers may be reluctant to award a repeat contract to a supplier even if performance has been excellent. Repeat contracts tend to lessen the survival rate of competitors. Those falling by the wayside tend to empty the pot.

This uncertainty fosters the growth of certain professions. For instance, an award of a three-month contract gives the marketing department of a supplier exactly three months to obtain the next contract. The shorter the term of the contract, the more who have to be employed in marketing to keep those employed in production busy. The system of managed instability provides many employment opportunities in the buyers' purchasing departments. The relatively rapid turnover of contracts means that plenty of invitations to bid have to be thrown to the corporate peons, many responses have to be evaluated, many negotiations have to be initiated and concluded, many details have to be tidied up, and many contracts have to be monitored for compliance. The shorter the term of the contract, the greater the number of those who have to be employed in purchasing to keep the assembly lines in operation.

The system of intentional insecurity for suppliers, and the concomitant lack of confidence in the future, also encourages the growth of large numbers of consultants who would be more appropriately described as intelligence gatherers for suppliers. Who won the contract to supply ten thousand bendable gadgets to a particular division of Gigantean Corporation? When will the XYZ plant of Behemoth Manufacturing be in the market again for fasteners? Is the MNO plant of Leviathan Industries satisfied with its current supplier? What were the details on the contract won by Acme Parts, a competitive supplier? And, most important, what are the prices being submitted by competitors on a particular piece of business that the supplier is bidding on?

Top management of the customers believes that the turmoil of the system serves their interests best by providing them with the lowest price for the many parts and components purchased from outside suppliers. Therefore, they understand the need for large purchasing department staffs who, in turn, believe in playing one supplier against another to cut the best deal for their employers. The marketing departments of the suppliers are up to their collective ears in preparing and submitting bids. They believe in winning a sufficient number of short-term contracts to ensure the long-term job security of those who keep the production lines running. And the market intelligence apparati believe in wining and dining and bribing to gather every crumb of rumor and every tidbit of juicy information that they can sell to the highest bidder.

SINGLE SOURCING

Computer integrated manufacturing coupled with flexible manufacturing systems (FMS) provides a means of lowering the cost not of the manufacture of a part, but the manufacture of a whole family or grouping of parts. But these savings cannot be realized unless a huge number of parts can be manufactured.

Low cost of manufacture requires high volume and long-term contracts with customers—the very antithesis of traditional purchasing practices. Nevertheless, if customers would single source their need not just for a part, but for a family of parts, and not just for one plant, but for all, or most, plants, then suppliers can deliver the parts as customers need them at a substantial cost savings.

These savings come about from the productivity of a flexible manufacturing system where parts can be manufactured in large quantities day and night with no human involvement other than watching to make sure that the robot moving the part from one machine to the next does not become confused and start moving the machine rather than the part. The labor input is low because FMS is programmed to handle every detail of the manufacturing process. Any required labor is considered a fixed cost of operation rather than a variable cost. Labor is treated as a fixed expense similar to the rental on the building. Labor is not hired and fired as production levels change because, in essence, very little labor is required. Maybe only 5 percent of the manufactured cost of a part is represented by labor. If that is the case, there is no real reason to get too excited over labor costs or to search for the lowest-paid workforce.

The degree of automation is poignantly dramatized when the manufacturer of flexible manufacturing systems has everyone leave its demonstration plant at 6:00 P.M. each night. The last one out the door flicks off the lights. The first one in the next morning can tell if anything has gone wrong the night before when the lights are turned on. Nine hundred and ninety-nine times out of a thousand, everything is humming along just as it was when the lights were flicked off. There may be a reason on the one thousandth time to justify having a janitor keep his eye on things in an operating plant. But in a demonstration plant, it is better for marketing purposes to flick off the lights.

Automated retrieval and storage systems move the appropriate steel shape from storage to the FMS, and the finished product is transferred from the FMS to its designated bin. The computer driven system can easily accommodate the shifting of manufacture from one member of a family of parts to another with no real interruption in production. Laser light "inspectors" and other forms of automated quality control devices monitor a part at each step of the manufacturing process. This is the ultimate in 100 percent inspection since each part is inspected three to five times in the course of the production cycle. Perhaps, this should be considered 300 to 500 percent inspection. Computer feedback loops make necessary adjustments to the individual machines in the flexible manufacturing system to correct unfavorable trends in the production process. Robots pick out those parts that fail to pass inspection and toss them into a garbage pail that rarely needs emptying. The new way is a big step to the realization of the concept of zero defects.

All that has to be done to achieve the substantial cost savings and higher quality standards of computer integrated manufacturing coupled with flexible manufacturing systems is a radical change in what might be called acquisitions management. There is, however, an enormous incentive not to change current practices because traditional thinking has accepted as an article of faith that the lowest cost can be achieved in a laissez-faire marketplace of many suppliers and few customers. Those in purchasing would not be apt to challenge tradition because a contract, once awarded, puts them out of business. A contract won may be won forever. There is no need for further marketing efforts once the production floor is busy for the next ten to twenty years. As a matter of fact, there is not much need for marketing, and purchasing for that matter, because long-term contracts of such a magnitude are usually negotiated, and administered, between the customer's and the supplier's production managers, not through normal marketing and purchasing channels. Quality assurance and delivery schedules take precedence over price. Integration of the supplier's production schedule with the customer's assembly schedule is also more important than price. And how much dickering is there going to be about price when the price of the new way is already lower than the lowest price of the old way?

No matter how much resistance there may be to change, the old must give way to the new once the new has established a foothold, or a toehold for that matter. Certain manufacturing companies have already taken the leap to single sourcing and found that costs have actually fallen by a greater degree than what had been anticipated. This places these companies at a competitive advantage over those which insist on sticking with the old way. The old way must give way to the new. A company that insists on staying with the old way will be wiped out in the competitive free marketplace. Change will inevitably occur in a free marketplace no matter now entrenched purchasing and marketing personnel and marketing spies may be against change if change means greater profits for those who switch.

One of the strongest arguments against single sourcing is the upper hand that a supplier supposedly has over the customer. In the pot-churning ways of yore, suppliers were purposely kept in a weak negotiating position by making sure that there were plenty of them in the pot. They were truly at the mercy of the customer. When a supplier is the single source of not just a part, but a whole grouping or family of parts, and not to just one plant, but to all, or most of the plants of a customer, what keeps him from jacking up the price 300 or 400 percent? What ensures maintenance of a certain quality standard? In other words, what stops the supplier from behaving like the customer?

Those who think this way conveniently forget that the long-term contract may represent 90 percent of the business of a supplier. Few suppliers would be so stupid to pull such a stunt as jamming the price through the ceiling or delivering junk rather than a quality product when their entire livelihood depends on not behaving this way. No customer is going to idly pay the price premium and calmly accept the unworkable parts for the duration of a multiyear contract. No contract would permit the supplier to take such unilateral action and no contract would continue to be honored if the supplier were acting, or even hinting of acting, in such a fashion. Contracts are not written in such a one-sided way. Contracts give the customer the right to break with the supplier if the supplier is not living up to the provisions of the contract.

The single-source contract is such an important piece of business for the supplier that the supplier does everything possible to ensure that the customer is satisfied. It is the supplier who visits the customer's factory. It is the supplier who suggests changes either in the product or the process of doing things within the customer's factory, that reduces the cost of manufacturing even more than what had been anticipated. It is the supplier who is concerned that quality parts are delivered in a timely fashion. It is the supplier who cannot financially survive the repercussions of poor performance.

Single sourcing promotes an attitude change on the part of suppliers. Before suppliers were subject to the capriciousness of those in purchasing who fostered chaos as a means of obtaining the lowest bid. Now they are indispensable and integral members of the customers' corporate family. They think not only in terms of the importance of the contract for personal financial survival, but the importance of the role that they fill within the customers' operations. They are responsible for supplying an entire spectrum of parts to all the plants of the customer as needed by the customer delivered just in time for their incorporation in the assembly of a product. They view the customer's success and their own welfare as being one and the same. They view themselves, not as independent suppliers, but as subsidiaries of the customer. For indeed, that is exactly what the supplier has become because without the single source contract, he is nothing.

THE LOAN REQUEST

Let us suppose that a subsidiary of a conglomerate has won its first long-term single-source contract for a small grouping of parts to be shipped to a single plant of an automobile manufacturer. This contract utilizes 20 percent of the capacity of one flexible manufacturing system. In order to achieve the greatest impact of the economy of scale of computer integrated manufacturing, the subsidiary has proposed the building of a plant that can accommodate four flexible manufacturing systems. The $18 million investment includes the building, the automated retrieval and storage system to handle four FMSs, and a central computer system to support all four FMSs. However, only one FMS is to be initially installed. The second, third, and fourth FMSs will not be purchased until a sufficient number of contracts have been garnered to justify their acquisition. Each successive FMS costs $4 million.

The conglomerate has approved the subsidiary proceeding with this project on the condition that a substantial portion of the financing required is obtained by the management of the subsidiary. If management can arrange proper banking support, the conglomerate will then inject the necessary equity and working capital requirements. The management of the subsidiary makes contact with several banks, including those that do major business with the conglomerate itself. The following summary of salient facts is presented to the various banks.

The conglomerate will not be responsible for repayment of the principal of the loan or the payment of the interest in any manner whatsoever. The conglomerate's maximum extent of liability is the initial equity and working capital requirements. Banks involved with this project can only look to the financial performance of the project itself as the source of repayment of the loan. The conglomerate reserves the right to sell the subsidiary to whomever it desires. As an example of the leeway the conglomerate demands, the conglomerate may sell the subsidiary to an empty shell of a corporation for one dollar as a prelude to the subsidiary declaring itself bankrupt if the loan cannot be repaid. The bank has no recourse whatsoever to the conglomerate.

Banks responding to this request are expected to lend a substantial portion of the $18 million cost of the project, which includes the first FMS, plus the $4 million for the second FMS. The only condition on financing the second FMS is that the first one is fully utilized before the second one is purchased. The responding banks are not putting themselves on the line for the third and fourth FMSs. The banks could finance these, but they are not obligated to do so as they are with the second FMS. Therefore, from the point of view of evaluating the project, the third and fourth FMSs can be assumed to be financed by the conglomerate. But the banks are obligating themselves for the second FMS, with the proviso that the first is fully employed, should they decide to support the project.

The nominal contract size is assumed to utilize 20 percent of the capacity of one FMS. One FMS can handle five contracts and the plant has a maximum capacity of twenty contracts (five contracts for each of four FMSs). The first contract lasts for thirty-six months and generates a gross margin (sales price less all variable costs of production) of $48,000 per month. Management projections assume that the average contract will generate $50,000 in gross margin per month and will be renewed on its termination date. Any contract, once awarded, is presumed to run forever.

At $50,000 per month, a contract is worth $600,000 on a yearly basis with each FMS capable of handling five contracts. In the first year, the projection calls for 2.5 contracts generating $1.5 million in gross margin. The second year has an average of 7.5 contracts for $4.5 million in gross margin; the third year has 12.5 contracts generating $7.5 million. At the start of the fourth year, the plant is assumed to be at full capacity, with 20 contracts generating $12 million in gross margin. With a fixed annual cost of $500,000 per year, there is plenty of money being generated for a bank to fund 100 percent of the project with complete confidence of payback in short order.

The proposal is presented in a way that gives the bankers the impression that management expects that something close to an $18 million check plus one undated check for $4 million will be in the return mail along with a note apologizing for the fact that the loan does have to be repaid, but that the timing of repayment can be at management's discretion.

Some of the banks throw the proposal in the wastebasket once the wining and dining session is over. Some do so because there is no collateral in the loan outside of the asset itself being financed. Therefore, if the payment or credit underlying the loan fails, so will the protection or collateral support. If $10 million is lent on the project and there is an insufficient number of contracts to generate the cash flow necessary to pay off the loan, there will be little chance that the asset, the collateral supporting the loan, can be sold for $10 million to pay off the loan. As the foundation of payment and credit crumbles, so will the external supporting structure of protection and collateral. Without the protection afforded by a guarantee from the conglomerate, some banks will not even consider the loan request.

Others consider the loan request without a parent company guarantee, but take an extra hard look at the payment or credit aspects of the project itself. There is only one signed contract that stipulates certain performance criteria. The bankers' thoughts turn to assessments of the minimum, most likely, and maximum outcomes of the venture with much, if not all, of the thought process dedicated to an assessment of the minimum outcome. With no collateral support for this loan, one cannot blame the bankers for taking a rather jaundiced view of the prospects of repayment of the loan request.

If bankers desire to avoid loan losses as their first order of priority, what will be their assessment of the minimum outcome? One possible minimum assessment is that the system will fail to meet the performance conditions imposed by the initial contract. This will void the initial contract leading to a total failure of the project. A variation on this dismal theme would include a nonrenewal of the initial contract plus no new contracts. This is three years of partial disaster before total disaster strikes. Another cacophonic tune of doom to be played with the minimum outcome assessment might be the renewal of the initial contract, but no other contracts being awarded for the life of the factory.

This latter case is the best of the three catastrophes. The gross margin from the initial contract is $48,000 per month for twelve months, or $576,000 per year. Fixed expenses are $500,000. If this contract is renewed for twenty years, there is only $76,000 available to support a loan of $6, $8, or $10 or so million. This is far short of meeting even the interest payments. If these assessments of a minimum outcome are in a banker's mind, no one can question the rejection of the loan proposal. Only those bankers who have a more optimistic assessment of the worst case can seriously consider this loan. This is not to say that those banks who throw the proposal in the wastebasket are wrong. But their assessments of worst-case scenarios are of such a nature that further consideration of the request is out of the question.

Assuming for the moment that the present operations of the parts making subsidiary does not provide any meaningful collateral support—in fact, may well be abandoned if the new factory is built—we may wonder why bankers would proceed in considering this loan. They may be thinking in terms of the conglomerate surviving for its entire existence without guaranteeing obligations for any of its subsidiaries, yet having none of its subsidiaries ever default on an obligation. The fact that no subsidiary ever defaulted on an obligation is an important point in considering whether to proceed with this loan without a parent company guarantee. Freedom from guaranteeing obligations allows the parent to wheel and deal with subsidiaries, but that freedom would be severely tested if a subsidiary ever defaulted on an obligation—even after being sold by the conglomerate.

Some financial institutions might proceed without parent support on the condition that the subsidiary carries the parent's corporate name and that there are restrictions on the ability of the parent to dump the subsidiary. Carrying the name of the corporate flagship does affect the decision of whether the dinghy should be cast adrift in the midst of a financial storm. The willingness of banks to support subsidiaries without a parent guarantee must be matched by the reluctance of the parent to permit a subsidiary from walking away from its obligations.

Moreover, the conglomerate has nothing to lose by insisting that the subsidiary ask for terms that are favorable to the borrower. If all financial institutions balk at financing the subsidiary operations without a parent guarantee, the conglomerate may have to, or be forced to, rethink its policy. On the other hand, financial institutions that do proceed without a parent guarantee have a competitive advantage over those that insist on having such collateral support in their dealings with the subsidiary.

Any banker proceeding with the evaluation of this loan proposal would have a perception that the following set of conditions are true:

1. The character of the professional staff in the subsidiary is impeccable. They have the necessary technological, managerial, marketing, and engineering skills to make this venture a success. If the trend toward single sourcing and flexible manufacturing systems materializes to any meaningful extent, this is the group of people to be associated with from the point of view of funding the debt.

2. The purpose of the loan is not just to finance one of the first "factories of the future," but to place the bank in a position to finance others. There is a marketing aspect to this loan—approve this one, and others are sure to follow.

3. This loan might contain less risk than financing conventional suppliers in that there is no way that the latter can compete with the "factory of the future" on a cost basis. If the concept of single sourcing with grouping of parts to be manufactured and delivered just in time to multiple plants catches on, the risk will not be in financing the "factory of the future," but in financing suppliers who stay with the factory of the past. One "factory of the future" reduces the size of the market for conventional suppliers. A series of "factories of the future" can obliterate the market for high-volume parts, leaving the traditional suppliers with the scraps and crumbs.

4. Without any outside support in the form of a parent company guarantee, or an interest in assets other than the factory itself, the collateral and protection aspects of this loan proposal are weak. This can be compensated, in part, by ensuring that the equity investment by the conglomerate is of such significance to make walking away from this project a painful experience. Therefore, financing above 80 percent should not be considered. On the other hand, financing below 30 percent should not be proposed because the conglomerate is attempting to garner as much outside financial support as possible. The trick is to advance as much funding as possible without taking on undue risk, while at the same time advancing as much funding as necessary to be awarded with the deal. The amount to be advanced is, in turn, determined by the credit and payment aspects of the loan proposal. Every banker entertaining this loan must think in terms of what size loan can be put against the projected cash flow for a given level of risk of the bank being stuck with a bad debt.

One banker, desiring to be part of the trend toward the realization of the "factory of the future," meets with an industry expert and a simulator builder. The initial response of the industry expert is that the request is ludicrous. His principal objection is that single source contracting is done slowly and carefully on the part of the customer. The customer cannot afford to make a mistake. His whole operation is truly at the mercy of a single source supplier if that supplier, for any reason, does not deliver the right quantity of goods of the right quality to the right plant at the right time. The expert feels either the management of the subsidiary is blindly optimistic or that the proposal is written in such a way that it blinds the bankers to the potential risk of delay in obtaining the necessary contracts. Other than a few other modifications of lesser significance, the industry expert is in favor of the banker proceeding with the proposal as long as the banker does not accept the subsidiary's optimistic forecast on garnering contracts.

The discussion among the banker, the expert, and the simulator builder evolves around the development of a model based on assessments that the expert feels are reasonable for the circumstances. The simulator builder focuses on ensuring that the expert provides the necessary information for him to build a simulation model of the situation. The banker focuses on the payment and credit ramifications of the industry expert's remarks.

The expert cautions that negotiating for contracts, and the terms of the contracts, are affected by business conditions. Good times are much more conducive to concluding long-term transactions than bad times. The expert feels that negotiating long-term contracts during the bad times of a business cycle is very difficult. He feels that the chance of concluding these contracts during recessions is low. He also thinks that the management of the subsidiary cannot possibly negotiate four contracts per year during the most buoyant of times considering the effort required to nail down a single source contract. Assuming contracts to be of the same size as the one already awarded to the subsidiary, the industry expert, with some prompting from the simulator builder, constructs the following table on the annual number of contracts that he thinks can be successfully concluded by the management of the subsidiary.

Probability of Obtaining Indicated Number of Contracts per Year

NUMBER OF CONTRACTS	GOOD TIMES	BAD TIMES
0	15%	70%
1	35	25
2	35	5
3	15	0
Total	100%	100%

The expert feels that contracts will have a minimum length of three years, most likely a length of four years, but with an outside chance of five or six years depending on business conditions.

Length of Contract in Months

ASSESSMENT	GOOD TIMES	BAD TIMES
Minimum	36	36
Most likely	48	48
Maximum	72	60

The expert disagrees with management that a contract, once awarded, is awarded forever, although he thinks that the probability of continuance is quite high. He feels that there is an 80 percent chance that a contract will be renewed during the good times. If renewed, the gross margin will remain the same. He believes that it is very difficult to enhance the gross margin on a contract once it is initially established. The primary reason for this is that there are provisions within the contract to protect the supplier from certain risks, such as fluctuations in the price of steel. The contract price of the parts to be manufactured contains adjustments for the rise and fall of the price of steel. The supplier does not benefit if the price of steel falls during the course of the contract but neither does the supplier suffer if the price rises. The contract does much to preserve gross margin. Therefore, the supplier is in a weak position to improve upon initial gross margin because of the provisions within the contract that help to preserve gross margin from the vicissitudes of the marketplace. The best the supplier can do during the renewal phase of a contract is to recoup any uncompensated escalation of costs caused by inflation. If this is the best he can do, the expected outcome from contract renewal negotiations is the preservation of the initial gross margin of a contract.

For the 20 percent chance that the contract will not be renewed, however, the expert feels that there will be a delay of only one to six months before the next one can be attained if business conditions are robust. Generally speaking, the expert is in agreement with management that once a contract is awarded, and regardless of the number of years stipulated in the contract, contracts are for the lifetime of the plant.

The expert notes that large manufacturers do not truly single source right off the bat, but double or triple source on their way to single sourcing. This way manufacturers can evaluate a few suppliers before selecting the final single supplier. Alternatively, the volume of parts might be so large that customers can divide the contract between two or among three suppliers and still achieve the full economies of large-scale computer integrated manufacturing. Having a few suppliers provides the competitive pressure to ensure that an individual supplier lives up to his obligations. It is also easier for management to adopt single sourcing by first going from many suppliers to few suppliers.

The expert cautions that customers might prefer to stay with a few suppliers and not truly single source even if there is a marginal economic incentive to go from two or three suppliers to a single supplier. Sometimes the comfort of having what essentially amounts to a backup for a single supplier might override the economic consideration of a slight cost differential of having more than one supplier. Therefore, there is a risk that a contract might be interrupted at its renewal time for any number of reasons with the customer depending on the other suppliers to satisfy demand for parts.

The expert feels that contract renewals during bad times have only a 60 percent chance of being renewed without delays or adjustments in the gross margin. Otherwise, there is anywhere from a six- to eighteen-month delay in obtaining a new contract. Although the renewed contract will probably be with the original customer, the customer might use the hiatus in the contract to reduce the flow of parts to factories. Again, this presumes that the manufacturer is relying on a few suppliers. In a true single source situation, the manufacturer would continue the contract but at reduced volume. This would have the same effect on revenue as an interruption during the renewal phase of a contract.

Although the expert generally agrees with management's assessment of $50,000 per month in gross margin, he feels that there is a chance that they can improve on this figure in negotiating succeeding contracts during good times. If times are bad, however, they will have trouble topping $50,000 per month. With some prodding from the simulator builder, the expert provides the following assessments:

Monthly Gross Income per Contract

ASSESSMENT	GOOD TIMES	BAD TIMES
Minimum	$40,000	$30,000
Most likely	50,000	40,000
Maximum	70,000	50,000

The expert reviews the fixed costs and concludes that $500,000 is low. He is more comfortable with an estimate between $600,000 and $700,000. He also thinks that fixed costs should rise with the number of contracts, although the gross margin contains provision not only for variable costs, but also some cost elements generally associated with fixed costs. It is agreed to add $10,000 in annual fixed costs for each negotiated contract.

The banker notes that the expert is hesitating while the simulator builder is summarizing the assessments. When queried, the expert notes that the gross margins are linked to the inefficiencies associated with the manufacturing facilities of traditional suppliers. He is uneasy about their permanence.

"Suppliers have to be short-term oriented because conventional wisdom on the part of customers is to give them short-term contracts. This makes suppliers very hesitant to purchase new equipment. They would rather stay with outmoded and inefficient machinery that has already been paid for and hire and fire workers as required by the contracts they win and lose. They are really high cost producers even with their low profit margins. This factory is living off the high costs of existing suppliers because their costs are setting the base level of prices.

"This isn't going to hold over the next twenty years. As the more forward looking suppliers convert to flexible manufacturing systems, they are going to force the conventional suppliers out of business. At some point, the flexible manufacturing system companies will begin competing against themselves. Then we will see gross margins erode just as we have seen gross margins erode in any new technology after it has liquidated the old."

This time the banker is doing the prodding. The expert concludes that gross margins in year 20 should be reduced by one-third of the initial gross margins. He also feels that the erosion of gross margins will not start for about ten years as it will take at least that long for the new technology to penetrate the market to a sufficient degree that FMS companies will be competing against FMS companies rather than against conventional suppliers. The simulator builder notes that he intends to first establish gross margins without any long-term correction as previously discussed. He then states his intention to have the aggregate annual gross margin for all contracts erode by 3 percent per year cumulatively, starting in the tenth year. Neither the industry expert nor the banker objects to his approach.

The simulator builder first develops a model to simulate gross income as requested by the banker. The banker wants to gauge the growth and magnitude of the projected gross income before running financial simulations. The gross income is the gross margin less the fixed costs. It is the cash flow available for servicing the debt—the payment or credit aspects of a loan which form its foundation and which are of foremost concern to the banker. The simulator builder provides Table 4.1 summarizing the worst, average, and best of the one thousand simulations of annual gross income (figures in thousands of dollars).

The banker quivers as he looks at the worst of the one thousand simulation runs. The simulator builder is prepared to answer the banker before the banker has a chance to react to the worst-case scenario.

"You see, we have set up a system where there is a 70 percent chance that no contracts can be won if times are bad and a 15 percent chance that no contracts can be won if times are good. The chance that one good year follows another, or one bad years follows another, is 80 percent. This models business cycles in that good and bad times come in groups of years. We are looking at the one chance in a thousand of having not only primarily bad years, but also drawing out of a bag of ping-pong balls the 70 percent of all balls indicating no new contracts. We have some good years in there, but then we were drawing from the 15 percent portion of ping-pong balls that signified that no new contracts would be awarded. Only that can explain winning three contracts in twenty years with the third being won in the twentieth year."

"How about the fourth year where there is a loss of $653,000?"

"Well, it takes one contract to cover fixed costs. Roughly speaking, the annual

Table 4.1
Simulation of Gross Income

	WORST SIMULATION		AVERAGE OF ALL SIMULATIONS	BEST SIMULATION	
YEAR	NUMBER OF CONTRACTS	GROSS INCOME	GROSS INCOME	NUMBER OF CONTRACTS	GROSS INCOME
1	1	-$131	$ 191	4	$1,330
2	1	-87	715	6	2,303
3	1	-92	1,229	8	4,015
4	1	-653	1,621	11	4,747
5	1	-370	2,206	12	6,307
6	1	-161	2,709	14	7,275
7	2	247	3,159	16	8,740
8	2	230	3,615	17	10,031
9	2	-137	4,145	17	9,745
10	2	208	4,464	18	9,884
11	2	242	4,751	19	10,245
12	2	168	4,953	20	9,840
13	2	212	5,141	20	10,007
14	2	-160	5,334	20	9,443
15	2	25	5,447	20	9,135
16	2	101	5,510	20	8,772
17	2	126	5,527	20	8,265
18	2	66	5,472	20	8,047
19	2	9	5,388	20	7,768
20	3	-68	5,281	20	7,336

gross income from one contract is about equal to annual fixed costs. Looking at the numbers, it appears that the first contract of three years was not renewed. That must have been bad times because it looks like we took another direct hit of eighteen months of delay before the contract was renewed. With no contract, year 4 has no gross margin to counteract $653,000 in fixed costs. Year 5 has about six or so months of gross margin to counteract the fixed costs. The loss in year 6 of $161,000 indicates that the new gross margin was on the low side of the $30,000 to $50,000 range permitted during bad times."

"You may say that this particular run was hitting us, financially speaking, with the worst hits we could take. I would say we were striking out every time we were up at bat."

"Well, that's another way of looking at it. Then we can say that the best simulation out of the one thousand simulations could be interpreted as home run hits every time we came up to bat."

"Yes, but look how long the succession of home runs took to get up to twenty contracts—twelve years! And that's the best!"

"You're probably right, although the best, and worst, simulations were selected on the basis of aggregate or total gross income over the twenty-year span, not on the number of contracts. Nevertheless, it looks like it is going to take ten or more years to get up to full capacity—even under favorable conditions."

"And they tell us four years in their proposal. What poppycock! Any credit analyst who can read would doubt that and any banking officer worth his salt would challenge that assertion."

"Why do they make such optimistic forecasts? All they seem to be doing is casting doubt on the validity of the whole project."

"Well, in the world of business, strange things happen. What was presented to us is not necessarily what was presented to the board of directors of the conglomerate. Let's face facts. There are some tough boys in that conglomerate who have a habit of asking some mean and nasty questions. Maybe the conglomerate decided that ten years might pass before this plant would realize its full potential. For all we know, maybe that was what management told the board of directors. But that is not necessarily what they are going to tell us when they are sniffing around our moneybags. It's up to us to do our own appraisal of the situation and come up with our own conclusions."

"That means that management tends to oversell a project both internally and externally."

"Well, certainly externally . . . and we tend to undersell a project because we are concerned with the risk of loss while management is more keyed to the reward of profit. A manager and a banker look at the same cash flow—but at opposite ends of it. Management salivates over the high end and what that means in profits while we have anxiety attacks over the low end and what that means to us in losses. I tell you, if I believed your worst case, I would stop considering this loan right now. It is a disaster."

"It happened once in a thousand runs."

"Well, it happened because we ended up with twenty years of mostly bad times. None of my loans could withstand that long of a stretch of depression. This would simply be another loan going bad."

"Then you have little choice but to stay with the average gross income projection."

"We have a problem here, too. The cash flow in the early years of the project can't support much in the way of debt financing charges."

"What do you want me to do now?"

There is some give and take between the simulator builder and the banker as to the nature of the final model. The banker wants the model to reflect reality as closely as possible. The simulator builder is concerned with the overall programming effort of what the banker wants. They both agree that the model need not be too complex. They also agree that the whole model rests on the validity of the expert's assessment on the garnering of new contracts. The banker considers the possibility of obtaining another opinion to substantiate this critical assessment. The final model consists of the following elements.

The initial loan amount to be considered is a $12 million loan with no principal repayment during the first three years. The loan will then be amortized with equal payment of principal over the succeeding seventeen years. The banker selects interest only during the first three years in recognition of the fact that the cash flow of the factory will reflect a gradual buildup of contracts and will not support much in debt retirement during the startup years. He also instructs the simulator builder to use a fixed rate of interest of 12 percent plus a risk premium of 1 percent for a total of 13 percent interest to be charged to the borrower.

The banker determines the 12 percent interest rate as follows: the bank can borrow the money at a fixed fate of 10.5 percent from a pension fund as long as the bank guarantees the payment of interest and amortization. The bank lends the money to the conglomerate, or to a subsidiary with a parent guarantee, at 12 percent. The 12 percent contains the typical markup for the bank's perception of the creditworthiness of the conglomerate. The 1 percent premium is selected as a trial risk premium to compensate the bank for the possibility that the subsidiary will not successfully conclude a sufficient number of contracts to support the financing charges associated with the loan.

The initial amount of the loan of $12 million will increase automatically to $16 million when the sixth contract is obtained. The sixth contract will necessitate the acquisition of the second flexible manufacturing system. The banker assumes a seven-year payout of the $4 million loan for the second FMS. A considerable amount of time is spent by the banker ensuring that the simulator builder understands the mechanics of the cash flow.

Tables 4.2–4.4 are printouts of an actual simulation run. The simulation program is contained in the appendix. The purpose of the tables is to explain the mechanics of the generation and disposition of the cash flow. Note that some rounding errors are present in the tables as all figures are expressed to the nearest thousand dollars. In this simulation run, the sixth contract is awarded in the eighth year, necessitating the investment of $4 million in the second FMS. This can be seen in the face amount of the loan and in the amortization, interest, and depreciation schedules.

The payment of 12 percent interest is calculated by applying the interest rate to the average outstanding amount at the end of the previous and current years. For instance, the interest payment for year 4 is based on the average outstanding loan balance of $11,647. This is calculated from the outstanding balance at the end of year 3, which is also the outstanding balance at the start of year 4 ($12,000) and the amount outstanding at the end of year 4 ($11,294). The average of these two figures ($11,647) is multiplied by 12 percent to obtain the interest payment and then by 1 percent to obtain what is called the risk premium on the loan.

The subsidiary is paying 13 percent interest. The bank is charging an extra 1 percent above its normal 12 percent interest charge and will set this aside in a special account to be used as a source of funds if the subsidiary cannot pay off the loan. This is the initial attempt to determine the degree of compensation that is necessary because of the greater risk of loss associated with the absence of a parent guarantee.

Table 4.2
Financial Charges

YEAR	LOAN FACE AMOUNT	PRINCIPAL REPAYMENT	AMOUNT OWED	INTEREST PAYMENT	RISK PREMIUM ON LOAN	DEPRECIATION OF ASSETS
1	$12,000	$ 0	$12,000	$1,440	$120	$ 900
2	12,000	0	12,000	1,440	120	900
3	12,000	0	12,000	1,440	120	900
4	12,000	706	11,294	1,398	116	900
5	12,000	706	10,588	1,313	109	900
6	12,000	706	9,882	1,228	102	900
7	12,000	706	9,176	1,144	95	900
8	16,000	1,277	11,899	1,265	105	1,300
9	16,000	1,277	10,622	1,351	113	1,300
10	16,000	1,277	9,345	1,198	100	1,300
11	16,000	1,277	8,067	1,045	87	1,700
12	16,000	1,277	6,790	891	74	1,700
13	16,000	1,277	5,513	738	62	1,700
14	16,000	1,277	4,235	585	49	1,700
15	16,000	706	3,529	466	39	1,700
16	16,000	706	2,824	381	32	1,700
17	16,000	706	2,118	296	25	1,700
18	16,000	706	1,412	212	18	1,300
19	16,000	706	706	127	11	1,300
20	16,000	706	0	42	4	1,300

The depreciation consists of $900 ($900,000) for the twenty-year writeoff of the $18 million investment in the factory. Each succeeding $4 million FMS is written off during the subsequent ten years at a rate of $400 ($400,000) per year. For this particular simulation run, the sixth contract is awarded in the eighth year necessitating an additional $400 charge that continues for the next ten years. The eleventh contrast is awarded in year 11. This necessitates the purchase of the third FMS and another $400 charge to depreciation for the succeeding ten years.

The additional charges to depreciation for the third and fourth FMS have no effect on the outstanding loan amount because the bank is not obligated to fund the third and fourth FMS, although it may decide to do so at the appropriate time. For evaluation purposes for the initial loan, the third and fourth FMS are assumed to be financed by equity funds from the conglomerate. In this simulation run, the fourth FMS was not added, indicating that there were between eleven and fifteen contracts negotiated over the twenty-year period. This is far from management's assessment of twenty contracts within four years.

The banker intends to require that an escrow account be set up by the subsidiary with an initial balance of $1 million. The escrow account must accumulate another $1 million from earnings before money can pass to the conglomerate. The escrow account earns 9 percent on a before tax basis, reflecting the good business practice of banks giving less in interest to depositors than what they

Table 4.3
Before Tax Profit

YEAR	ESCROW ACCOUNT EARNINGS	INTEREST EXPENSE LINE OF CREDIT	RISK PREMIUM LINE OF CREDIT	ANNUAL GROSS INCOME	BEFORE TAX PROFIT	TAX LOSS CARRY FORWARD
1	$ 90	$ 0	$ 0	$ 633	-$1,737	$1,737
2	14	0	0	1,640	-805	2,542
3	23	0	0	1,771	-666	3,208
4	44	0	0	1,177	-1,193	4,401
5	0	61	5	1,869	-519	4,920
6	0	100	8	2,004	-334	5,255
7	0	117	10	1,380	-885	6,140
8	0	200	17	1,714	-1,173	7,312
9	0	338	28	2,462	-667	7,979
10	0	415	35	2,592	-455	8,434
11	0	467	39	3,853	515	7,919
12	0	354	30	4,667	1,617	6,302
13	0	109	9	5,182	2,564	3,738
14	180	0	0	5,332	3,178	560
15	180	0	0	5,191	3,166	0
16	180	0	0	4,816	2,883	0
17	180	0	0	4,369	2,528	0
18	180	0	0	4,135	2,786	0
19	180	0	0	3,977	2,720	0
20	180	0	0	3,646	2,480	0

charge borrowers even though the subsidiary is both a depositor and a borrower. In addition, a line of credit is to be established by the bank to fund the subsidiary to prevent its insolvency. All interest and amortization payments on the loan itself will be paid as originally scheduled, but any cash shortfalls in accomplishing this will be drawn from the line of credit account. The line of credit account can be likened to the "rich uncle" in the previous chapter. The line of credit carries an interest rate of 13 percent, consisting of 12 percent for the regular payment of interest had there been a parent guarantee plus a 1 percent risk premium to compensate for the fact that there is no parent guarantee. The risk premium charges on both the loan and the line of credit are to be deposited in a special bank risk account.

Table 4.3 is a continuation of the previous table, showing the derivation of before tax profits and the tax loss carryforward account. The calculation of the escrow account earnings and interest charges on the line of credit will be dealt with shortly.

The gross income is the gross margin from operation less the fixed operating costs. The before tax income is the sum of the gross income plus the interest income on the escrow account, less the interest and risk premium on the loan, and less the interest and risk premium on the line of credit. In the first year, the

Table 4.4
Disposition of Cash Flow

YEAR	TAXES PAYABLE	CASH FLOW	BALANCE ESCROW ACCOUNT	BALANCE LINE OF CREDIT ACCOUNT	PAYOUT TO PARENT	BALANCE BANK RISK ACCOUNT
1	$ 0	$-837	$ 163	$ 0	$ 0	$ 120
2	0	95	258	0	0	247
3	0	234	492	0	0	382
4	0	-999	0	507	0	521
5	0	-325	0	832	0	667
6	0	-140	0	972	0	818
7	0	-691	0	1,663	0	972
8	0	-1,150	0	2,813	0	1,152
9	0	-644	0	3,457	0	1,362
10	0	-432	0	3,890	0	1,578
11	0	938	0	2,952	0	1,799
12	0	2,040	0	912	0	2,011
13	0	2,987	2000	0	74	2,202
14	0	3,601	2000	0	3,601	2,383
15	912	3,248	2000	0	3,248	2,565
16	1,009	2,868	2000	0	2,868	2,750
17	885	2,637	2000	0	2,637	2,940
18	975	2,405	2000	0	2,405	3,134
19	952	2,362	2000	0	2,362	3,333
20	868	2,206	2000	0	2,206	3,536

escrow account earnings of $90 ($90,000) is the 9 percent interest earned on the $1 million that the subsidiary is required to fund. The gross income plus the escrow account income totals $723. This, less the depreciation of $900 and interest expense of $1,440 on the loan and the risk premium of $120, yields a before tax income of −$1,737. Tax losses are accrued to a tax carryforward account.

The tax carryforward account works the same way as described in the previous chapter: it grows when there is a negative before tax income and is depleted when there is a positive before tax income. In year 13, the gross income is $5,182 with no earnings from the escrow account. The interest charges are $738 on the loan, plus a risk premium of $62 and $109 on the line of credit, plus its risk premium of $9, for a total of $918. The gross income less the interest charges and depreciation charges of $1,700 results in a before tax profit of $2,564. No taxes are payable because the tax loss carryforward of $6,302 at the end of the previous year shields the profits from taxation. But the tax loss carryforward account is thereby reduced from $6,302 to $3,738. Actual tax liabilities occur in year 15, when the tax loss carryforward account has been exhausted.

Negative cash flows drain the escrow account until it is emptied of funds.

Table 4.5
Line of Credit Account with No Cash Earnings

YEAR	AMORTIZATION OF LOAN	INTEREST ON LOAN	INTEREST ON LINE OF CREDIT	YEAR END STATUS OF LINE OF CREDIT
1	$ 0	$1,560	$ 0	$ 470
2	0	1,560	61	2,091
3	0	1,560	272	3,923
4	706	1,514	510	6,653
5	706	1,422	865	9,646
6	706	1,331	1,254	12,937
7	706	1,239	1,684	16,563
8	706	1,147	2,153	20,569
9	706	1,055	2,674	25,004
10	706	964	3,251	29,924
11	706	872	3,890	35,392
12	706	780	4,601	41,479
13	706	688	5,392	48,265
14	706	596	6,274	55,842
15	706	504	7,259	64,312
16	706	413	8,361	73,791
17	706	321	9,593	84,411
18	706	229	10,973	96,320
19	706	138	12,522	109,685
20	706	46	14,259	124,696

Then the line of credit is drawn down to ensure the solvency of the company. There is no limit to the amount of the line of credit because its purpose is to act as a barometer of the ability of a company to pay off a loan. If there is a balance in the escrow account, the account earns interest. If there is a balance in the line of credit account, the account generates an interest charge.

The escrow account is initially funded at $1 million, but it must reach a level of $2 million before any excess cash generation can be passed on to the parent. The cash flow is the sum of the gross income and earnings on the escrow account less taxes payable, amortization of the loan, and all interest charges associated with the loan and the line of credit. Positive cash flows are first applied to the line of credit account until it is paid off. Then the flows are directed to the escrow account until its balance reaches $2 million. When this has been achieved, any further cash generation is passed on to the parent in the form of a dividend payment.

Referring to Table 4.4, the first year's before tax income is −$1,737, resulting in no tax liability. Adding back in the noncash expense of depreciation ($900) and subtracting the real cash after tax expense of amortization ($0 in the first three years), the cash flow is −$837, which reduces the initially funded escrow account from $1 million ($1,000) to $163. The bank risk account received the proceeds of the risk premium associated with the loan ($120) and with the line of credit ($0). This money is set aside, earning a 6 percent after tax return. It will be used to compensate for shortfalls in paying off the line of credit should such a condition exist at the end of the twentieth year.

The next two years are positive cash flows that build up the escrow account to $492 by the end of the third year. The return of the escrow account in the fourth year is the previous year's balance multiplied by 9 percent, or $44. The fourth year results in a negative cash flow of −$999. This is derived by adding the noncash depreciation expense of $900 to the before tax profit of −$1,193 less the amortization of $706. Alternatively, the cash flow is the sum of the gross income and the escrow account earnings ($1,221) less all interest charges ($1,514), taxes ($0), and amortization of debt payments ($706), or −$999. This wipes out the balance of $492 in the escrow account, resulting in drawing down the line of credit by $507.

The fifth year is another year with a negative cash flow. The deficit of $325 is funded by another drawdown of the line of credit from $507 to $832. The interest charge on the line of credit is 12 percent of the previous end-of-year balance of $507, or $61. The risk premium on the line of credit is 1 percent of $507, or $5. The bank risk account for the previous year is $521, which is presumed to grow at a 6 percent after tax return to $552. Then the risk premiums associated with the loan ($109) and the line of credit ($5) are added to the bank risk account, bringing the end-of-year balance up to the indicated $667 (rounding error).

There is a positive cash flow in the thirteenth year of $2,987 of which $912 is used to pay off the line of credit, $2,000 to replenish the escrow account up to its prescribed limit, leaving $74 (rounding error) to be paid to the parent in the form of a dividend. The subsequent positive cash flows are passed directly to the parent because the escrow account is fully funded.

Taxes are first payable in the fifteenth year. The before tax income of $3,166 (Table 4.3) is only partially shielded by the tax carryforward of $560, leaving $2,606 exposed to taxation. The tax bill is 35 percent of $2,606, or $912 (Table 4.4). The cash flow is $5,191 in gross income, plus $180 in earnings on the escrow account, less total interest charges of $505, less taxes of $912 and amortization of $706, or $3,248. All of this can be passed directly to the parent because the escrow account is fully funded.

There is no residual value calculation because the business is presumed to continue beyond the projection period. There is no need to "wrap up" the project at the end of the twentieth year because the internal rate of return is not being calculated. The banker is not interested in the internal rate of return for the equity owners, but in the prospects of repayment of the loan and the payment of its associated interest charges. Although a low return on the equity investment may mean trouble with respect to repayment of the underlying debt, the banker is not overly concerned about the return on investment that the equity owner earns. His concern is that the subsidiary makes enough money to pay back the loan.

INCORPORATING DEBT IN MEASURING REWARD

The evaluation of the return on the project in the previous chapter did not contain any provision for financing the project with debt. Financing was done through equity funds. There has been much debate over incorporating debt in evaluating potential investment situations from the point of view of the equity owners. A greater reliance on debt means a smaller equity investment. Generally speaking, the return on equity can be enhanced by the use of debt. Therefore, there is a question whether the use of debt in financing projects should be part of the process of evaluating the return on investments.

For example, suppose that there is a $10 million investment and banks are willing to fund up to 80 percent of the cost of the project. Should the equity owners evaluate the project on the basis of a $10 million or a $2 million investment? The return on investment will be significantly different. Some argue that since the equity owners are putting up $2 million in cash, the project should be evaluated on the basis of a $2 million investment. However, one point is inescapable. The equity investors must guarantee the repayment of the $8 million loan. Although they put up $2 million, they are on the line, so to speak, for $10 million—their investment plus the repayment of the loan to the bank. Therefore, the investment should be evaluated on the basis of $10 million even though the equity owners are putting up only $2 million.

Another way to approach this issue of whether this project should be evaluated on the basis of a $2 million or a $10 million investment is to proceed from the sublime to the ridiculous. Suppose that a bank is willing to advance $9,999,999. Should a $10 million investment be evaluated on the basis of a $1 equity investment? Suppose that the bank advances $10 million; now there is no equity investment and some degree of confusion over how to interpret the rate of return on a zero investment. Going one step further, suppose the bank advances $10,000,001. Is the project to be evaluated on the basis of a negative dollar investment? Perhaps it is more consistent for management to evaluate a project, or compare projects, on the basis of equity funding. Once a project is approved, then thought can be given as to how the project should be financed.

MEASURING THE DEGREE OF RISK

Returning from this digression, the banker wants the simulation set up on the basis that the original loan is paid off under all circumstances. If the line of credit balance is zero at the end of the twentieth year, the loan has been paid off by the gross income generated from the operation of the factory. The extra interest increment charged to the loan, called the risk premium, to compensate for the added risk of not having a parent guarantee, is kept by the bank. If the line of credit balance is not zero, however, the loan has not been amortized through operations, but by further borrowings from the bank. The original loan has been paid off by creating a new loan called the line of credit. The ending balance of the risk account is applied against the ending balance of the line of credit to gauge the potential loss in making this loan.

To illustrate the calculation of the potential loss, and to gauge just how large it can be, suppose that the gross margin from the single contract is just sufficient to offset the fixed costs and that this condition continues throughout the twenty-year period. There is no cash generated from operations to satisfy financing charges. The original loan of $12 million is paid off by continued borrowings from the line of credit. The line of credit sinks deeper into the abyss as the years go by. To simplify the calculations, let us assume that the interest on the loan and the line of credit is 13 percent. This avoids the necessity of separating the risk premium from the interest payments. Table 4.5 shows the balance in the line of credit after twenty years of no cash earnings.

The initial figure of $470 in the line of credit is derived from the deficit of $1,560 in financing charges being partly satisfied from the $90 in earnings from the $1 million escrow account plus the liquidation of the escrow account. This provides $1,090 in funds that are paid to the bank as partial compensation for the interest charges. The remaining $470 is borrowed from the line of credit.

The rest of the table is constructed using the following methodology. Arbitrarily selecting year 9, the bank is owed $706 in amortization and $1,055 in interest payments on the original loan. In addition, the bank is owed interest on the line of credit, which at the end of year 8, or at the start of year 9, totals $20,569. The interest on the line of credit is 13 percent of $20,569, or $2,674. The financing charges for the original loan and the line of credit total $4,435. The gross margin from operations is just sufficient to cover fixed costs. This means that there is no cash generation from operations that can be applied against the $4,435 owed to the bank. The company then borrows this amount from its unlimited line of credit, bringing its new end-of-year amount outstanding up to the indicated $25,004.

The simulator builder is incredulous that a company could borrow $12 million and end up owing $125 million.

"Well, that's the nature of compounding of interest. Look at the interest payments at the end of the twenty-year period. The annual interest payment is greater than the original loan."

"You bankers are making a fortune. You lend out $12 million and you are owed $125 million. Not a bad business to be in."

"Actually, we have collected nothing from this loan. This is a liability that will never be paid. Meanwhile we have been paying out real cash at 10 to 11 percent to the pension fund that originally advanced us the money."

"Then the pension fund is making a fortune."

"The pension fund is getting 10 to 11 percent on the funds it advanced to us— not much more money than investing in government bonds."

"I am looking at a bill for $125 million on an initial investment of one-tenth that amount, and you are telling me that no one is making money?"

"Fine, let's make a receivable out of it. I'll sell it to you. How much are you willing to pay for it?"

"Pay for it!?"

"Yes, pay for it. Here is a factory that in twenty years has not made one red cent over operating costs. Everything is twenty years old and probably falling apart. It never has—and probably never will—make a penny. It owes us $125 million. There is no uncertainty over what it owes us. It's all in black and white. Now what are you going to pay for it?"

"Nothing more than what I could sell the factory for."

"Then, that is what it is worth. Maybe that something is nothing."

"But if you sell it to me for nothing, so to speak, don't you have to take a $125 million writeoff on an original loan of $12 million?"

"Would you believe that we can't write off $125 million and survive the fiasco? Besides, we haven't lost $125 million. It is mostly a bookkeeping entry. We lost what we actually paid to the pension fund. We lost $12 million in principal and all the interest. If I add up the interest on the loan, the total is . . . nearly $18 million. But that is at 13 percent . . . if I just ratio that for, say, 11 percent . . . that looks like it is slightly over $15 million for a total of $27 million."

"Then what does the $125 million mean?"

"If that factory can start operating profitably in the twenty-first year, it owes us $125 million. If not, we write off $27 million, which is our cash out-of-pocket loss."

"And what about the $100 million difference?"

"Beat's me. I'm only a banker. Sounds like an accounting problem to me. It certainly isn't a real $100 million loss in terms of cash. It is simply a book-keeping entry. I really don't know how this would be handled. This reminds me of an international loan to a third world nation. If we lent $12 million to Upper Volta, and if we wait long enough, they will owe us $125 million simply because they don't generate the dollars to pay the interest on the original loan. Yet much of that $125 million is unreal, just as the ending balance of $125 million in the line of credit is unreal."

"What would you do if you were the factory owner and things started looking better after the twentieth year?"

"If I were the factory owner, and things looked like we might have a profit after the twentieth year, I would declare bankruptcy—clear the deck so to speak—and go on from there. How can the factory even begin to pay the interest on a $125 million debt? Actually this situation would not be allowed to degenerate to this state. We would never wait until the twentieth year to pull the plug on this loan. For instance, we might abandon all hope after ten straight years of not generating any funds to pay the financing costs. Then our total loss would be repaying the remaining principal of the $12 million loan, and all interest payments up to that point, say around $11 or $12 million, or a total of $22 or $23 million. And if we could get $2 or $3 million from selling the factory—someone might be able to make a go at it at that level, or use the facilities for something else—then our total loss could be contained to about $20 million. Even this is on the high side. Five years of no earnings would be more than adequate justification for us to pull the plug. Then our losses wouldn't be as large as $20 million."

"Applying what you're saying to Upper Volta, the best thing you can do for yourself and Upper Volta is wipe its debt off your books."

"Not my books, but somebody's books. Think about it. If Upper Volta does not have any dollar income, and its debt repayment and interest arrears are simply rolled over into a new loan where the interest keeps compounding away year after year, it is a matter of time until its total debt is ten times higher than the original debt and where the annual interest payment is equal to the amount of the original loan. Think about it. You borrow $1. You end up owing $10 and you have received nothing for the $9 difference. When you are talking in terms of billions of dollars, it is clearly an impossible situation. Even though I am a banker, I think that there is a lot of wisdom in the Old Testament on handling unpayable debts."

"Which is?"

"After seven years, if a debt cannot be paid off, it is liquidated from the books. Gone forever. No compounding of interest mushrooming indebtedness until it fills the solar system with outstanding balances representing hardly anything other than the cost of the red ink to print the figures. Anyway, when do you think I'll be able to see the results of the simulation?"

"Soon."

"Well, I think we have another Upper Volta, with plenty of opportunity for writing off debt. Want to see the results?"

"Isn't that what we are paying you for?"

"I ran the simulation one thousand times. In 742 runs, the balance in the line of credit at the end of the twentieth year was zero. This means that the factory was able to generate sufficient funds to pay off the debt."

"And we keep the balance in the risk bank account."

"Yes, which amounted to about $3 to $3.5 million depending on the use of the line of credit during the projection period. Then there were another 21 runs where the balance in the line of credit account at the end of the twentieth year was less than $3.5 million. Because the deficit in the line of credit account could be satisfied by the balance in the risk premium account, everything is fine."

"Except we made 12 percent on the return on the investment, and not 13 percent."

"True, but remember, you were satisfied with 12 percent if you had a parent guarantee. The 13 percent contains a 1 percent risk premium to cover losses, and for these 21 runs, it was sufficient to perform its function. For these 763 runs, you made 13 percent most of the time. Only a few runs, 21 to be exact, consumed the balance in the risk account. Anyway, you are 76 percent safe in going ahead with this loan."

"And 24 percent at risk of a loss."

"Twenty-six of the runs had losses as measured by an ending balance in the line of credit account of between $3.5 million and $20 million, and 211 runs had losses in excess of $20 million. But according to you, your maximum loss would be limited to $20 million."

"So, I have a 21 or so percent chance of being wiped out if I proceed along the lines indicated by management."

"That's what the model says."

"Well, I tell you, that kills the loan. There is no way I can get this through management. And even if I did, what good does it do me? If the loan works out, we can keep the risk premium account. If it doesn't work out, my career goes down the drain. No upside for me, and all downside. I am not going to lose any sleep on this loan."

"Then, it's dead."

"No, it's not dead. All I have to do is start acting as a banker, and there may still be a possibility for us to do some business here. I want you to do the following. Can you change the model to handle the following situation: I will advance $20 million in the fifth year—provided that there are two or more contracts on the books. Do that for three or more, and for four or more, contracts. If this condition of a minimum number of contracts is satisfied, simulate my putting the money into the operation during the fifth year and amortize the loan over the subsequent fifteen years of the project. Keep the initial balance in the escrow account at $1 million. Don't make any other changes. I just want to see the results, and then we can go from there."

"But that is going against the rules of the game as proposed by management."

"Hey, I'm not obligated to dance to their tune. I am not going to participate in any loan where, for openers, I have over a 20 percent chance of losing everything. If someone else wants to take the risk, it's a free country. But why should any bank take what is so clearly an equity risk? Let the conglomerate face the risk of the plant not functioning, the nonrenewal of the first contract, the inability to obtain any other contracts, and anything else we can throw into the equity risk pot. I'm a banker. I should be advancing funds on the basis that these hurdles have all been cleared. Companies do their betting with equity money before the race starts. Banks do their betting with debt money after it is reasonably clear that the horse has left the starting gate and is at least in the race. We really don't know if the new factory can even function. But, once it demonstrates that it can function somewhere near management's expectations with two, three, or four contracts under its belt, then maybe it is time for us to jump in with what amounts to a total refinancing of the project. But I need some measure of the risks I am taking in setting up minimum performance criteria of two, three, or four contracts. So, can you do what I asked for?"

"Yes, and I'll get back to you."

Exhibit 4.1
Line-of-Credit Ending Balance (1,000 Simulation Runs)

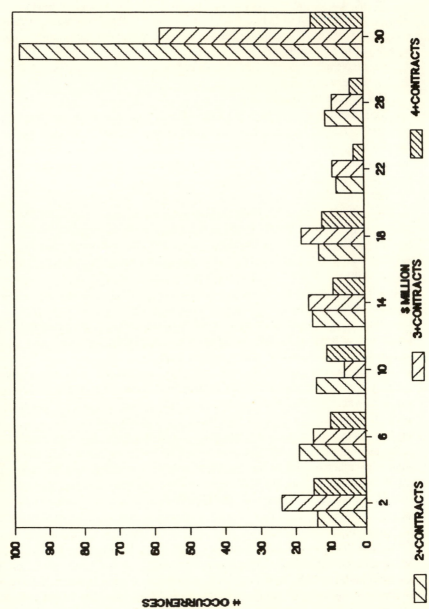

"Well, I got the results you requested."

"That didn't take long. How did you do it so fast?"

"The modifications weren't that significant. Then I found three personal computers that weren't being used and ran the three simulations simultaneously. The results are, in short, better, and you are on the right track of making them even better. In the one thousand runs that I made, about 200 occurrences, or 20 percent of the simulation runs, resulted in a loss when funding was done on the basis of at least two contracts being in place. That dropped down to 16 percent when funding was dependent on having three contracts in place, and another drop to 8 percent when four contracts were in place before the $20 million was advanced. This graph [exhibit 4.1] illustrates the nature of the losses. I kept the maximum loss to $30 million by assuming that you will pull the plug before losses exceed that amount."

"But why are you concerned with this when you don't intend to respond to the loan request along the lines indicated by management?"

"Oh, but I do want to respond. I do want to keep the door open. I do want to appear constructive in my attitude toward their proposal. I do want to make this loan. Management has given me their preference; I'll give them mine. There is, at this time, an unbridgeable gap between us. If no other banker responds the way they want him to, then they can start talking to me because I have given them something to respond to. I have not thrown their proposal into the wastebasket as, I hope, all my competitors have done. I'm even going to tell them about your simulation model. You're going to do a writeup on this project. We are going to tell them about the expert's assessment on their getting new contracts. I am really interested in what they have to say about his assessment. We are going to have a constructive interplay that may end up becoming a loan. But it is going to be a type of loan that won't disturb my sleep. And I have a tool where I can fool around with what year to make the loan, the amount of the loan, what conditions have to be met with both the required funding of the escrow account and the number of contracts that have to be on the books. Believe me, you are as much a part of my marketing effort as you are a part of my credit evaluation effort."

APPENDIX

The simulation in this appendix is modeled after the discussion contained in the chapter. It is a single purpose program that would have to be rewritten to be a generalized program for evaluating loan proposals. It does contain the principal provisions that would have to be incorporated into a generalized program.

SIMONE was run to generate the simulators associated with the length of the contract in good and bad times and the monthly gross margin of the contract negotiated during good and bad times. These are entered into the arrays L(1,I), L(2,I) and the arrays D(1,I), D(2,I), respectively, in statements 100 to 160. The simulation begins at statement 170 by erasing the results of previous runs (statements 180–190) and in determining whether good (Z = 1) or bad (Z = 2) times prevail at the start of the simulation (statements 200–220). For the subsequent twenty years (statement 230), business conditions are determined on the basis that there is an 80 percent chance that they will remain the same as the previous year (statements 240–280).

The initial contract is entered in statement 290 and all other contracts during the twenty-year period are set up in statements 300 to 380 and the associated subroutines. The C(I) array contains the number of contracts and an internal check is made in statements 390 to 410 to ensure that there are no more than twenty contracts. The M(1,I) array in statement 420 translates the number of contracts to the required number of FMSs. The M(2,I) array in statement 430 keeps track of the timing of additional FMSs that will determine the timing of the incremental $4-million loan for the second FMS and the incremental depreciation schedules for each additional FMS. Statement 440 establishes the fixed operating cost. The monthly revenue figures for each individual contract are stored in the R(I,J) array and are reduced to an annual gross margin in the M(3,I) array in statements 450 to 460. Statement 470 reduces the annual gross margin by 3 percent per year cumulatively, starting in the tenth year. By eliminating the GOTO 540 at the end of statement 470 the aforementioned arrays can be printed.

Statement 540 determines the gross income by subtracting the fixed operating costs from the gross margin. Removal of the GOTO 620 at the end of statement 540 and the REM in statement 600 permits the generation of the worst, best, and average gross income simulations shown in the chapter. The worst and best are selected on the basis of the lowest and highest aggregate gross income over the twenty-year period (statements 550–590) and the results are printed out in statement 610.

The incremental depreciation associated with each additional FMS is calculated in statements 620 to 660 and stored in array A(7,I). The incremental loan for the second FMS is determined in statements 670 to 700 and stored in array M(2,I). The incremental seven-year amortization of the loan on the second FMS is stored in array M(1,I) (statements 710–750). The total depreciation schedule in statement 760 is the twenty-year depreciation of the factory itself plus the incremental depreciation for additional FMSs. The amortization of the loan in statements 770–780 is the seventeen-year amortization of the first loan on the factory itself starting in year 4 plus the incremental amortization of the second loan for the follow on FMS. Statement 790 keeps track of the maximum face amount of the loans being extended to the subsidiary and is recorded in array M(5,I). Array M(6,I) in statement 800 is the outstanding balance of the loan. It is calculated by comparing the face amount of the loan with the total amortization payments that have already been made. Statement 810 calculates the interest and the risk premium on the basis of the average outstanding amount and stores the results in arrays M(7,I) and M(8,I).

Statements 820 to 830 record the interest income of the escrow account in array M(9,I) and the interest expense of the line of credit in array M(10,I). Statement 840 calculates the risk premium on the line of credit and stores the results in array M(11,I). The same statement also calculates the balance in the bank risk account and stores the results in array A(11,I). Before tax income is determined in statement 850 and recorded in array A(2,I). Statements 860 to 920 handle the tax loss carryforward account, which is stored in array A(3,I), and taxes, which are stored in array A(4,I).

Statement 930 records the net cash flow in array A(5,I). Statements 940 to 1060 dispose of the cash flow in terms of the escrow account in array A(9,I), line of credit in array A(10,I), or payout to the equity owner in array A(6,I). Removing the GOTO 1200 at the end of statement 1070 permits printout of the various arrays determining the net cash flow

and its disposition as shown and described in the chapter. Statements 1210 to 1260 record
the results of each simulation internally, while statements 1270 to 1360 store the aggregate
results of all the simulations externally.

In response to the banker's request to run simulations for a minimum number of
contracts, certain modifications had to be made. The simulation was not permitted to
proceed beyond statement 410 if the value of $C(5)$, the number of contracts in the fifth
year, was not above the stipulated minimum number. The statements determining the
financing of the second FMS were bypassed and the financing proceeded on a subsequent
fifteen-year payout of the $20 million loan made in the fifth year. A counter was installed
in statement 1260 to ensure that one thousand simulations were run with the requisite
minimum number of contracts before the recording of the data starting in statement 1270.

```
10  REM NAME OF PROGRAM IS FMS
20  DIM R(20,240):DIM L(2,100):DIM D(2,100):DIM Y(240)
30  DIM C(20):DIM M(15,20):DIM F(20):DIM A(15,20):DIM P(2000,500)
40  C1=4000:C2=18000:A1=12000:P=1000:E1=12:U=2000:E2=1:GOTO 90
50  PRINT:INPUT "AMOUNT OF LOAN: ";A1
60  PRINT:INPUT "INITIAL FUNDING ESCROW ACC'T: ";P:E1=12
70  PRINT:INPUT "MAXIMUM BALANCE ESCROW ACC'T: ";U
80  PRINT:INPUT "INT RATE DIFF FOR RISK MGT:   ";E2
90  Z8=1000000!:Z9=0:OPEN "I",#1,"GLENGTH"
100 FOR I=1 TO 100:INPUT #1,L(1,I):NEXT:CLOSE #1
110 OPEN "I",#1,"BLENGTH"
120 FOR I=1 TO 100:INPUT #1,L(2,I):NEXT:CLOSE #1
130 OPEN "I",#1,"GDEAL"
140 FOR I=1 TO 100:INPUT #1,D(1,I):NEXT:CLOSE #1
150 OPEN "I",#1,"BDEAL"
160 FOR I=1 TO 100:INPUT #1,D(2,I):NEXT:CLOSE #1
170 FOR S=1 TO 1000
180 FOR I=1 TO 11:FOR J=1 TO 20:M(I,J)=0:A(I,J)=0:NEXT:NEXT
190 FOR I=1 TO 20:FOR J=1 TO 240:R(I,J)=0:NEXT:NEXT
200 X=RND(X):IF X<.5 THEN 210 ELSE 220
210 Z=1:GOTO 230
220 Z=2
230 FOR I=1 TO 20
240 X=RND(X):IF X>.8 THEN 250 ELSE 280
250 IF Z=1 THEN 260 ELSE 270
260 Z=2:GOTO 280
270 Z=1
280 FOR J=12*(I-1)+1 TO 12*I:Y(J)=Z:NEXT:NEXT
290 FOR I=1 TO 36:R(1,I)=48:NEXT:C=1:M1=36:GOSUB 1560
300 FOR Y=1 TO 20:Z=Y((Y-1)*12+1)
310 GOSUB 1370:IF N>0 THEN 320 ELSE 380
320 FOR N1=1 TO N:X=RND(X):M1=12*(Y-1)+INT(1+X*11+.5):GOSUB 1530
330 L=INT(L(Z,T)+.5):GOSUB 1530:R=D(Z,T):C=C+1:IF C>20 THEN 370
340 IF M1+L>240 THEN 350 ELSE 360
350 L=240-M1
360 FOR J=M1 TO M1+L:R(C,J)=R:NEXT:M1=M1+L:GOSUB 1560
370 NEXT
380 C(Y)=C:NEXT
390 FOR I=1 TO 20:IF C(I)>20 THEN 400 ELSE 410
400 C(I)=20
410 NEXT
420 FOR I=1 TO 20:M(1,I)=INT((C(I)-1)/5):NEXT
430 FOR I=2 TO 20:M(2,I)=M(1,I)-M(1,I-1):NEXT
440 FOR I=1 TO 20:X=RND(X):F(I)=600+X*100+10*C(I):NEXT
450 FOR I=1 TO 20:A=0:FOR C=1 TO 20:FOR J=12*(I-1)+1 TO 12*I
460 A=A+R(C,J):NEXT:NEXT:M(3,I)=A:NEXT
470 FOR I=10 TO 20:M(3,I)=(100-3*(I-9))*M(3,I)/100:NEXT:GOTO 540
480 FOR I=1 TO 20:PRINT I;C(I),M(2,I),M(3,I),F(I):NEXT:INPUT Z$
490 FOR I=1 TO 240:PRINT I;R(1,I),R(2,I),R(3,I),R(4,I):NEXT:INPUT Z$
500 FOR I=1 TO 240:PRINT I;R(5,I),R(6,I),R(7,I),R(8,I):NEXT:INPUT Z$
510 FOR I=1 TO 240:PRINT I;R(9,I),R(10,I),R(11,I),R(12,I):NEXT:INPUT Z$
```

```
520 FOR I=1 TO 240:PRINT I;R(13,I),R(14,I),R(15,I),R(16,I):NEXT:INPUT Z$
530 FOR I=1 TO 240:PRINT I;R(17,I),R(18,I),R(19,I),R(20,I):NEXT
540 FOR I=1 TO 20:A(1,I)=M(3,I)-F(I):NEXT:GOTO 620
550 FOR I=1 TO 20:A(2,I)=A(2,I)+A(1,I)/1000:NEXT
560 A=0:FOR I=1 TO 20:A=A+A(1,I):NEXT:IF A<Z8 THEN 570 ELSE 580
570 FOR I=1 TO 20:A(3,I)=A(1,I):A(5,I)=C(I):NEXT:Z8=A
580 IF A>Z9 THEN 590 ELSE 600
590 FOR I=1 TO 20:A(4,I)=A(1,I):A(6,I)=C(I):NEXT:Z9=A
600 REM NEXT:S=S-1
610 FOR I=1 TO 20:PRINT I;A(5,I);A(3,I),1000*A(2,I)/S,A(4,I);A(6,I):NEXT:END
620 FOR I=1 TO 20:IF M(2,I)=0 THEN 660 ELSE 630
630 FOR J=I TO I+9:IF J<=20 THEN 640 ELSE 650
640 A(7,J)=A(7,J)+C1/10
650 NEXT
660 NEXT
670 A=0:FOR I=1 TO 20:A=A+M(2,I):IF A>1 THEN 680 ELSE 690
680 M(2,I)=0
690 NEXT
700 FOR I=1 TO 20:M(2,I)=C1*M(2,I):M(1,I)=0:M(3,I)=0:NEXT
710 A=C1/7:FOR I=1 TO 20:IF M(2,I)>0 THEN 720 ELSE 750
720 IF I<15 THEN 730 ELSE 740
730 FOR J=I TO I+6:M(1,J)=M(1,J)+A:NEXT:GOTO 750
740 K=I-14:FOR J=I TO 20:M(1,J)=M(1,J)+A:NEXT:M(1,20)=M(1,20)+K*A
750 NEXT
760 FOR I=1 TO 20:M(3,I)=C2/20+A(7,I):NEXT
770 FOR I=4 TO 20:M(4,I)=A1/17:NEXT
780 FOR I=1 TO 20:M(4,I)=M(4,I)+M(1,I):NEXT
790 A=0:FOR I=1 TO 20:A=A+M(2,I):M(5,I)=A1+A:NEXT
800 A=0:FOR I=1 TO 20:A=A+M(4,I):M(6,I)=M(5,I)-A:NEXT:M(6,0)=M(6,1)
810 FOR I=1 TO 20:A=(M(6,I-1)+M(6,I))/2:M(7,I)=E1*A/100:M(8,I)=E2*A/100:NEXT
820 A(3,0)=0:A(9,0)=P:A(10,0)=0:A(11,0)=0:FOR I=1 TO 20
830 M(9,I)=(E1-3)*A(9,I-1)/100:M(10,I)=E1*A(10,I-1)/100
840 M(11,I)=E2*A(10,I-1)/100:A(11,I)=1.06*A(11,I-1)+M(8,I)+M(11,I)
850 A(2,I)=A(1,I)-M(3,I)-M(7,I)-M(8,I)+M(9,I)-M(10,I)-M(11,I)
860 IF A(2,I)<0 THEN 870 ELSE 880
870 A(3,I)=A(3,I-1)-A(2,I):A(4,I)=0:GOTO 930
880 IF A(3,I-1)=0 THEN 890 ELSE 900
890 A(4,I)=.35*A(2,I):GOTO 930
900 IF A(3,I-1)>A(2,I) THEN 910 ELSE 920
910 A(3,I)=A(3,I-1)-A(2,I):A(4,I)=0:GOTO 930
920 A(4,I)=.35*(A(2,I)-A(3,I-1)):A(3,I)=0
930 A(5,I)=A(1,I)-A(4,I)-M(7,I)-M(8,I)+M(9,I)-M(10,I)-M(11,I)-M(4,I)
940 IF A(5,I)>0 THEN 950 ELSE 1040
950 IF A(10,I-1)>0 THEN 960 ELSE 1000
960 IF A(10,I-1)>A(5,I) THEN 970 ELSE 980
970 A(10,I)=A(10,I-1)-A(5,I):GOTO 1070
980 B=A(5,I)-A(10,I-1):A(10,I)=0
990 A(9,I)=A(9,I-1)+B:IF A(9,I)>U THEN 1010 ELSE 1020
1000 A(9,I)=A(9,I-1)+A(5,I):IF A(9,I)>U THEN 1010 ELSE 1030
1010 A(6,I)=A(9,I)-U:A(9,I)=U:GOTO 1070
1020 A(6,I)=0:A(9,I)=A(9,I-1)+B:GOTO 1070
1030 A(6,I)=0:A(9,I)=A(9,I-1)+A(5,I):GOTO 1070
1040 B=-A(5,I):A(6,I)=0:IF A(9,I-1)>B THEN 1050 ELSE 1060
1050 A(9,I)=A(9,I-1)-B:GOTO 1070
1060 B=B-A(9,I-1):A(9,I)=0:A(10,I)=A(10,I-1)+B
1070 NEXT:GOTO 1200
1080 PRINT "LOANS","AMOUNT","AMORT","INTEREST","RISK PRE"
1090 PRINT "MADE","OWED","OF LOAN","ON LOAN","ON LOAN"
1100 FOR I=1 TO 20:PRINT M(5,I),M(6,I),M(4,I),M(7,I),M(8,I):NEXT
1110 INPUT Z$:PRINT " ","INTEREST","INTEREST","RISK PRE","BK RISK"
1120 PRINT "YEAR","ESCROW","LOFCRE","LOFCRE","ACCOUNT"
1130 FOR I=1 TO 20:PRINT I,M(9,I),M(10,I),M(11,I),A(11,I):NEXT
1140 INPUT Z$:PRINT "GROSS"," ","BEFORE","TAX"
1150 PRINT "INCOME","DEPREC","TAX","CARRYFORW","TAXES"
1160 FOR I=1 TO 20:PRINT A(1,I),M(3,I),A(2,I),A(3,I),A(4,I):NEXT
1170 INPUT Z$:PRINT " ","CASH","ESCROW","LINE OF","PAYOUT"
1180 PRINT "YEAR","FLOW","ACCOUNT","CREDIT","TO OWNERS"
1190 FOR I=1 TO 20:PRINT I,A(5,I),A(9,I),A(10,I),A(6,I):NEXT
```

```
1200 PRINT S;" LOFCRE: ";A(10,20);" RISKACT: ";A(11,20)
1210 B1=INT(A(10,20)/100+.5):B2=INT(A(11,20)/100+.5)
1220 IF B1>0 THEN 1230 ELSE 1260
1230 IF B1>B2 THEN 1240 ELSE 1250
1240 B1=B1-B2:B2=0:GOTO 1260
1250 B2=B2-B1:B1=0
1260 P(1,B1)=P(1,B1)+1:P(2,B2)=P(2,B2)+1:NEXT:S=S-1
1270 B1=0:B2=0:FOR I=0 TO 2000:B1=B1+I*P(1,I):B2=B2+I*P(2,I):NEXT
1280 B3=0:B4=0:FOR I=1 TO 2000:B3=B3+P(1,I):B4=B4+P(2,I):NEXT
1290 PRINT "EXPECTED LINE OF CREDIT BALANCE: ";100*B1/S
1300 PRINT "EXPECTED RISK ACCOUNT BALANCE:   ";100*B2/S
1310 A9=999:OPEN "O",#1,"RESULTS"
1320 B5=0:B6=0:FOR I=0 TO 2000:IF I=0 THEN 1330 ELSE 1340
1330 WRITE #1,100*I,P(1,I),A9,A9,A9,P(2,I),A9,A9:GOTO 1360
1340 C1=P(1,I):C2=P(2,I):B5=B5+C1:B6=B6+C2
1350 WRITE #1,100*I,C1,100*C1/B3,100*B5/B3,A9,C2,100*C2/B4,100*B6/B4
1360 NEXT:CLOSE #1:END
1370 X=RND(X):ON Z GOTO 1380,1460
1380 IF X<.15 THEN 1420
1390 IF X<.5 THEN 1430
1400 IF X<.85 THEN 1440
1410 GOTO 1450
1420 N=0:GOTO 1520
1430 N=1:GOTO 1520
1440 N=2:GOTO 1520
1450 N=3:GOTO 1520
1460 IF X<.7 THEN 1490
1470 IF X<.95 THEN 1500
1480 GOTO 1510
1490 N=0:GOTO 1520
1500 N=1:GOTO 1520
1510 N=2:GOTO 1520
1520 RETURN
1530 X=RND(X):T=INT(100*X+.5)
1540 IF T<1 THEN 1530
1550 RETURN
1560 M1=M1+1:IF M1>238 THEN 1730 ELSE 1570
1570 Z=Y(M1):X=RND(X):ON Z GOTO 1580,1590
1580 IF X<.8 THEN 1600 ELSE 1630
1590 IF X<.6 THEN 1600 ELSE 1640
1600 GOSUB 1530:L=INT(L(Z,T)+.5):IF M1+L>240 THEN 1610 ELSE 1620
1610 L=240-M1
1620 FOR I=M1 TO M1+L:R(C,I)=R(C,I-1):NEXT:M1=M1+L:GOTO 1560
1630 X=RND(X):D=INT(1+X*5+.5):GOTO 1650
1640 X=RND(X):D=INT(6+X*12+.5)
1650 IF M1+D>240 THEN 1660 ELSE 1670
1660 D=240-M1
1670 FOR I=M1 TO M1+D:R(C,I)=0:NEXT:M1=M1+D
1680 GOSUB 1530:R=D(Z,T):GOSUB 1530:L=INT(L(Z,T)+.5)
1690 IF M1+L>240 THEN 1700 ELSE 1710
1700 L=240-M1
1710 FOR I=M1 TO M1+L:R(C,I)=R:NEXT
1720 M1=M1+L:GOTO 1560
1730 IF M1>241 THEN 1770
1740 IF M1=240 THEN 1750 ELSE 1760
1750 R(C,240)=R(C,239):GOTO 1770
1760 FOR I=M1 TO 240:R(C,I)=R(C,I-1):NEXT
1770 RETURN
```

5

Self-Insuring a Loan Portfolio

Much of what goes on in the insurance business in assessing risks and determining premiums to cover such risks is done by actuaries. It is not the intention of this chapter to suggest that computer simulation be used alongside of, or be substituted for, actuarial calculations. Simulation should be considered only for those situations where actuarial calculations fail to provide a solution. This fits the philosophic thought of simulation being the last resort of mathematicians in attempting to obtain a quantitative solution to a problem. This may even avoid piquing the sensitivities of an established profession.

The calculation of risk premiums and adequate reserves to provide for some degree of intended coverage against a potential loss falls under the rubric of financial risk management. The presentation of risk management in providing protection against a potential loss is in terms of self-insurance, not in terms of the purchase of insurance from an independent insurance company. This choice should not be construed as an endorsement of such a course of action, but to simplify the description of insurance as it pertains to financial risk management. There is no confusion over who is benefiting and who is paying for laying off the risk of a situation when, for instance, banks band together to self-insure against potential defaults in a portfolio of loans.

Addressing the subject matter in terms of self-insurance avoids the issue of government regulation of the insurance industry. Other issues that are not addressed are the operating costs of an insurance company and the competitive nature of the insurance business. Insurance companies recoup their operating costs by an "add-on" to the premium rate. This "add-on" and the premium rate affect the competitiveness of an insurance company in its market environment. The derivation of a risk premium in this chapter is strictly from the point of view of providing sufficient protection against losses, leaving aside regulatory, political, operational, and competitive considerations.

SELF-INSURANCE AND SELF-DELUSION

The previous chapter introduced the concept of an incremental risk premium to be added to the normal interest rate to provide some degree of protection, or coverage, for a particular risk. The risk associated with the loan proposal was the speculative element not covered by a parent guarantee. An examination of the role of the risk premium in the previous chapter should destroy any illusion that the banker protects himself against the risk of loss. As structured, the risk premium utterly fails to perform its intended function. The illusion of self-insurance was a delusion.

The intended function of the risk premium is to insure against catastrophic loss. The risk premium, as applied in chapter 4, insures against a very minor loss. The actual loss was anywhere between $0 and $20-30 million depending on which situation was being analyzed. The risk premium provided coverage for losses whose magnitude was about $3 million. In reviewing the distribution of losses, the probability that a loss would be this small was quite low; in fact, most losses far exceeded $3 million. The most probable size of a loss, for those occasions where there were losses, was either $20 or $30 million for the respective situation under scrutiny. Increasing the risk premium will not provide necessary protection. In a case where a plant fails to garner the requisite number of contracts, no risk premium, no matter how high, will provide any degree of protection. If the plant itself cannot generate the funds necessary to pay off a loan, how can it generate the funds necessary to pay for the risk premium, whose purpose is to pay off the loan? Increasing the risk premium simply widens the deficit in the line of credit account at the end of the twentieth year. This does not provide one iota of protection for the banker.

This point of self-insurance being a self-delusion can be demonstrated in another way. Suppose that an individual cancels the fire insurance policy on his home. Instead of paying a premium to a fire insurance company, the individual deposits the same amount of money in a special account. Suppose that the premium to insure a home for $250,000 against loss by fire is $500. At the start of the first year, the $500 is placed in a special account rather than being paid to an insurance company. The account earns 6 percent after taxes. The actual amount of insurance protection at the end of the first year is all of $530. At the end of the second year, there is $1,092 in loss reserves to provide coverage against a loss by fire. If there is a fire during the second year and the damage can be contained to $1,092, everything is under control. If the house burns to the ground, however, the owner of the house has not self-insured his loss. An insurance company would have paid him $250,000; his self-insurance scheme has a reserve for losses of only $1,092. This is exactly the problem faced by the banker in having a risk premium on the interest rate of a loan. Unless the loss is minuscule in relation to the size of the loan, the accumulated value of all the risk premium payments does not perform its intended function, which is to provide protection against a catastrophic loss of principal and interest.

The purpose of an insurance premium, then, is to pay for someone else's losses, not one's own. One cannot self-insure his own home. The banker cannot self-insure a loan. Insurance works when many individuals band together to essentially provide protection for each other against catastrophic losses. In essence, insurance is a mutual cooperative association set up to share the risk of loss of a few members among the association's many members. If one thousand individuals took the $500 they had been paying to a fire insurance company and placed the money into a special loss reserve account, then there would be $500,000 in premium payments in reserves in the first year of operation. If two homes, each worth $250,000, burn to the ground during the first year, there will be enough loss reserve funds to compensate for the losses. Nine hundred and ninety-eight policy holders contributed to the loss suffered by two individuals. All but two paid insurance premiums to cover the losses of others, not themselves. If three houses burn to the ground, however, the self-insurance scheme will fail its intended purpose of providing adequate protection to its membership because the losses exceed the reserves set aside to provide protection against this catastrophe.

Bankers, in setting up risk premium accounts, cannot self-insure loans. But they can contribute the incremental interest representing the risk premium to a loan loss reserve account that acts as a depository of the risk premiums from a thousand other loans. The accumulation of risk premiums in excess of claims increases the amount of reserves set aside to offset the losses suffered from bad loans. If actual loan losses do not exceed the loan loss reserves, then the self-insurance arrangement is a success. If actual loan losses do exceed the loan loss reserves, the arrangement fails its intended purpose. This is no different than having three homes burn to the ground when the reserves for losses are sufficient to provide adequate coverage for only two homeowners.

Suppose that a banker obtains the cooperation of other bankers to set up a self-insurance arrangement for a maximum of one thousand loans. The bankers contribute office space and personnel support to operate the captive insurance company. The insurance company is considered a captive company because it has been created by the participating banks to serve their exclusive needs. The captive insurance company, however, must act as an independent entity with the right to refuse loans submitted to it by the banks owning the captive company. Otherwise, one bank may enter into extremely risky bank loans and attempt to pawn the risk off on the other participating banks by having these loans insured by the captive insurance company.

This provision of a captive company acting in an independent fashion is part of risk management. A banker with reasonable prudence in approving new loans does not want to end up supporting the reckless lending practices of another. A somewhat less than scrupulous banker, who knows that he can insure his unintentional, or intentional, errors of judgment against the risk of losses, might be tempted to vastly expand his portfolio with highly risky loans. As noted in the previous chapter, profits in the banking business can be enhanced by expanding the size of a portfolio of loans as long as the loans are creditworthy. A noncreditworthy loan can be made creditworthy if its potential for loss can be insured by a third party.

A somewhat less than scrupulous banker may load up on loans of dubious creditworthiness, loans that do not possess those qualities that inspire confidence of repayment. His objective is to have a large-sized portfolio contribute to the bank's overall profitability while at the same time passing the higher risk of default to the captive insurance company. In so doing, the banker may think that he is being street-smart. He may think in terms of paying a risk premium that represents the average loss rate of the portfolio of loans while his claims are representing those loans in the portfolio with the highest loss rate. He is entering into a mutual insurance arrangement with the intent of being a net beneficiary.

This may be street-smart, but it is insurance-dumb. One enters into an insurance arrangement on the basis of being a loser, not a winner. Does one purchase automobile insurance with the hope of being involved in a head-on collision with a forty-ton truck? Should one be disappointed that last year's fire insurance premium was wasted because one's home did not burn down to the ground? Does one really want to be a winner when it comes to collecting on a personal life insurance policy?

UNDERWRITERS AND ADJUSTERS

In a captive, or mutually owned, self-insurance arrangement on loans, there may be a temptation to place the riskiest loans into the self-insurance scheme with the purpose of having the other banks bear a disproportionate share of an individual banker's mistakes. The captive loan insurance company must be able to reject loans that its shareholders want to have insured. In addition, the loan insurance company must have its own workout team to deal with loans that fall into default. Both a credit evaluation team and a workout team are necessary for a mutually owned insurance company to reduce the cost of insuring bank loans for its clientele, who are the banks owning the insurance company. These twin efforts of weeding out the worst credit risks and salvaging those loans that become financial casualties have a much greater impact on the cost of insurance than setting up an operation with a low overhead.

The credit evaluation team, the underwriters deciding which loans to accept in the captive insurance company, control the cost of the operation by reducing the probability of a claim from a defaulted loan. The stronger the financial structure of a company responsible for repaying a debt, the less the chance of the insurance company paying a claim. The workout team provides the other means of controlling costs. When a claim does arise, the workout team, acting as an adjuster, does whatever it can to contain the magnitude of the loss. Any action taken to reduce the probability of a claim arising or the extent of the loss associated with an individual claim reduces the risk premium that has to be charged to protect the participating banks from loan defaults.

A SIMULATION PROGRAM

Simulating Underwriters

Suppose that a captive loan insurance company has been formed by a group of banks to insure up to a total of one thousand individual loans. An analysis of loans for this group of banks shows that the typical loan is expected to range in size from $2 to $40 million, with most loans being around $8 million. These loans are not individual loans as such, but represent the collective exposure to a particular company of all the participating banks. Several loans may have been made to the same company for various purposes by the participating banks. A company may have borrowed $4 million from bank A and $6 million from bank B. Both banks have insured these loans with the captive insurance company. From the point of view of the captive insurance company, these two loans would be treated as one of the thousand with a total exposure to loss of $10 million if the company begins to slide toward financial oblivion.

The mutual self-insurance company has a few sharp credit analysts who scrutinize loans being placed in the loan portfolio fund. No loan can be added to the portfolio, if—in the opinion of the credit evaluation group acting as underwriters—it has a loss potential profile that exceeds the following criteria:

	BUSINESS CONDITIONS		
RANGE OF PROBABILITY OF LOSS	WORST	EXPECTED	BEST
UPPER	5%	1%	0%
EXPECTED	10	2	1
LOWER	15	4	2

Most loans are good loans when times are good. When times are good, the prospects for companies are good and loans are booked with confidence that the borrowers can honor the terms and conditions pertaining thereto. Loans usually do not go bad during good times; their weak points are masked by a strong economy. Weak points in the financial structure of a loan become apparent during the bad times. Bad times test the expectations of the good times when the loans were booked.

By banking standards, these loss assessments might be considered high. If a banker really believed that there was a 15 percent chance of a default simply because business conditions had taken a turn for the worse, the loan probably would not be booked. The history of loan losses might reveal, however, that actual loan losses have a profile of probability of default as reflected in the table. Few lending officers would admit that this might be the case—particularly on the day that the loan documents are being signed. Their mission is to book loans—and all loans are good loans on the day they are booked. The day of signing of the loan documentation is usually a day of celebration, not a day to assess the probability of a dream turning into a nightmare. Lending officers are not in a good psychological position to assess the risk of loss because their mission is to build up a loan portfolio. This is why credit analysis is done by a different group of people, not by the lending officers. Those associated with credit analysis and workout situations are in a better position to judge the validity of loss assessments are as, for that matter, lending officers who no longer have a vested interested in adding loans to a bank's portfolio.

The formulation of the SIMTWO program in chapter 2 requires ascending values as business conditions progress from worst to best. Rather than rewriting the SIMTWO program to accommodate descending values, the problem can be avoided by expressing the probability of loss as the probability of *not* suffering a loss.

| | BUSINESS CONDITIONS | | |
RANGE OF PROBABILITY OF NO LOSS	WORST	EXPECTED	BEST
UPPER	95%	99%	100%
EXPECTED	90	98	99
LOWER	85	96	98

The restatement of the table with the lower, expected, and upper values ascending in value as business conditions progress to higher levels of activity makes it possible for the SIMTWO program to generate a two-dimensional simulator of the situation without having to rewrite the program.

Simulating Adjusters

When a loan goes bad, losses are not necessarily 100 cents on every dollar. The captive insurance company has a workout team that is activated when a loan goes into default, or possibly, when there is an anticipated default. Usually this team consists of members who are specialists in credit evaluation, accounting, the legal framework in securing the rights of the lender, and industry conditions. The latter specialist may be an outside consultant who is hired on an ad hoc basis.

The workout team consists of bankers, accountants, lawyers, and industry experts. When a loan is about to, or has just gone into default on its payment of principal or interest, the workout team generally prefers to work with management to stem the tide of losses and rectify the cause of these losses. If this is unsuccessful, it may be necessary for the workout team to find new management who are more amenable to minimizing the losses to the debt holders rather than saving the investments of the equity owners.

The objective of the workout team in its role as adjuster is to minimize the extent of the losses associated with a claim. Cost cutting in the company's operations and salvaging the best operating divisions while liquidating the rest is the usual prescription given to a sick company. The workout team might conclude that the best course of action is to keep the company in operation, restate the debt at a lower level, and accept stock as compensation for writing off a portion of the loan. In this case, the bank permits the company to continue operation without forcing it into bankruptcy.

The workout team may conclude that the best course of action is to force the company into bankruptcy by insisting on its satisfying an obligation to the bank that is beyond the realm of possibility. Now a bankruptcy court judge is administratively in charge of things. The bank, as one of the creditors, can propose anything from a continuation of operations to a cessation of operations and the liquidation of everything in sight. The lawyers on the workout team would do their best to ensure that the bank is standing as close to the front of the line as possible to collect the proceeds from the fire sale. In a bankruptcy proceeding, however, the bank has lost control over the situation in that it is now just one of a number of creditors. The bank can suggest, or propose, what it feels is in its best interest, but it is the bankruptcy judge who makes the final decision. And that decision is based on the claims of all those who are involved with the proceedings. Therefore, it is not necessarily true that the bank is at the front of the line. What a bank actually receives in a bankruptcy proceeding is, to a large extent, at the discretion of the judge in charge of the case.

Bankers can exert more control over a situation by using the threat of having the firm declared bankrupt as a heavy-handed means of persuasion to induce management to do its will. In this game of wills, however, management may use the threat of declaring bankruptcy as a heavy-handed means of persuasion not to do the will of the bankers. Both management and bankers lose a great deal of control over a situation by forcing, or by declaring, bankruptcy because, in bankruptcy proceedings, the presiding judge has the last word in the disposition of assets and funds.

There is only one conclusion from all this: the workout team acting as an adjuster can be expected to pursue a course of action that it deems to be most appropriate in containing the extent of losses. For purposes of illustration, suppose that it has been the experience of the banks that the percentage of losses for loans in default, with the same general creditworthiness as those in the self-insurance arrangement, has been as follows.

BUSINESS CONDITIONS

DEGREE OF LOSS IN CENTS PER DOLLAR OF LOAN	WORST	EXPECTED	BEST
UPPER	40	20	10
EXPECTED	60	30	20
LOWER	80	50	30

When loans go bad during the upswing of the business cycle, they can be kept partially afloat by the buoyancy of the times. Losses are more containable when there is general optimism in the air. The average loss rate during the best of times is one percent of the individual loans in the portfolio. When a loss is suffered, the average loss is 20 cents on the dollar, or 20 percent of the face value of the loan. During the best of times, the expected losses on a $10 billion loan portfolio would be 1% × 20% × $10 billion, or $20 million per year. During the worst of times, the average loss rate is 10 percent and the average loss is 60 percent of the face amount of the loan. The corresponding expected losses during the worst of times would be 10% × 60% × $10 billion, or $600 million. Although losses during the bad times are significantly worse than during the good times, an assessment of a likely loss on a single-year basis masks the true nature of the problem. Good and bad times are multiyear phenomena. A few bad years in a row can lead to substantial cumulative losses.

Business conditions influence the degree of loss on defaulted loans. The salvage effort of the workout team can be aided, or hampered, by business conditions much as the salvage effort directed toward a foundering vessel can be aided, or hampered, by the weather. Calm seas aid rescue efforts while stormy seas impede, or even prevent, the saving of life and property. Good times mean that the economy is more robust, giving bankers a greater opportunity to make good on a bad loan. Good times encourage entrepreneurial individuals to seek out the few companies having financial difficulties. These individuals are eager to make their presence known; their wallets are flush with cash from other successful ventures; their views of the future are optimistic; and they are willing to risk equity money in faltering operations.

When loans go bad during business recessions, however, the situation becomes a mirror image of what has been just described. The depressed nature of business conditions exacerbates those conditions giving rise to problem loans. There are far more companies in financial trouble. Bad times reduce the eagerness of risk takers to become involved. There is less loose change in their wallets because their business enterprises are also bearing the strain of bad times. The money that used to jingle in their pockets is socked away under mattresses rather than being exposed to the increased risk of loss through involvement with companies overburdened by debt and unpaid bills.

Because of the greater number of loans in trouble and the greater likelihood of large losses, bankers become less patient. They are more apt to pull the rug out from under the borrower rather than exert the requisite patience to work out a difficult situation. Conventional wisdom in good times to minimize loses when bankers have few problem loans to worry about is patience. Conventional wisdom in bad times to minimize losses when bankers are saddled with many problem loans is cut and run. To no one's surprise, banking losses are more severe during bad times than during good times.

The previous table is restated in terms of cents per dollar recouped rather than lost to accommodate the SIMTWO simulator generating program.

BUSINESS CONDITIONS

DEGREE OF RECOUPMENT IN CENTS PER DOLLAR OF LOAN	WORST	EXPECTED	BEST
UPPER	60	80	90
EXPECTED	40	70	80
LOWER	20	50	70

Simulating Demand for Loans

Loans tend to grow in size and number during good times and shrink in both dimensions during bad times. The aggregate exposure to individual companies grows by a maximum of 4 percent per year during the best of good times and declines by a maximum of 4 percent per year during the worst of the bad times. This reflects the fact that companies have a greater demand for credit when times are good. While it is true that loans are being amortized (i.e., are being paid off over the passage of time), other loans are being added to finance higher levels of sales and to support the expansion of productive capacity.

During bad times, demand for credit by companies becomes more subdued as business activity declines. Moreover, bankers prefer to have loans amortize as quickly as possible. This reduces their risk of exposure should a company start exhibiting symptoms of financial distress because of poor sales, weak profits, and reduced cash flows. Reduced cash flows impede the repayment of debt. Amortization of loans cannot proceed as scheduled or as quickly as the bankers may desire without bringing on the very difficulties the bankers are hoping to avoid. Bankers will advance money during bad times as long as they are confident that the underlying financial structure of a company is reasonably sound. Therefore, liquidation of loans during the worst of the bad times occurs at a rather modest pace as the proceeds of these "new" loans are being used to make the regularly scheduled payments on existing loans. The plug is pulled on a company when bankers are convinced that they are throwing good money after bad—when further support of the company will only increase the extent of their losses.

Simulating Loan Losses

During each year of the simulation, a number is drawn for every loan in the portfolio. If it is the "wrong" number, the loan is considered in default and is removed from the loan portfolio. Another number is drawn and the percentage of the loan that is salvaged by the efforts of the loan workout team is obtained from the appropriate simulator. The percentage of loss is 100 percent less the percentage of the loan that has been salvaged. The magnitude of the loss is determined by multiplying the degree of loss by the balance of the loan, or technically, the collective exposure of the participating banks to a company.

The simulation program strikes the loan off the books by reducing its balance to zero. Loans with a zero balance can be replaced by new loans to, presumably, other companies. If a loan goes bad during good times, there is a high probability of its being replaced by a large loan, or exposure, to another company. This reflects the good times ebullience of adding large-sized loans as quickly as possible to a portfolio of loans. When a loan is removed from the loan portfolio during bad times, the probability of its being replaced by a loan to another company is low. If the loan is replaced, the size of the commitment is relatively small. This reflects the bad times predilection of either avoiding or making small commitments to new customers.

Loans made to new borrowers during bad times are usually more inherently sound than loans made during good times. Good times mask weaknesses in a firm's financial structure; bad times expose them. Loans made in bad times are made to companies that can withstand the storm of weak demand, declining prices, and reduced cash flows.

Running the Simulation

The first program in the appendix (LOSSES) simulates a portfolio of the collective exposure to a thousand different companies to gauge the extent and timing of losses over a millennium of time for the conditions under discussion. Business activity is modeled as discussed in chapter 2 with a 75 percent chance that one good year follows another or one bad year follows another with the added proviso that good times and bad times cannot exceed a twelve-year duration.

In Exhibit 5.1, business activity fluctuates around a middle value of fifty with somewhat rare excursions into the best and worst of times. The simulator attempts to imitate reality in that bad times and good times are multiyear phenomena. (The century of time between 800 and 900 years of the thousand-year simulation has been arbitrarily selected for all the exhibits in this chapter.)

The average balance of the loan portfolio is $10.8 billion over the thousand-year simulation, with a maximum value of $15.6 billion and a minimum value of $7.2 billion. The value of the portfolio varies, reflecting growth during good times and shrinkage during bad times. As a company fails, the loan portfolio

Exhibit 5.1
Business-Cycle Simulator, 75 Percent Year-to-Year Bias

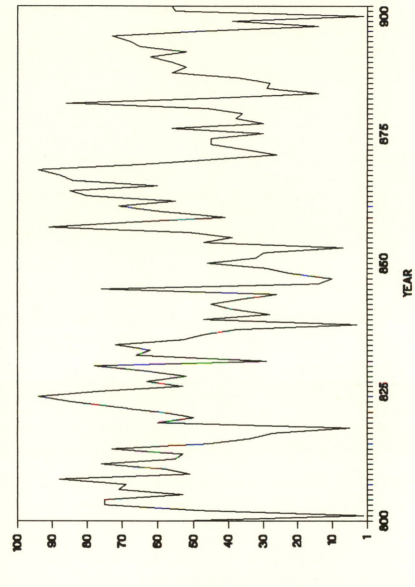

balance is reduced by the amount of the outstanding balance of the total credit exposure to the company by the participating banks. The reduction in the loan portfolio balance is not the same as actual losses. Actual losses have to take into account the salvaging efforts of the workout team. Both the probability of replacement and the size of a new loan are affected by the state of business activity. Exhibit 5.2 shows the insured, or total, balance of the loan portfolio.

The expansion and contraction of the loan portfolio follow the swings of business activity between good and bad times. The losses of the loan portfolio are determined by the SIMTWO simulator linking business conditions with the probability of not having a loss. The loss probability is 100 percent less the probability, percentage-wise, of not having a loss. Once a loan is tagged a loser, another draw is taken from the SIMTWO simulator linking the same business condition to the probability of salvaging a portion of the loan. The actual loss is the outstanding balance of the loan, or exposure to a company, multiplied by 100 percent less the probability, percentage-wise, of the degree of salvage of the loan through the efforts of the workout team. The actual losses over the century under consideration are shown in Exhibit 5.3.

The timing of losses in Exhibit 5.3 reflects the simulation of good and bad times not alternating with each passing year, but having a tendency to last for a number of years. The average loss is $129.4 million per year, with a peak loss year of $871 million. These figures mask the true nature of the exposure to loss because losses occur more frequently, and are larger in magnitude, during bad times.

The average five-year loss on a cumulative basis should be around $647 million (5 × $129.4 million). The possibility that the aggregation of five-year losses will be larger than this is shown in Exhibit 5.4, which illustrates the probability distribution of cumulative losses over every consecutive five-year span in the thousand-year simulation. There are 996 such spans of time. The first one is years 1 through 5, the second years 2 through 6, the third years 3 through 7, and so forth, with the last being years 996 through 1000.

About 35 percent of the five-year spans have cumulative losses around the expected value of $600 million. About one-third of the five-year spans have five-year cumulative losses around $300 million, representing the good years when losses are few in number and small in size. Slightly less than one-third of the five-year cumulative losses are spread over a wide range. As Exhibit 5.4 shows, it is possible that a string of bad years in business activity can generate considerable losses far in excess of what one expects when dealing with annual average losses. Average figures can be very misleading; one can drown crossing a river whose average depth is six inches. Although the average loss over five years is $647 million, there are individual five-year cumulative losses that are more than three times greater in size.

The distribution of losses in Exhibit 5.4 is not an ordinary normal curve, where losses are evenly spread around the mean of $647 million. The tail on the left side of the mean is shorter than the tail on the right side of the mean. The

Exhibit 5.2
Insured Value Loan Portfolio

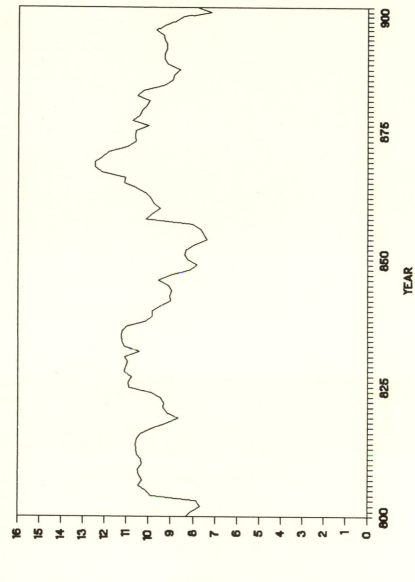

Exhibit 5.3
Loan Portfolio Losses

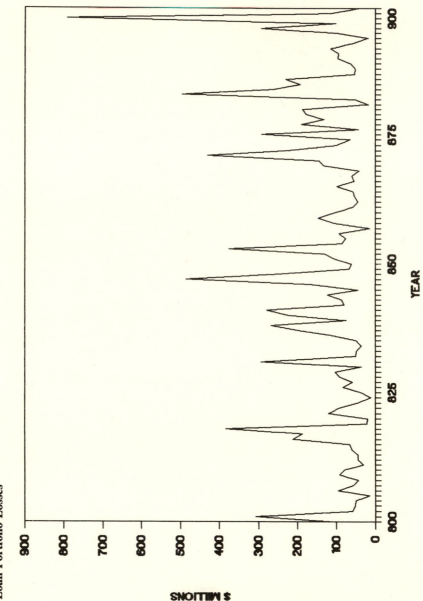

Exhibit 5.4
Five-Year Cumulative Losses (Probability Distribution)

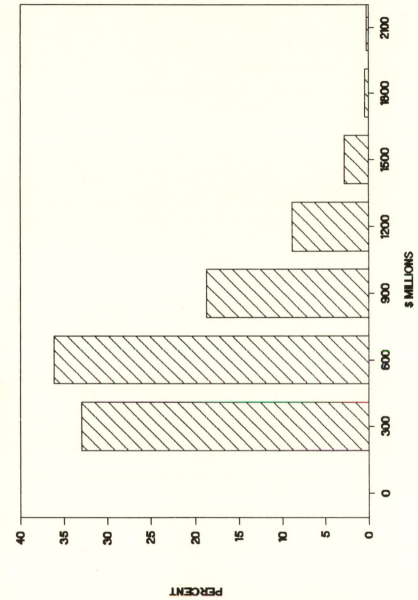

smallest cumulative five-year loss is $156 million, and the largest is $2,187 million. The probability distribution is skewed to the right. This means that there is a small chance that the loan insurance company can be exposed to claims on losses considerably greater than what we might expect from a cursory look at the assessments of risk. This reflects reality. When times are tough and loans go bad, loans go bad by the basketful.

Deriving a Risk Premium

The above exhibits were derived from running the LOSSES simulation program. Another program, named PREMIUM, was used to assess a risk premium that would be sufficient to cover the actual losses in the loan portfolio over the thousand-year simulation.

Exhibit 5.3 illustrates the actual losses over the selected century of the millennium. The average loss over the thousand-year simulation, as noted before, is $129.4 million. We might conclude that the average loss divided by the average loan portfolio value of $10.8 billion, or 1.2 percent, would be the appropriate risk premium to be applied to the loan portfolio over the thousand-year period.

A fixed premium rate, however, does not lend itself to satisfying the dynamics of this simulation of reality. During the good times, a risk premium of 1.2 percent is too high, causing loss loan reserves to accumulate to an amount that exceeds the value of the loan portfolio. There is no reason to continue paying a risk premium into a fund that already provides coverage for a 100 percent default rate coupled with a 100 percent loss rate. To continue paying a premium that builds up reserves in excess of the value of loans being insured can be compared to paying $100,000 in premiums for an insurance policy that provides $50,000 in protection. It is better to pay $50,000 into a special account to provide the necessary insurance than to pay $100,000 to a third party to provide the same protection.

Alternatively, a risk premium of 1.2 percent might prove to be insufficient to provide adequate coverage from losses during the bad times. Once loan loss reserves have been exhausted, we would expect the risk premium to rise to cover any further losses and to replenish the loan loss reserves. Otherwise, the insurance company would have to declare itself bankrupt because it cannot honor the legitimate claims of its policy holders. Therefore, the appropriate rate covering a millennium of time appears to be one that varies with business conditions—increasing when the loan loss reserves are depleted by defaults and decreasing once the loan loss reserves have been replenished to some desired level.

The initial risk premium is arbitrarily set at one percent. A capital infusion of $50 million is assumed to be put up by the participating banks. This capital account provides the initial loan loss reserves should the mutually owned insurance company be hit with significant losses during the first years of its existence. Good times prevail at the beginning of the simulation. Claims by policy holders for insured loans are less than the premiums being paid by the banks. This is an auspicious time to launch the captive loan insurance company because good times last long enough for the loan loss reserves to build up to their desired level before being hit by the first round of significant losses.

The simulation demonstrates the point that the best time to launch a new insurance company is when claims are few in number and small in size. This gives the company time to build up its reserves. The wrong time to launch a new line of earthquake insurance is just before the Big One strikes. This does not bode well for the shareholders or the policy holders.

The desired level of loan loss reserves is arbitrarily selected to be $1 billion, about one-tenth of the insured value of the loan portfolio. In the early years of the simulation, the risk premiums exceed losses allowing the loan loss reserves, which contain all surplus funds, to accumulate to the desired level of funding. The loan loss reserve account is the depository of the surplus between risk premium income and the payout of claims on losses incurred by the participating banks. There is no reason why loan loss reserves have to lie fallow, earning no interest. Loan loss reserves are presumed to be invested in high-quality bonds earning an annual interest rate of 9 percent. The captive insurance company is presumed to operate in a tax-free environment.

If there are substantial losses that deplete the reserves to cover loan losses, it is presumed that the participating banks will lend sufficient funds to keep the captive insurance company solvent to meet its obligations. Loans made to the captive insurance company are charged 12 percent interest. The loans will be repaid out of revenues derived from hikes in the risk premium rate. (Were this a truly independent insurance company without lines of credit to support those times when loss reserves were insufficient to satisfy claims, the insurance company would have gone out of business—much to the chagrin of the policy holders.)

At a fairly early point in the simulation, the loan loss reserves reach the arbitrarily selected desired level of $1 billion. The reason for this is that the premium rate, in following the preset rules to be described, rapidly climbs to 2 percent. A 1 to 2 percent premium rate on an expanding $10 billion loan portfolio with loan loss reserves compounding at 9 percent per year coupled with modest claims on loan losses does not require a great deal of time for the loan loss reserves to accumulate to $1 billion, roughly equivalent to 10 percent of the value of the portfolio. Any further generation of funds from the earnings of the loan loss reserves and the excess of premiums to claims on loan losses are dedicated to repaying the initial $50 million capital infusion. This is accomplished about six years after the formation of the insurance company.

The risk premium is permitted to vary between 0 and 3 percent, depending on the circumstances. For each year of the simulation, the earnings of the loan loss reserves, or charges thereto if there are negative reserves, are added to the risk premium income and then reduced by the extent of loan losses to obtain the net cash flow. The prior year's loan loss reserves are adjusted by the cash flow to determine the current state of the reserves. If loan loss reserves are negative, the risk premium is increased by an increment of one percent. Insurance companies exhibit little reluctance to raise rates when they are drowning in red ink. If loan loss reserves are less than half of the desired amount of $1 billion, the risk premium is increased by an increment of 0.2 percent. If loan loss reserves are more than half but still less than the desired amount, the risk premium is increased by an increment of 0.1 percent. When loan loss reserves exceed $1 billion, the risk premium is reduced by an increment of 0.5 percent. These somewhat simplistic rules generate the risk premium shown in Exhibit 5.5.

Changes in the risk premium are dependent on the magnitude of the loss suffered by the loan portfolio when bad times follow good times. Hikes in risk premium take place after losses have drained loan loss reserves below the desired level of $1 billion. Rate hikes are necessary to replenish the depleted loan loss reserves. The state of depletion of the reserves determines the magnitude of the rate hikes: the greater the depletion of loan loss reserves, the less the degree of protection against future claims and the larger the rate hikes.

The risk premium income is the risk premium rate multiplied by the value of the loan portfolio. Risk premium income is shown in Exhibit 5.6.

The average risk premium income over the thousand-year simulation is $92.1 million. This divided by the average loan portfolio being insured of $10.8 billion gives an average risk premium of about 0.9 percent. This is less than the initially assessed 1.2 percent because of the contribution of the earnings of the loan loss reserves in helping to cover losses in the loan portfolio.

Loan loss reserves are not simply the subtraction of loan losses from risk premium income because the loan loss reserves earn 9 percent income on investments. Exhibit 5.7 shows the loan loss reserves during the century under scrutiny.

The average amount of loan loss reserves is $743.8 million over the millennium. There are no negative balances during the hundred years under examination, but there is a maximum negative balance of $532.9 million at one point in the thousand-year simulation. Negative balances are covered by loans from participating banks who charge 12 percent to keep their captive insurance company solvent.

During good times, loan loss reserves exceed the desired balance of $1 billion. Exhibit 5.8 illustrates the refunding of the risk premium, which is the surplus of funds above $1 billion in loan loss reserves.

The refund of all monies in excess of the desired level of $1 billion in loan loss reserves maintains the upper limit of $1 billion in loan loss reserves in Exhibit 5.7. Over the thousand-year simulation, the average refund is $29.4 million per year, paid back to the participating banks. This represents any surplus of funds above the stipulated level of $1 billion in loan loss reserves.

Over the thousand-year simulation, the average risk premium is $92.1 million less the refund of $29.4 million, for a net figure of $62.7 million. The effective risk premium rate is not the original assessment of 1.2 percent to cover expected losses, nor the 0.9 percent (which reflects the earnings of loan loss reserves), but

Exhibit 5.5
Risk Premium

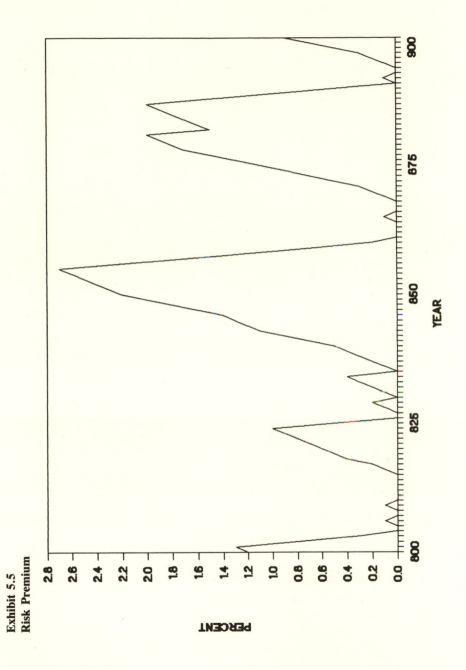

Exhibit 5.6
Risk Premium Income

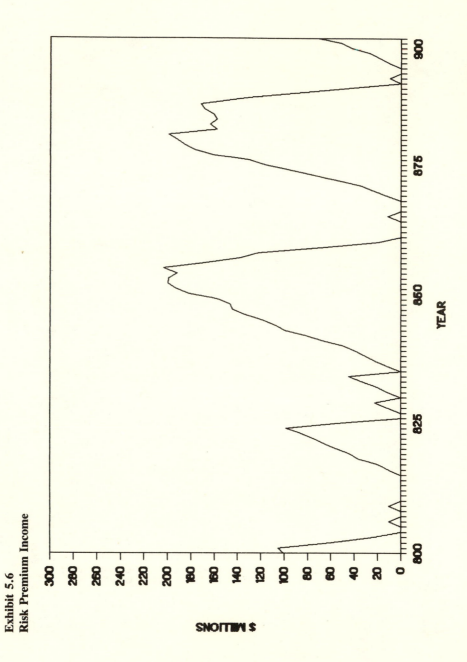

Exhibit 5.7
Loan Loss Reserves

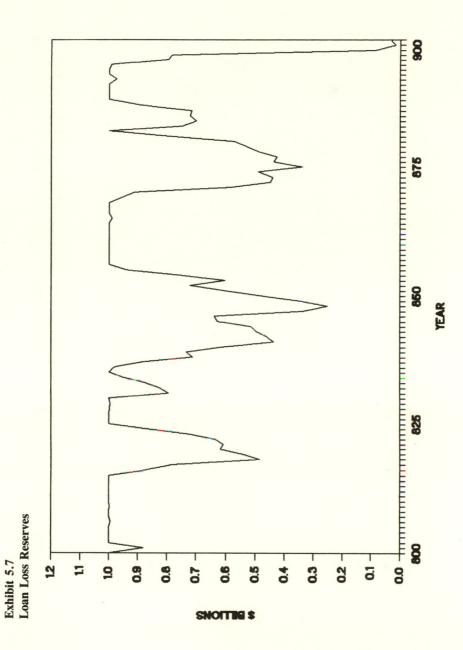

Exhibit 5.8
Risk Premium Refund

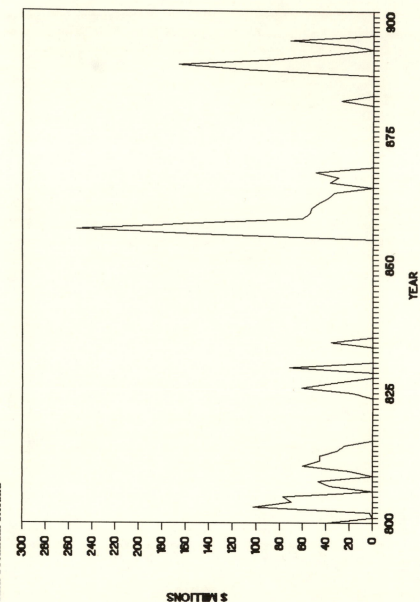

0.6 percent (which reflects both the earnings of the loan loss reserves and refunds for balances in reserves in excess of $1 billion). This, plus the "add-on" to cover operating costs, is the average risk premium charged on the face amount of loans placed into the captive insurance company over the millennium.

The rules for changing the risk premium in timing and degree, the range of the permissible risk premium, and the desired level of loan loss reserves are all arbitrarily selected to demonstrate the principles of self-insurance to cover the risk of bad loans. There may, and probably is, a better set of rules. Perhaps a maximum of a 3 percent premium is too high of an incremental charge to compensate for a given perception of risk. It might be difficult for lending officers to market loans with this magnitude of a risk premium added to the normal rate of interest for more creditworthy borrowers. A lower maximum premium rate could be selected, but this might necessitate a different set of rules concerning incremental changes to the risk premium rate to avoid potentially larger negative balances in loan loss reserves than those experienced in the simulation. Perhaps this problem can be better approached by selecting a higher level of loan loss reserves. The optimal set of rules is determined by trying out different sets of rules concerning changes to the premium rate and different maximum levels of loan loss reserves and examining the results. This is the trial and error methodology of obtaining the optimal solution inherent in simulation. If the computer itself is programmed to select the optimal decision rules for determining the rate premium, this might be considered an application of artificial intelligence to simulation.

LOAN LOSS RESERVES

It is tempting to think of loan loss reserves as a capital infusion from banks. Nothing can be further from the truth. The banks put up $50 million, which in the simulation, is recouped in about six years. The source of loan loss reserves is the risk premium, or incremental interest rate, that is added to the normal interest charge that applies to more creditworthy borrowers. Who pays for the risk premium? Certainly not the banks! The borrowers pay for it. The borrowers who survive, who are the overwhelming number of borrowers, make the banks whole for the occasional borrower who goes under. Borrowers cannot make good on their own borrowings by paying a risk premium. Many borrowers can make good on a bad debt, however, by pooling their risk premiums. This, in effect, is what the banks accomplish by adding a risk premium to the normal rate of interest charged to more creditworthy customers and depositing the premium into a captive insurance company.

Perhaps it would be wiser for borrowers to band together to form a mutual loan guarantee association. If the borrowers are going to pay the risk premium, why not directly benefit from the insurance? Borrowers are paying the risk premium. If they get into financial difficulty and go bankrupt, their loans to the bank are made good by the insurance company. This being the case, borrowers should band together, self-insure themselves using the same precautions banks do, and reap the benefit for themselves. As it now stands, firms go under and banks are made whole. Why not make both the banks and the companies whole by redirecting the inflow of risk premiums and the outflow of claims settlements?

JUNK BONDS

Junk bonds were sold on the basis that their higher interest rate covered the higher risk of default. The higher risk of default was openly acknowledged by the underwriters of junk bonds, who reinforced the generic nature of these bonds by calling them "junk." The implication of buying a junk bond is that it is, from a credit standpoint, junk. If an individual buys one twenty-year junk bond for $1,000, can the higher rate of interest cover the risk of default? By definition, a loan cannot guarantee its own principal repayment. Suppose that a twenty-year junk bond carries a coupon rate of 5 percentage points higher than a quality bond where repayment can be reasonably expected. At what point can the junk bond pass into default with the holder being compensated for the loss of principal? The premium in interest of 5 percent can be set aside to cover for the possibility of default. Ignoring taxes and compounding of funds held in bond loss reserves, twenty years of a risk premium of 5 percent might provide sufficient coverage if bankruptcy occurs about five minutes before the bond matures. An earlier default would not be covered by the higher rate of interest.

The only feasible way for the extra interest to provide protection against a higher risk of default would be for the buyer of junk bonds to invest in one hundred different issues. Suppose that the investor did buy $1,000 in bonds for one hundred different issues of junk bonds (different issues meaning different companies). That would be a $100,000 investment in junk bonds where the 5 percentage points in extra interest are to compensate for the higher risk of default. Suppose the investor takes this risk premium and sets its aside as a self-insurance policy against defaults. This is $5,000 per year in protection against defaults. Five bonds defaulting each year is break even with making a comparable sized investment in quality bonds. Four defaults per year and the investor is ahead of the game. Six defaults per year and the investor is behind. According to "The Biggest Scam Ever?" in the February 19, 1990, issue of *Barron's*, default rates are estimated to reach 10 percent per year. For this hypothetical one hundred junk bond portfolio, the investor is clearly behind the eight-ball.

Rather than give the investor a higher rate of interest to compensate for a higher rate of default, the issuers of the junk bonds could have paid a normal interest rate to the investors and deposited the 5 percent premium in a junk bond insurance company owned by the buyers of the bonds, not by the issuers of the bonds. If the risk premiums were adequate to cover the risk of loss, then the bond loss reserves would build up over the years. If these reserves exceeded certain stipulated levels, then the bond holders, as owners of the insurance company, would receive a dividend on a pro rata share with the size of their bond holdings to reduce the bond loss reserves to the desired level. At the end of the maturity period of all the junk bonds, the bond loss reserves would be divided among the participants. This would have been an effective way for the risk premium to act as insurance against a higher rate of default.

This would not have worked, however, because the loss rate far exceeded the premium rate. No insurance scheme will work if the outflow to compensate for losses is larger than the inflow from premiums and earnings on the reserves. This is the key point in the *Barron's* article—the risk premium in the form of a higher interest rate was not even close in covering the risk of loss.

CREDIT CARD SELF-INSURANCE

An interesting application of self-insurance, from the banker's point of view, is credit cards. An individual bank issues thousands of credit cards, and, as anyone who borrows on these cards well knows, the interest charge is quite high. Credit cards may be one of the most profitable activities in the banking business. If the cost of funds for a bank is, say, around 8 percent, and the interest being charged to those who elect to pay off the balance of their credit purchases over time is on the order of 18 percent, there appears to be a gross margin of about 10 percent on these lines of credit. Moreover, the banks charge about 5 percent to merchants on reimbursing credit card purchases. Merchants, naturally, pass this cost along to customers in terms of higher prices.

Of course, banks do have administrative expenses associated with issued cards. Among these expenses are the losses associated with those who run up charges to the maximum possible extent before leaving town with no forwarding address. Millions of card holders pay what essentially amounts to a risk premium that is included in the interest rate on their credit card balances to cover the risk of default by others. Bankers are the beneficiaries of the risk premiums in that they are being made whole for those who default on their credit card purchases. Bankers have little recourse to those who do walk away from their credit card obligations, as credit cards represent a form of unsecured lending.

Nevertheless, the general approach to determining the risk premium to cover the risk of default of credit cards would be the same as already discussed concerning insuring loans to companies. The differences would be in the tables of assessments as to the probability of loss and recoupment. The probability of loss is fairly high for new recipients of credit cards as compared to those who have a long history of honoring their credit card obligations. Risk management reduces the degree of loss by limiting the amount of credit to new recipients of credit cards and by having some control over the selection process for new credit card holders. If banks are using mailing lists, they may prefer a mailing list of recent college graduates over a listing of those just released from prison, although this may not be that effective in screening out potential deadbeats.

The underwriting function is more important than the adjusting function in containing losses because of the difficulty in collecting on delinquent accounts.

The probability of recoupment on a defaulted line of plastic credit is much less than indicated for a loan portfolio because loans usually have some form of collateral protection. Plastic credit is essentially unsecured lending because the loan may have been used to finance a junket to Jamaica. Fond memories have little collateral value.

THE SAVINGS AND LOAN CALAMITY

The distress in the savings and loan industry is different from the fiasco in junk bonds. A fiasco is, in some respects, brought on by the folly of certain individuals. A general distress in an industry, or an economic calamity, is something else. Insurance presumes that the general principle of the relative many paying for the losses of the relative few holds true for a given situation. In our example of the captive bank loan insurance company, the worst that was anticipated to happen was a highly unlikely 12 percent loss rate. The thousand loans being insured presumed that each loan, or exposure to a single company, was independent. In other words, each year a number was drawn for each individual loan. That number determined whether the loan ended the year in good standing with the bankers. The simulation did not contain a time bomb, or a wild card, in the form of a default by one particular loan triggering the automatic default of one hundred others.

Loans in a dynamic, free market, competitive economy are not independent. They are all, to some degree, tied to others. Some years ago when Chrysler was on the brink of bankruptcy, the government rushed in to bail the company out of its difficulties. One of the compelling reasons for doing so was that the collapse of Chrysler would have taken with it thousands of independent suppliers for whom Chrysler represented a primary, if not the sole, source of their revenue. The collapse of these would, in turn, have triggered the collapse of certain large regional banks that financially supported the suppliers. If minimizing losses was an incentive to act, then saving Chrysler was the desired course of action.

The collapse in oil prices during the 1980s in relation to the price in the late 1970s, did not cause distress for one drilling company, but for all drilling companies. A diversified portfolio of loans to oil-drilling companies would not suffer a single casualty, but a multitude of casualties far beyond what any self-insurance arrangement could be expected to provide in protection. One bad drilling loan meant that there were thousands of others because the same economic conditions that ruined one company destroyed the whole industry.

Once the underpinning of one industry is torn asunder, the rest of the economy is in great danger. As an industry retrenches, for example, people have to move to obtain jobs elsewhere or to raise cash to feed their families. A flood of "Home for Sale" signs causes prices to fall. This, in turn, wipes out the collateral value on mortgages and halts building activity. It also removes liquidity from the market because everyone is playing the role of seller while no one is playing the role of buyer. The determination of market value requires the presence of both buyers and sellers interacting with one another. A market made up of only sellers is not a market. Therefore, the collateral value protecting mortgages on homes does not decline, but disappears. The appraised value of a house when there are no buyers is fictitious.

Thus a problem in the oil field becomes a problem for everyone in real estate. It becomes a problem for merchants who sell their wares to those involved in the oil industry and in the real estate business. It becomes a problem for those who run the municipal government when they cannot collect property taxes from those whose livelihoods depend on the oil industry, real estate, and local businesses. Then it becomes a problem for school teachers who are laid off because the school budget has to be cut back to balance the municipal budget. Finally, it becomes a problem for the financial institutions who have lent money to individuals and businesses that are being wiped out by the downturn in oil prices. Therefore, everyone is affected by the collapse in oil prices even though their paychecks are not actually written by companies in the oil business.

It is interesting to note that individuals and firms under financial pressure may take on an unusual degree of risk at the very time when they should not be doing so. An individual without a job and with $10,000 cash might not keep that money in a safe 5 percent savings account. With the prospects of employment being nil, the individual might be tempted to invest that money in a highly risky venture. If he leaves the nest egg alone, he can calculate to the minute when he will be unable to feed his family. He is not that much worse off if he risks the money in some sort of venture that only has a remote chance of success. If the venture goes bust, he merely files bankruptcy earlier than anticipated. If the venture is a success, he has survived the financial holocaust.

Corporations do the same thing. There is no reason why corporations should behave any differently than individuals because corporations are run by individuals. Corporations which sense the writing on the wall may take on very risky undertakings for the same reason. Doing nothing does not delay the inevitability of liquidation. Plunging into risky undertakings at least has the prospect of avoiding the inevitable.

APPENDIX

Two programs are used to generate the exhibits shown in this chapter. The LOSSES program generates a simulator for a thousand years of losses and the PREMIUM program determines an appropriate risk premium to address these losses. A more general purpose program can be written to measure the performance of different sets of rules in adjusting the premium rate and various levels of loan loss reserves to arrive at an optimal choice of a set of rules and a desired level of reserves.

LOSSES

This program simulates the losses inherent in a portfolio of one thousand loans. The SIMTWO program is run twice to generate the two tables in the chapter concerning the probability of not suffering a loss for various levels of business activity and of the cents per dollar salvaged by the efforts of the workout team. Statements 40 to 70 feed these simulators into the program. Statement 80 enters the simulator of the growth of the portfolio from −4 to +4 percent as business activity progresses from an activity index value of 1 to 100. The loan portfolio growth simulator is created by running SIMONE for a distribution of one hundred values from −4 to +4 with a median value of 0 and a scaling factor of 20 percent.

Statement 90 enters the distribution of loans in the portfolio. This is created by running SIMONE for an output of one thousand loans ranging in value from $2 to $40 million, with a median value of $8 million and a scaling factor of 20 percent. Statement 100 enters the business activity simulator that is generated by operating the SIMONE program with minimum, expected, and maximum values of 1, 50, and 100, respectively, and a scaling factor of 30 percent.

The initial loan portfolio, as created by SIMONE, is stored in array $L(1,I)$. The actual loan portfolio is recorded in array $L(2,I)$ and is assigned the initial distribution of loans contained in the array $L(1,I)$ in statement 120. The results of the simulation as far as the size of the portfolio, the extent of the losses, and the level of business activity are stored in the arrays $Y(1,I)$, $Y(2,I)$, and $Y(3,I)$, respectively. These arrays are initially set to zero in statement 130. Statements 140 to 150 determines whether the simulation starts with good times ($Z = 1$) or bad times ($Z = 2$).

The thousand-year simulation starts in statement 170. Statements 180 to 280 create a business cycle where there is a 75 percent chance that one good year follows another, which is indicated by a B value of greater than 50. There is also a 75 percent chance that one bad year follows another where the value for B is less than 50. An internal counter ensures that good or bad times do not exceed twelve years.

Statement 290 controls the actual loan portfolio growth or shrinkage as dictated by business conditions. The total size of the loan portfolio is determined in statement 300 and recorded in the array $Y(1,I)$, and the corresponding business activity is recorded in the array $Y(3,I)$. Statements 310 to 330 detect all loans that have previously gone bad, indicated by $L(2,I)$ having a value of zero. These loans are replaced on the basis that there is a greater probability of replacement with a larger loan for higher levels of business activity (statements 340–460). New loans are drawn from the array $L(1,I)$. The number and size of loan losses are determined in statements 470 to 490 and loan losses are stored in the array $Y(2,I)$. Statement 500 shows the results while the simulation is running and statements 510 to 520 record the results of the thousand-year simulation in an external data file.

```
10 REM NAME OF PROGRAM IS LOSSES
20 DIM P(10,100):DIM M(10,100):DIM Y(3,1000)
30 DIM L(2,1000):DIM G(100):DIM B(100)
40 OPEN "I",#1,"LPROB"
50 FOR I=1 TO 100:INPUT #1,P(1,I),P(2,I),P(3,I),P(4,I),P(5,I),
P(6,I),P(7,I),P(8,I),P(9,I),P(10,I):NEXT:CLOSE #1
60 OPEN "I",#1,"LMAG"
70 FOR I=1 TO 100:INPUT #1,M(1,I),M(2,I),M(3,I),M(4,I),M(5,I),
M(6,I),M(7,I),M(8,I),M(9,I),M(10,I):NEXT:CLOSE #1
80 OPEN "I",#1,"GROW":FOR I=1 TO 100:INPUT #1,G(I):NEXT:CLOSE #1
90 OPEN "I",#1,"SIZE":FOR I=1 TO 1000:INPUT #1,L(1,I):NEXT:CLOSE #1
100 OPEN "I",#1,"BUSACT":FOR I=1 TO 100:INPUT #1,B(I):NEXT:CLOSE #1
110 FOR I=1 TO 100:B(I)=INT(B(I)+.5):NEXT
120 FOR I=1 TO 1000:L(2,I)=L(1,I):NEXT
130 FOR I=1 TO 3:FOR J=1 TO 1000:Y(I,J)=0:NEXT:NEXT:A1=0
```

```
140 X=RND(X):IF X<.5 THEN 150 ELSE 160
150 Z=1:GOTO 170
160 Z=2
170 FOR Y=1 TO 1000
180 X=RND(X):IF X<.75 THEN 220 ELSE 190
190 IF Z=1 THEN 200 ELSE 210
200 Y1=0:Z=2:GOTO 220
210 Y1=0:Z=1
220 GOSUB 530:B=B(T):ON Z GOTO 230,240
230 IF B<50 THEN 220 ELSE 250
240 IF B>50 THEN 220
250 Y1=Y1+1:IF Y1<=12 THEN 290 ELSE 260
260 Y1=0:IF Z=1 THEN 270 ELSE 280
270 Z=2:GOTO 220
280 Z=1:GOTO 220
290 FOR I=1 TO 1000:L(2,I)=(100+G(B))*L(2,I)/100:NEXT
300 A=0:FOR I=1 TO 1000:A=A+L(2,I):NEXT:Y(1,Y)=A:Y(3,Y)=B
310 N=0:FOR I=1 TO 1000:IF L(2,I)=0 THEN 320 ELSE 330
320 N=N+1
330 NEXT
340 IF B<25 THEN 370 ELSE 350
350 IF B<50 THEN 380 ELSE 360
360 IF B<75 THEN 390 ELSE 400
370 X1=.2:X=RND(X):X2=INT(1+X*600):GOTO 410
380 X1=.4:X=RND(X):X2=INT(100+X*600):GOTO 410
390 X1=.6:X=RND(X):X2=INT(300+X*600):GOTO 410
400 X1=.8:X=RND(X):X2=INT(400+X*600)
410 IF N=0 THEN 470
420 FOR I=1 TO 1000:IF L(2,I)=0 THEN 430 ELSE 460
430 X=RND(X):IF X<X1 THEN 440 ELSE 460
440 L(2,I)=L(1,X2):N=N-1:IF N=0 THEN 450 ELSE 460
450 I=3000
460 NEXT
470 GOSUB 570:L=100-P(V,B)
480 FOR I=1 TO 1000:X=RND(X):IF 100*X>L THEN 500 ELSE 490
490 GOSUB 570:C=100-M(V,B):Y(2,Y)=Y(2,Y)+L(2,I)*C/100:L(2,I)=0
500 NEXT:A1=A1+Y(2,Y):PRINT Y;Y(3,Y);N,Y(1,Y),Y(2,Y),A1:NEXT
510 OPEN "O",#1,"RESULTS":FOR I=1 TO 1000
520 WRITE #1,I,Y(1,I),Y(2,I),Y(3,I):NEXT:CLOSE #1:END
530 X=RND(X):T=INT(100*X+.5)
540 IF T=0 THEN 550 ELSE 560
550 T=100
560 RETURN
570 X=RND(X):V=INT(10*X+.5)
580 IF V=0 THEN 590 ELSE 600
590 V=10
600 RETURN
```

PREMIUM

The purpose of this program is to evaluate a rule-based mechanism to protect against the thousand years of losses. The external data file containing the losses and the size of the portfolio is fed into this program in statements 30 to 40. Statements 50 to 100 derive Exhibit 5.4 and are bypassed in running the rest of the program.

Statement 110 sets the program up to examine a desired level of loan loss reserves from \$1 to \$2 billion in steps of \$0.2 billion. All exhibits are derived on the basis of an arbitrarily selected level of \$1 billion in loan loss reserves. Statement 120 erases any previous data. Statement 130 establishes an initial capital infusion of \$50 million to cover potential early losses prior to building up adequate loan loss reserves and fixes the initial premium rate at 1 percent. The simulation starts in statement 140 and is followed by statement 150, where the income is determined by multiplying the premium rate by the size of the loan portfolio. The balance in loan loss reserves is first examined for a negative value in statement 160. If the negative value is in excess of $1 billion, the run is terminated (statements 170–180). This is done because there would be some limit to the support banks would provide to a captive insurance company. As long as the balance is less than $1 billion in the red, the interest charge of 12 percent is applied against the balance representing the banks' compensation for keeping their captive insurance company solvent (statement 190).

If the loan loss reserves are positive, the reserves are invested in quality debt instruments bearing a rate of interest of 9 percent (statement 200). Note that all calculations are performed on a before-tax basis. Insurance companies are permitted to keep a portion of their "profits" in reserve to satisfy claims up to limits provided by government regulation. Some captive insurance companies are incorporated in tax havens such as Bermuda. (The taxation of insurance companies is a complex subject that goes beyond the scope of the discussion of risk management in this chapter.)

After determining interest charges or interest earnings, the loan loss reserves are adjusted for the inflow of premiums and the outflow of compensation for claims on loan losses (statement 210). If, at this point, the loan loss reserves are negative, the risk premium rate is increased by one full percentage point with an overall maximum of 3 percent (statements 350–360). If the balance in the loan loss reserve account is over the desired level, all excess funds are returned to the participating banks first in the form of returning the initial capital infusion (statements 230–260). Once this has been accomplished, the risk premium rate is reduced by one half of a percentage point (statements 270–280) and all excess funds are returned in the form of a risk premium refund (statement 290).

The remaining condition to be addressed is a balance in the loan loss reserves that is neither negative nor above the desired limit. In this case, the risk premium is increased by 0.2 percentage points if the balance is less than half of the desired level and by 0.1 percentage points if the balance is more than half of the desired level subject to an overall maximum of 3 percent (statements 300–340). No attempt is made to select an optimal set of rules for governing the amount of the risk premium or the desired level of loan loss reserves.

The amount of loan loss reserves, the status of the initial capital account, the risk premium, and the refund of excess loan loss reserves are recorded internally in statement 370. At the end of each individual run, the most negative value in the loan loss account is calculated and the operator is given a choice of whether to continue (statements 380–420) or to stop the run and store the results in an external data file (statements 440–450).

```
10 REM NAME OF PROGRAM IS PREMIUM
20 DIM L(2,1000):DIM R(3000):DIM Y(4,1000)
30 OPEN "I",#1,"RESULTS"
40 FOR I=1 TO 1000:INPUT #1,A,L(1,I),L(2,I),B:NEXT:CLOSE#1:GOTO 110
50 FOR I=1 TO 996:A=0:FOR J=1 TO 5:A=A+L(2,I-1+J):NEXT
60 A=INT(A+.5):R(A)=R(A)+1:NEXT
70 OPEN "O",#1,"LOSS":FOR I=1 TO 3000
80 IF R(I)=0 THEN 100 ELSE 90
90 WRITE #1,I,R(I)
100 NEXT:END
110 FOR F=1000 TO 2000 STEP 200
```

```
120 FOR I=1 TO 4:FOR J=1 TO 1000:Y(I,J)=0:NEXT:NEXT
130 C=50:P=1:W=0:
140 FOR I=1 TO 1000
150 R=P*L(1,I)/100:E=0
160 IF W<0 THEN 170 ELSE 200
170 IF W<-1000 THEN 180 ELSE 190
180 I=1000:GOTO 370
190 W=1.12*W:GOTO 210
200 W=1.09*W
210 W=W+R-L(2,I):IF W<0 THEN 350 ELSE 220
220 IF W>F THEN 230 ELSE 300
230 IF C>0 THEN 240 ELSE 270
240 D=W-F:IF D<C THEN 250 ELSE 260
250 C=C-D:W=W-D:GOTO 370
260 W=W-C:C=0:GOTO 370
270 P=P-.5:IF P<0 THEN 280 ELSE 290
280 P=0
290 E=W-F:W=F:GOTO 370
300 IF W<F/2 THEN 310 ELSE 320
310 P=P+.2:GOTO 330
320 P=P+.1
330 IF P>3 THEN 340 ELSE 370
340 P=3:GOTO 370
350 P=P+1:IF P>3 THEN 360 ELSE 370
360 P=3
370 Y(1,I)=W:Y(2,I)=C:Y(3,I)=P:Y(4,I)=E:PRINT I,W,P:NEXT
380 A=10000:FOR J=1 TO 1000:IF Y(1,J)<A THEN 390 ELSE 400
390 A=Y(1,J)
400 NEXT:PRINT "LOW POINT IN INSURANCE FUND IS: ";A:PRINT
410 INPUT "CONTINUE RUNS  YES-1  NO-2: ";Z1:ON Z1 GOTO 430,420
420 F=2000
430 NEXT
440 OPEN "O",#1,"RESULTS2":FOR I=1 TO 1000
450 WRITE #1, I,Y(1,I),Y(2,I),Y(3,I),Y(4,I):NEXT:CLOSE #1:END
```

6

Determining the Safe Load
of Debt

Underwriters in Chapter 5 have to assess the risk of a loan going into default before it can be admitted into the captive insurance company. This assessment of loss has to be made while the ink is still drying on the loan documents. While the lending officer and the financial officer of the borrowing company are clinking glasses at some swank restaurant celebrating the closing of the loan, underwriters are attempting to gauge how much may be lost in insuring the loan. The banker and the financial officer are celebrating the birth of a loan; the underwriters are contemplating its demise. Undertakers deal with the certainty of death, underwriters deal with the probability of death, and neither gets invited to the birthday party.

The decision to underwrite the risk of default in guaranteeing the principal of a loan should follow the same general process of making the loan to a borrower. The underwriter is in the same boat as the lender. Both lose if a loan gets into trouble. The underwriter must put up funds to guarantee the remaining principal of the loan. The lender may seem on the surface to be made whole because the insurance company has covered the loss. However, the lender will eventually pay for the folly of being involved in the default through the risk premium. The risk premium is determined by the loss record and increases as losses escalate. Insurance shares the losses among those seeking the solace of not having to face a catastrophic loss by shifting the cost of the loss from one individual to many. The loss does not disappear; it is merely redistributed. Neither the lender, the guarantor, nor the originator of the loan can escape the consequences of a loan in default.

Therefore, it does not really matter whose perspective is taken in determining the safe level of debt in the capital structure of a company. Neither the lender, borrower, nor the guarantor is interested in becoming involved with a loan that may destroy a company. No one benefits. The only difference in perspective occurs after a loan has gone into default as each jockeys to minimize his respective loss.

THE CONVENTIONAL EVALUATION OF RISK

Although the chief financial officer starts the process of seeking outside sources of capital in the form of debt, it is the lender's decision on booking the loan that actually creates the loan. At some point in the process, a credit analysis group views the company with a jaundiced eye and attempts to assess risk by examining financial ratios such as the debt to equity ratio, the ratio of cash flow to interest payments, and the ratio of current assets to current liabilities. The chance of a favorable decision to book a loan or to buy a debt instrument varies inversely with the debt to equity ratio and directly with the ratio of cash flow to interest and the ratio of current assets to current liabilities. In other words, borrowers have a greater chance of having a loan approved or a debt issue purchased if they have little existing debt in relation to the equity in the capital structure of a firm, a great deal of cash generation in relation to the size of the interest payments, and a large checking account balance in relation to the bills that have to be paid. In addition, the final decision to approve a loan is influenced by the degree of brightness of the overall outlook of the company, its associated industry, and the economy as a whole. The quantitative analysis of the financial ratios and the qualitative judgments of a company's management team, the company's prospects in its respective industry, and the outlook of the industry and the economy are the elements of the decision-making process in the booking of loans and the purchase of debt issues.

These are the rules of the game set by those who control the purse strings. Successful financial officers make sure they abide by the rules. If lenders are making loans based on more or less prescribed standards, then astute financial officers will do what they can to ensure that their company meets those standards. If lenders are sensitive to the general economic climate before becoming involved with an industry, one can be confident that financial officers start their business days by checking the temperature of the economy. Warm temperatures in economic activity are conducive for deal making. Financial officers also check the barometer of the financial market for the right time to float another batch of stocks or bonds. The financial weather must be balmy with calm seas for the launching of a new issue of stocks and bonds. One indication of a rising barometer, indicating fair weather on the financial horizon, is the number of unsolicited calls from commercial and investment bankers.

What are these individuals from commercial and investment banks looking at when they pay a call on a company? They would like to see a history of three or more years of rising profitability. They would like to see the financial ratios with some semblance of respectability. They want to have a feeling that all is well with an industry. Usually these three conditions go together. All going well with an industry means prosperous times. Three or more years of profitability generates the cash necessary to restore some modicum of respectability to the financial ratios. Respectable-looking financial ratios, in turn, reinforce the illusion that all is well with a company and its industry. The time to raise capital is when lenders have the confidence that there is no risk of default. As already discussed, the best time to raise capital is when the lenders perceive that the money is not needed.

The floating of a bond issue or the closing of a loan is done when the timing is right, which may or may not coincide with the timing of the need for capital. A financial officer anticipates the demand for outside sources of capital and realizes that garnering external funds is not done on the basis of need, but on the perception of not needing the funds. These perceptions include a feeling among those buying the debt instruments or making the loan that the financial ratios are reasonable, that the prospects of the industry appear promising, and that the company seems well positioned to take advantage of promising prospects.

THE CHALLENGE OF RISK ASSESSMENT

Generally speaking, financial officers do not seek to raise capital in the form of debt until they feel that conditions are such that their requests will not be refused by banks and other lending institutions. Loans, generally speaking, are booked during the good times for an industry when the probability of a default is nil. And the probability remains nil until the bad times arrive. Then the probability of the company averting some sort of financial crisis may no longer be nil.

Underwriters guaranteeing loans face a challenge. They must evaluate the chance of a default at the very time when the financial ratios are, by definition, in line with commonly accepted practices and the outlook for the industry and for the company within that industry is auspicious.

For the most part, loans, bonds, and other forms of debt financing collapse during bad times when the volume of goods sold falls off precipitously, prices plummet, profits disappear, cash flow dries up, and red ink appears. If doom and gloom last too long, financial obligations cannot be satisfied and it is all over for the company. During this transition from calm to rough financial weather, a change also occurs with respect to the financial ratios, which were in such good order when the debt obligations were placed on the books.

When bad times arrive, the debt to equity ratio, so modest when a loan was booked, soars. During good times, financial officers set up lines of credit that are not intended to be drawn down. They are put in place as a precaution against a possible squeeze in funds. These lines of credit are considered temporary, to be rapidly repaid once the condition causing a momentary squeeze on liquidity has passed. The banks put these lines of credit on their books on the basis that their use is infrequent and of short duration. Again, there is a perception that lines of credit are not needed in the normal course of events at the time that they are established. Bankers are partial toward lines of credit because they can charge a fee for a line of credit, which, presumably, is most likely not to be drawn upon. Lines of credit are a nice source of income during good times. There is no risk on an undrawn line of credit and, at the same time, the banks are collecting a fee for the right of the firm to draw down on the line of credit. This is like paying a doctor or a dentist for the privilege of not seeing him.

But in bad times these lines of credit are drawn down, ballooning the amount of debt in relation to equity. This behavior is no different than an individual who, in losing his livelihood, draws down on his credit card lines in his attempt to keep his family fed. It would be highly unusual for an individual to declare bankruptcy without having already drawn down every line of credit within his grasp. His personal debt to equity ratio climbs to new heights just before his financial house collapses. A corporation behaves no differently.

During hard times, cash flow diminishes from falling prices and decreasing volume of sales while interest payments rise because of increasing debt. This destroys the once favorable ratio of coverage of cash flow to interest. The ratio of current assets to current liabilities, a favorable measure of liquidity when the loan was made, is no longer so favorable. Current assets in the form of cash are drawn down to meet the payroll expenses because of a shortfall in revenue. Current assets in the form of receivables are down because sales have evaporated. Current assets in the form of inventories may be up because the company cannot sell what it is producing. Unsold, and unsalable, inventories should not be considered a current asset unless they can be easily liquidated to generate cash, which is usually not the case during business slowdowns. Nevertheless, true liquidity represented by current assets in the form of cash and receivables declines while current liabilities in the form of unpaid bills climb. The ratio of the two deteriorates at what can be an alarming rate.

Various models have been constructed to analyze trends in the financial ratios of companies for the purpose of assessing the prospects, or probability, of these companies failing at some point in the future. A company's probability of failure is assessed by comparing its financial ratios, and the rate of their deterioration, with the financial history of companies that have failed. If there is sufficient statistical fit between the deteriorating financial status of a company in comparison with those that have failed, then the model can assess a probability of failure. In addition to trying to fit two situations together in a statistical sense, the model may incorporate rules where it can more "intelligently" compare the current status of a company to those already consigned to the graveyard. These rules are based on in-depth interviews with experts in the field of failing or failed companies. If the statistical comparison and the "judgmental" rules are valid, and continue to hold their validity with the passage of time, then the model may be useful in identifying companies on the road to financial oblivion. This would be considered an application of artificial intelligence in the form of an expert, or knowledge-based, system to the world of corporate finance.

This model would be useful to stockholders and owners of publicly traded debt. Both can salvage a portion of their investment by selling stocks or bonds prior to a company becoming insolvent and having to declare bankruptcy. Bankruptcy destroys most, if not all, of the value of equity in a firm and significantly diminishes the worth of its debt holdings. Much of the debt in a company, however, is in the form of loans, lines of credit, mortgages, and leases for which there is no secondary market. These lenders cannot get out of a deteriorating situation. They are like those stranded onboard the sinking *Titanic* after all the lifeboats have been launched. There is nothing to do but promenade the first-class deck and watch the approaching ocean. Some loans permit lenders to insist on immediate payment if the financial ratios deteriorate beyond a stipulated point. Lenders demanding immediate payment, because deteriorating financial ratios permit them to do so, may bring on the very condition that the lenders are attempting to avoid—a declaration of bankruptcy.

Underwriters, lenders, and borrowers have a real challenge on their hands when they attempt to judge the ability of a company to weather a financial storm when the seas are calm. Of the three perspectives for determining the safe loading of debt on a company's capital structure, the preferred one may be that of the chief financial officer. Chief financial officers are, by the nature of their decisions on raising new capital, determining the degree of financial risk a company faces if there is a slump in business activity. If they err and pump too much debt into a company's capital structure, they create the very risk that lenders are trying to avoid—the risk of a default. It is their decision to pursue a loan over an issue of stock that starts the sequence that could lead to a default and the demise of a company. If a loan goes bad, all fingers point to the financial officer who initiated the loan process. That being the case, the best vantage point for viewing the process of assessing the risk of default in loading debt on a company's capital structure is that of the chief financial officer.

RAISING CAPITAL

Why is it necessary for financial officers to be concerned about whether new capital should be in the form of equity (stock) or debt (loans, bonds, mortgages, leases)? If a company needs capital to fund a new factory, why not turn to profits? Indeed, if profits are large enough, companies do not have to sell shares of stock, or enter into loan arrangements, or float bonds. If a company needs $10 million to fund a project, and there is $10 million in the petty cash till, there is no need to seek outside sources of capital.

Despite certain notable exceptions, funding capital projects through self-generated profits is a rarity in the world of business. For the most part, profits are not sufficient to fund capital projects. One reason for this is that companies do not retain all their profits. Retained earnings are not profits, but after-tax profits net of dividends. Suppose that a company earns $1,000 in profits. The federal government takes about a 35 percent cut of the pie with the state governments, plates in hand, wanting their share of the largesse. Right off the bat, a company is left with $650, or less, after paying $350, or more, to various federal and state income tax authorities. In other nations, the tax cut is even more severe.

Now the shareholders, with plates in hand, want their slice of the pie. A dividend paid on a share of stock provides the slice of pie. It is not unusual for the shareholders of a mature company to receive something on the order of one-third of the after-tax profits, or about $220 of the $650 left over from Uncle Sam's cut of the action. This leaves $430 out of the original $1,000 to be retained by the company. Retaining 40 or 45 percent of the profits may still be sufficient to fund the capital projects of a company if after-tax profits net of dividends are large enough. For many companies, they are not. Continued operation of a firm, particularly in the renewal of its asset base and the expansion of its productive capacity, requires outside sources of capital. A review of publicly available financial information on companies shows that the capital structure of most companies, the total of equity and debt, grows faster than what can be credited to the accumulation of retained earnings. Most companies are net borrowers of capital, be it in the form of equity by issuing stock or in the form of debt by floating bonds or arranging loans.

Inflation forces companies to resort to the capital markets because the profitability of the existing facilities cannot pay for their replacement. Airlines that have flown their $10 million planes for twenty years and have to replace them with $50 million aircraft are forced to seek outside sources of capital. Their capital structures grow because the needed funds to replace their assets are not forthcoming from airline ticket sales. Electric utilities are enormous sinks of capital because rates are determined by regulatory authorities on the basis of a modest return on investment. The capital for investing in new electric-generating plants is not forthcoming from monthly utility bills. Utility rates are based on a return on investment. The investment itself is funded from an almost continual offering of stocks and bonds. Steel companies in the midst of a thirty-year retrenchment had to rebuild their plants to match low-cost producers if they desired to survive. The money to build state of the art low-cost steel-producing plants did not come from selling steel in a shrinking market.

This is an interesting counterexample where raising capital is accomplished with the perception of a company needing the funds. No one lends to a retrenching industry on the basis that the probability of a default on a new loan is nil. Retrenchment does not provide the security of growth. The lending is done on the basis that the probability of default on existing loans is inevitable if further financing is not forthcoming. Lending institutions are forced to finance the modernization of a steel company because the alternative of doing nothing means that the existing loans will most probably end up in default. By pouring in more money, a steel company can transform its antiquated high-cost plant facilities into modern, low-cost steel mills. This allows the company to produce steel with a positive margin between price and cost even during times when the steel industry is less than robust. The alternative of continued operation of plants with a high variable cost of production is drowning in red ink because the cost of production is greater than the price of steel. This makes defaults on existing debt inevitable. The new loans are made to save the old.

In contemplating this lending philosophy, we have to bear in mind the adage that industries do not go bankrupt; companies go bankrupt. The only industry that went under as an industry was the canal companies. The canal companies that survived were those that invested in the railroads before the railroads wiped out the canal companies. Apparently, many canal companies did not hedge their bets. Some might say that the buggy whip industry went out of business when the automobiles came on the scene. Some probably did. But Fisher Brothers transformed their business from manufacturing horse carriages to horseless carriages, prospered and grew, and became part of General Motors.

The Great Depression did not result in the bankruptcy of industries, although many individual companies in an industry went under. The surviving companies in an industry were the low-cost operators. Realizing this, we can appreciate the reasons why lenders might pour money into a particular steel company to build new facilities even though the industry as a whole is retrenching. After all, steel still plays a vital role in modern industrial life. If the industry is not going bankrupt, then, by definition, there will be surviving companies.

With some exceptions, most companies must raise capital from outside sources. The questions that a financial officer must answer is how much, when, and in what form. The answers to these questions are easier to find in a single-product company than in a company whose activities span a dozen different industries. An extreme example is estimating the need for capital in a conglomerate with one hundred subsidiaries in diverse fields of endeavor, from servicing travelers' needs to producing electric motors. How can the parent organization project future capital needs under such complex circumstances? Estimating future capital needs is part of the control mechanism that has been developed for a relatively small parent organization to keep track of a large number of subsidiaries in unrelated businesses.

One way for the parent organization to handle the situation of many different subsidiaries is to reduce the number of decisions to be made. In most conglomerates, the operating decision-making process has been thoroughly decentralized. No parent company, no matter how decentralized its operations, lets an operating division or subsidiary run amuck doing its own thing. No subsidiary goes its own way without reporting back to headquarters on what it is doing. Decentralization really means that management of the subsidiary is allowed to make whatever operational decisions are necessary without having to obtain permission from someone higher up in the organization as long as these decisions do not have a meaningful financial impact on the subsidiary. Management of a subsidiary in a decentralized decision-making environment cannot purchase new equipment, take on new obligations, add to staff, or institute a new marketing program if its cost exceeds some stipulated amount. Then the management of the subsidiary needs permission from someone of higher authority. These are the rules of the game. Middle management—the managers of the subsidiaries—must play the game by the rules, or not play the game at all.

The rules of the game require, as a minimum, a flow of information that permits the parent to evaluate the activities of the subsidiary. Reports between a subsidiary and its parent usually take the form of a description of overall activities in marketing, production, and other operating particulars, plus detailed financial reports. The financial reports provide measures of performance such as profit margins, return on assets, and return on investment. Financial ratios and indicators of profitability are universal in nature and can be used to judge the relative performance of an operating subsidiary in the diaper disposal service with one that produces grass seed.

Part of this process of communication between a subsidiary and its parent is the financial forecast. One purpose of the forecast is to give those in headquarters a feeling as to how much of a source of capital, or demand for capital, the subsidiary may be in the grand scheme of things. If the subsidiary is a source of capital, then a decision has to be made on how to deploy the excess funds, that is, which of the capital-consuming subsidiaries will benefit from the largesse of the capital-generating subsidiaries. If the subsidiary is a sink for capital, that is, requires capital for expansion purposes or some other use, then the chief financial officer of the conglomerate must be aware of this fact. This information is essential in the decision-making process on the selection of the capital-consuming projects that are to be funded and the when, where, and how to raise the cash required for their funding.

Therefore, no matter how large a conglomerate may be and no matter how diverse its operations, it is organized in such a fashion that the requisite information on each unit of operation is made available to those at the top of the pyramid. This information is used to judge the efficacy of management and to come to a decision regarding the funding of pet projects of the management of the subsidiary. Decentralization may mean that no one from headquarters is watching the day-to-day operations of the subsidiary, but that does not mean that no one in headquarters is watching!

The forecast of profitability is the result of forecasting, or projecting, revenue and costs. The revenue forecast is often an extrapolation of the recent history of revenue generation. The revenue forecast is accompanied by some sort of explanation substantiating the reasons behind the typically rising sales volume and prices. Accompanying the forecast on revenue is a forecast on costs. Costs are divided into variable and fixed costs. Variable costs are the labor, material, inventory, and shipping costs that can be directly associated with the production of goods or the providing of a service. Although labor may be more of a factor than material in providing a service than in producing goods, variable costs are common to both providing services and producing goods.

Fixed costs represent those items in overhead that do not change with varying levels of providing a service or producing goods. The costs of support personnel in terms of information systems, engineering, research and development, accounting, marketing, supervisory, and maintenance, and the costs of supplies, rents, property taxes, and insurance are part of fixed costs. Although fixed costs are generally thought of as being fixed, that is not strictly true. There is some variation in fixed costs as a factory, or a service, goes from being very idle to being very busy.

Netting the forecast of costs from that of revenue yields a forecast of gross income. Combining the gross income forecast from one hundred different subsidiaries, and taking into account depreciation, taxes, financing charges on existing debt, and dividend payouts results in a cash flow projection of the company that can be dedicated to satisfying capital projects. Combining the approved capital expenditures and netting out the internally generated funds provides the chief financial officer with the magnitude and the timing for raising capital from outside sources. Then it becomes a matter of how to raise the new capital necessary to support investments in plant and equipment.

AN ALTERNATIVE APPROACH

Simulation provides an alternative approach to the conventional method of projecting cash flow. The questions of what sales, prices, and costs are expected to be over the next few years are not going to be asked. For those who have to answer such questions, this should generate a sigh of relief. The questions that are going to be substituted by top management of the parent to each of its one hundred subsidiaries, and to be answered by middle management of each of these subsidiaries, are in the form of assessments to a hypothetical situation, in fact, three hypothetical situations. In considering the feasibility of the alternative approach, place yourself in charge of a subsidiary. Do you feel that you, immersed in the operations of a subsidiary, can make the following assessments?

Regardless of how much you are selling at this time, and regardless of how much you expect to sell over the next few years, what volume of sales would fairly represent the median over this period of time? Put another way, were you to select a volume of sales that half the time you expect to beat, and half the time you don't, what is that volume? If this question cannot be answered by a discrete, or single, value, then provide the range of sales that you feel contains the median sales volume. For the volume that represents the median in future sales, what price do you expect to obtain? If a discrete value is not possible, what range would most likely contain the median price?

This exercise has to be repeated for the best and worst business conditions. All of these are hypothetical. Although these assessments are for hypothetical business conditions, the assessments need not be pure pie in the sky. For instance, during the best of times, the volume assessment would probably be at, or near, the maximum capacity of production. This assessment should not be a difficult one to obtain. For the maximum volume, three prices are necessary: the expected, and the high and low estimates, or limits, surrounding the expected price during the best of times. This can be reduced to two prices which delineate the end points of a range. The most likely price can be assumed to be the middle value of the range.

Actual historic prices may not be applicable unless the best of times was a recent happening. Therefore, these assessments are not made relying on fond memories as a guide. If recent history does not provide data to support the best of the good times, then a little imagination is required. A little imagination is always required whenever anyone is forecasting or planning for the future.

During the worst of times, volume assessments may be more difficult than price assessments. Managers may have different ideas on how bad bad times can be in terms of volume. Volume assessments may be given with the thought that there is only one chance in a hundred that the expected volume will be as low as indicated. The lower limit associated with the expected volume for the worst of times takes care of a situation that one does not even want to contemplate whereas the upper limit takes into account that happenings need not be as bad as a nightmare can make them out to be.

Price estimates for the worst of times should be easier to obtain than the estimates on volume. The expected price during the worst of times is what the low-cost producer in the industry would price goods bearing in mind the adage that industries do not go bankrupt, but companies in an industry do. The price of goods during the Great Depression was at a level to ensure the survival of an industry. In fact, no industries went bankrupt during the worst depression in this nation's history. Many individual companies were buried in the debris of the Depression, but not industries. Low-cost producers are not going to price goods at a level that bankrupts themselves along with an entire industry. The expected price should be at, or near, the price that maintains the solvency of low-cost producers. This observation should serve as a guide for assessing the range of prices during the worst of times.

If management is confident of its assessments, there may be three assessments on volume or on price, one for each hypothetical business condition. Lacking that confidence, management may elect to supply a range rather than a discrete value of its assessments of volume and price for each of the three business conditions. Therefore, there may be nine assessments on volume, or on price, rather than three assessments for each. These nine assessments can be reduced to six if the upper and lower limits of a range are being provided and the expected value is assumed to be in the middle of the range. Whatever the number, these assessments are essential if the proposed methodology is going to work. If these assessments cannot be made, then the old way of doing things will have to do. After all, the old way has worked in the past, and can be expected to work in the future. The fact that the old way does not seem to be a reliable indicator of the safe level of debt to avert bankruptcy or financial difficulties should not be a mitigating factor against its continued usage. There is no guarantee that this alternative approach will make things any better.

Unfortunately, the job is not yet done. Associated with a volume of production is a variable cost of production. Unless a company hires and fires with changing levels of production, there may be an advantage in not including labor in the variable cost of production. Then the size of the labor pool need only be considered for three levels of business activity. Material and shipping costs are certainly variable, as are other costs that are proportional to the level of production. Usually these costs are fairly well defined. One can obtain unit gross margin by netting the sales price of variable costs.

It does not matter if the assessments are made in terms of unit price, volume of sales, unit variable costs, or unit gross margin and volume of sales. Unit gross margin is price less variable costs. One industry that assesses its future prospects in terms of unit gross margin is the oil-refining industry. The oil-refining industry uses the refiner's margin to judge the health of its market. The refiner's margin is the cents per gallon difference between the price of oil products sold less the variable cost of crude oil purchased for production.

The refinery manager would have to assess the utilization of the refinery for the worst, expected (median), and best of times. For example, the expected (median) utilization may be 80 percent. This means that the refinery is expected to operate at 80 percent or more half of the time and at 80 percent or less half of the time. For the best of conditions, the refinery cannot be over 100 percent utilization. For the worst of conditions, the refinery manager cannot envision sustained operation below 50 percent utilization.

For the expected volume of production, the refiner's average margin on an annual basis may be assessed at 2 to 4 cents per gallon. Dreaming about halcyon days in the oil business, a refinery manager may lick his chops over the prospects of the margin being anywhere from 4 to 7 cents per gallon. During the midst of a depression, a refinery manager may despondently contemplate operating in a market where the margin is only 0 to 1 cents, which leaves little, if anything, to cover his fixed costs. The refinery manager has no recent history of operations for these extremes of business conditions. Years of experience in the oil business is the basis of these assessments.

If these assessments are beyond the realm of imagination, then the refinery operator can revert to the usual forecast: over the next three years, refinery utilization will be 80 percent, 82 percent, and 84 percent, with the refiner's margin being 2, 2.5, and 3 cents per gallon, respectively. The dream content in this form of forecast should not be any more than what is required in making assessments. Actually, the refinery manager spends less time in dream land making assessments than forecasts because forecasts require explicit statements concerning refinery utilization and the refiner's margin. A refinery operator makes this forecast with some degree of bias depending on how the forecast affects preconceived notions about future operations. The forecast is also influenced by the realization that it may be revisited on him as a goal that determines his longevity with the company. One thing the refinery manager cannot escape, he must say something about the future, otherwise planning becomes an impossibility.

The real question is whether the contemplation of the future should be in terms of a discrete forecast for an assumed level of business activity or in terms of assessments for three hypothetical levels of business activity. Assessments involve more figures and information than conventional forecasting, but do not require making a definitive statement about the future level of business activity. Although nine figures for the assessment of the refiner's margin may sound high, there are really only six. The expected value is midway between the high and low estimates. The expected value when the refiner's margin is expressed as 2 to 4 cents per gallon is, presumably, 3 cents per gallon.

This technique can be equally adapted to the service industry. A service industry sells a unit of service. This unit of service may be one hour of a lawyer's, doctor's, dentist's, accountant's, or consultant's time. The median volume of hours of service to be sold and the unit gross margin, which is the difference between pricing and costing of an hour's worth of professional time, has to be assessed for the three hypothetical business conditions. If the service is platters of hors d'oeuvres, one has to assess the expected volume with an assessment of the range of the markup, or unit gross margin, per platter of chopped liver and smoked salmon. During the best of times, when everyone is celebrating, volume and unit gross margin soar. During the worst of times, when everyone is in the throes of belt tightening, one can well imagine the impact on sales of platters of boiled shrimp and crab claws. But this impact, no matter how severe, has to be assessed in order to obtain the safe load of debt in an operating company.

The unit of measure for a dry cleaning establishment may be in terms of a standard suit, a dress, or a shirt. The unit of measure for a fast food restaurant may be in terms of a hamburger, a box of fried chicken, or a pizza. For a communications company, a volume and gross margin evolve around units of time and distance. The assessments for a liquor establishment would require the rewriting of the SIMTWO simulator generator program if alcohol consumption rises as business conditions crumble.

For the expected (median), best, and worst business conditions, assessments have to be provided for fixed costs. These could be in terms of three assessments for each of the three business conditions or simply one assessment for each business condition. The former would require the running of SIMTWO and the latter the running of SIMONE in order to generate the applicable simulator. The selection of which to use has to do with management's degree of confidence in its assessment of fixed costs.

Fixed costs include every cost that has not been included in variable costs. While some of these are fixed, such as rentals on buildings, property taxes, insurance premiums, and utilities, other components may contain some degree of variability. During the best of times, the cost of labor increases from overtime premiums and temporary hirings for the blue collar types. For the white collar types, executive bonuses, first class business travel, and expensive entertainment allowances rise with the level of business activity. During the worst of times, the cost of labor for blue collar types falls with layoffs, but usually not in direct proportion to the falloff in production activity. A company may prefer a labor force with some element of idleness despite layoffs in order to be able to respond positively to an increase in demand. Less white collar types are employed, bonuses are gone along with first class travel, and entertainment is reduced to dinner parties at home. Blue and white collar labor costs vary with production levels and is not as precise as other factors in fixed costs.

Maintenance is another component of fixed costs that has a tendency to vary as business conditions change. Maintenance is often deferred when times are bad as part of a company's efforts to reduce costs. Catchup time for deferred maintenance occurs when the cash is pouring into a company's coffers. Although maintenance is considered a part of fixed costs, it varies with the level of business activity and its estimates also contain some degree of approximation.

All costs associated with the financing of a company should be excluded from fixed costs. Mortgages on buildings, lines of credit, and debt and lease payments should be segregated and accounted for separately by the parent organization. After all, the purpose of the exercise is to measure the ability of the company to carry various loads of debt. Leaving debt hidden within the fixed costs of the subsidiaries defeats this purpose. The exclusion of financing costs from fixed costs may not be as simple as it seems. Questions will arise whether a short term rental on a building or a lease on a truck should be included in the fixed costs of a subsidiary or in the financing costs of the conglomerate. The chief financial officer is going to have to provide guidance on this matter.

Capital expenditures are associated with the expansion of productive capacity or the replacement of existing plant and equipment as these capital assets are worn away from use and transformed from something bright and shiny to dust and ashes. Capital expenditures are reserved for big ticket items or a large number of small ticket items whose aggregate cost make them a big ticket item. This means that minor capital expenditures, such as the replacement of a single typewriter, may be buried in the fixed costs of a subsidiary. The timing and size of major capital expenditures net of internally generated funds are what sends the chief financial officer out looking for funds.

Capital expenditures are similar to maintenance expenses in one respect: capital expenditures are deferrable. During the worst of times, companies may reduce their capital expenditures to next to nothing. If something breaks, it is fixed even though it should probably be replaced. If it has to be replaced, substitute equipment is sought from a plant with spare equipment. If no substitute is available and every other means of avoiding a capital expenditure has been exhausted, then the item is purchased. If the capital expenditure is a new factory, the planned go ahead for its construction will be postponed as long as times remain less than robust.

During good times, management is eager to replace equipment or build a new factory, because profitability can easily accommodate their desires. Besides, any good manager realizes that a marginal piece of equipment may as well be replaced when times are good because it is not going to be replaced when times take a turn for the worse. The same can be said for building a new factory. Strike while the iron is hot is a good rule of thumb because management knows the repercussions on decisions to buy new equipment or build a new factory once the market softens. Companies tend to go to extremes in capital expenditures as business conditions swing between good and bad times. There is no more cyclical industry than those companies that supply machinery and equipment to manufacturing plants.

For purposes of illustration, suppose that a company consists of one subsidiary that makes a number of models of electric motors. For planning purposes, the management of the subsidiary reduces the several models to one aggregate model that fairly represents the weighted average of all the models sold from the point of view of consumption of manpower and material. The variable costs in terms of casings, wiring, other material components, and other costs such as average shipping costs are known with a good degree of confidence. Price and volume, however, are sensitive to business conditions. Management has made the following assessments concerning the key variables influencing profitability (see Table 6.1).

These assessments do not come from a century-long review of historic data. It would be unusual if more than five years of history are included in these numbers. Furthermore, historic data is not very useful in determining these assessments because no five-year period will encompass both extremes, and the median, of business activity. These are management's best assessments of how expected and extreme business activity will affect the key variables of sales, prices, and variable and fixed costs.

Table 6.1
Subsidiary I: Management Assessments of Key Variables

	BUSINESS CONDITIONS		
	WORST	EXPECTED	BEST
PRICE			
HIGH	$125	$175	$250
EXPECTED	100	150	175
LOW	75	125	150
VOLUME			
HIGH	70,000	170,000	210,000
EXPECTED	50,000	150,000	200,000
LOW	30,000	130,000	190,000
VARIABLE COSTS	$60	$62	$65
FIXED COSTS			
HIGH	$2,500,000	$4,250,000	$4,750,000
EXPECTED	2,000,000	4,000,000	4,500,000
LOW	1,500,000	3,750,000	4,250,000

The variance in the range of assessments indicates that management does not have an absolutely clear idea about the median values for price, volume, or fixed costs. Rather than give a discrete or single value for each of these variables, management has given a range with or without the expected value. For instance, management suspects that the median volume is around 150,000 units, but is not absolutely confident that sales higher than 150,000 will occur exactly half of the time nor that sales lower than 150,000 will occur exactly half of the time. But they are confident that the range of 150,000 plus or minus 20,000 does contain the median. The same is true for the median price. It is somewhere between $125 and $175 per motor. This is actually a rather wide range, but presumably, this is the best assessment management can provide. This same thought process applies to the assessments of price and volume for the best and worst levels of business activity. The degree of variance in price and volume suggests that the company is selling its motors to the highly cyclical capital goods market.

Management is reasonably comfortable with its assessments of variable costs, which are provided by three discrete values. Fixed costs are another area of uncertainty as is seen by the need to give nine assessments, or possibly six with the expected value being midway between the upper and lower limits of the range. In this example, fixed costs include the cost of the labor force. Management is unsure how the labor force will be laid off during weak times in the market. The wider band on fixed costs when the market is weak reflects this uncertainty.

These assessments are only tangentially related to historic data. The connection between assessments and actual data is in the cognitive process by which a manager reviews historic data and mentally digests, integrates, and translates actual figures to assessments of future values. This is the essential difference between man and machine. The machine mechanically transforms inputs to outputs. Man supplies the input, and the rules for transforming the input to output, and then interprets the output through a cognitive thought process little understood by man himself. The computer's appearance of being a thinking machine merely reflects the ability of the thinking man to provide the programming instructions that create such an illusion.

The proposed methodology is not a variation on conventional forecasting. Conventional forecasting is based on actual historic data and an assumed level of future business activity. In essence, most forecasting is accomplished by taking past data and historic trends and adjusting the trends to fit the perception of future business activity. Then the adjusted trends are extrapolated into the future to obtain the forecast. The proposed methodology asks management to make assessments of values for the key variables of sales volume, price, and variable and fixed costs for three hypothetical levels of business activity without asking for a forecast of business activity. Business activity will be simulated because no one knows the future level of business activity. If management can truly forecast future sales price, volume, and fixed and variable costs accurately, then they would be better off buying a seat on the New York Stock Exchange and trading the stock of the company rather than running the company. Management is answering the question of what three business conditions in the form of the expected (median), the best, and the worst, mean in terms of price, sales volume, and variable and fixed costs. If these assessments cannot be made in discrete, or single-value, terms, then management is permitted to provide a range that would most likely include the expected values.

Although past data certainly is part of the process in a manager's formulation of these assessments, past data does not determine these assessments. Data over five years old is probably useless. Data less than five years old does not provide a sufficient basis to assess the key variables for three business conditions because it is highly unlikely that five years of data contain even one of these three business conditions. The assessor looks into the future with relatively little guidance from past data other than providing a focal point in the thought process. Assessments rely on a manager's experience in a field of business and on the ability to intuitively translate this experience, which includes past data, into what this means in values for those variables that determine future profitability.

Looking into the future is always guesswork as any businessman knows. A manager is left with three choices. One choice is to make assessments for three levels of business activity without forecasting the level of business activity or relying extensively on past data. Another choice is forecasting price, volume, and cost to obtain a projection of profitability using past data as the primary means of determining future values. There is one remaining choice: recognize the inscrutability of the future and conduct business on an ad hoc basis. If managers are incapable of forecasting, or of making assessments, then they are unable to plan much more than a day or two into the future. If a company cannot lay out any plans for the future, then the need for management is vastly diminished. Stock boys and sales girls can run a shop on a day to day basis.

GROSS INCOME

Gross income before depreciation, interest, and taxes is price less variable costs multiplied by sales volume less fixed costs. Before performing any simulations on gross income, it may be useful to first estimate the outcome of the expected gross income and its associated range. For the median, or expected, business condition, one would not be overly surprised if the expected gross income is a sales price of $150 less $62 in variable costs multiplied by a volume of 150,000 less fixed costs of $4 million, or $9.2 million. These values are the expected values for each of the key variables. The best gross margin for this business condition is a highest sales price of $175 less $62 multiplied by a highest sales volume of 170,000 less the lowest fixed cost of $3.75 million, or $15.46 million. The worst is a lowest sales price of $125 less $62 in variable costs multiplied by the lowest sales volume of 130,000 less the highest fixed cost of $4.25 million, or $3.94 million. This is a rather wide range of results for the gross income for a single business index value, but this is the consequence of

Table 6.2
Subsidiary I: Gross Margin Range Limits

	BUSINESS CONDITIONS		
	WORST	EXPECTED	BEST
SUBSIDIARY I			
GROSS INCOME BEFORE DEPRECIATION, INTEREST AND TAXES			
HIGH	$3.05 MM	$15.46 MM	$34.60 MM
EXPECTED	–	9.20	17.50
LOW	-2.05	3.94	11.40

management's assessments of the key variables. A narrower range of gross income would be possible if management opted for a narrower range of assessments.

By taking the highest price, the highest volume, and the lowest fixed costs, we obtain the high end estimate of gross income for each of the hypothetical business conditions. By taking the lowest price, the lowest volume, and the highest fixed cost, we obtain the low end of the estimate of gross income (see Table 6.2).

Although there is a wide range of gross income for the three indicated business conditions, the extreme values are highly improbable. Taking the expected (median) business condition as an example, the chance that price is at its highest value of $175 per unit is one in ten. The chance that volume is at its highest value of 170,000 units is also one in ten. Although there is not much variation in fixed costs, the chance that it is as low as $3.75 million is, again, one in ten. There is only one chance in a thousand that these three specific values will be simultaneously selected. Therefore, there is only one chance in a thousand of a gross income of $15.46 million actually occurring in a simulation. This is true of the extreme points for gross income for each index value of business activity. The consequence of extreme values of the gross income being relatively rare events means that middle values of gross income have a greater chance of occurring. The resulting probability distribution of gross income peaks around the expected value and tails off as one approaches either extreme of the range.

We might be tempted to simulate the gross income by running the SIMTWO simulator using the previous table of values for the gross income as inputs. This would lead to a gross overstatement of the probability of the extreme ends of the permissible range. The SIMTWO simulator, as presently programmed, provides a 10 percent chance that an extreme value will be randomly selected for a given level of business activity. As just calculated, one in a thousand is a better estimate of the likelihood of an extreme gross income actually being experienced. The tails of the SIMTWO simulator are too fat. Therefore, without rewriting the SIMTWO simulator to reduce its overweighted tails, the preferred way of obtaining the probability distribution of gross income for this subsidiary is to create two-dimensional simulators for price, volume, and fixed costs, and a one-dimensional simulator for variable costs, and then write a special purpose program to generate a simulator of gross income.

In running a simulation for gross income, a business activity index number is first selected. This establishes the low, median, and high values for the range of price, volume, and fixed costs. These, in turn, have been previously determined by running the SIMTWO program for each of the nine applicable assessments of price, volume, and fixed costs. At this point, a number between 1 and 10 is randomly selected. The discrete value for price is determined by entering the SIMTWO simulator for price at the given level of business activity and for the selected random number. Another number between 1 and 10 is randomly selected, and the process is repeated to establish a value for volume; and again, to establish a value for fixed costs. In this example, variable costs are determined directly from the selected value of business activity. Gross income is then derived by netting the sales price of variable costs, multiplying the resulting unit gross margin by the sales volume, and subtracting fixed costs. Repeating this process an innumerable number of times should result in the extreme values of gross income not being beyond those indicated in the table. Were this to happen, there would be something wrong either in the derivation of values in the table or in the programming of the simulation. It is impossible for the extreme values generated by the simulation to be above the upper limits or below the lower limits. Moreover, the simulation should generate an expected value being about what is indicated in the arithmetically derived table on gross income.

In order to demonstrate the resulting probability distribution of gross income and to illustrate the nature of the probability distribution from combining the gross income from two different subsidiaries, a second subsidiary has to be introduced into the analysis. The conglomerate now consists of two subsidiaries with the second being in a different line of business than the first. The nature of the line of business is immaterial in the analysis of gross income because financial analysis is a universal means of evaluating the performance of a company independent of the nature of its business. Suppose that the management of the second subsidiary has provided the assessments in Table 6.3.

Management has already netted price of variable costs by providing its assessments in terms of unit gross margin. Using the same arithmetic methodology as before, we obtain the range of gross income, and the estimate of the most likely value for the three business conditions (see Table 6.4).

What would we anticipate to be the result of running a simulation combining the gross incomes of the two subsidiaries? The high for any business condition cannot be more than the sum of the two high estimates of gross income. The low cannot be less than the sum of the two low estimates. There may, or may not, be a question of whether the most likely value for gross income would be the sum of the two individual expected estimates of gross incomes. Were this true, then the

Table 6.3
Subsidiary II: Management Assessments of Key Variables

	BUSINESS CONDITIONS		
	WORST	EXPECTED	BEST
UNIT GROSS MARGIN			
HIGH	$30	$45	$55
EXPECTED	25	40	50
LOW	20	35	45
VOLUME			
HIGH	120,000	210,000	320,000
EXPECTED	100,000	200,000	300,000
LOW	80,000	190,000	280,000
FIXED COSTS			
HIGH	$3,500,000	$6,500,000	$9,500,000
EXPECTED	3,000,000	6,000,000	9,000,000
LOW	2,500,000	5,500,000	8,500,000

table of values for gross income of the two subsidiaries is simply the combination of the two individual tables of values for gross income (see Table 6.5).

In comparing this table of gross income of the two subsidiaries with the individual gross income tables, we see that the range between the upper and lower limits has widened. The probability of the extreme values of the range occurring has diminished, however. Focusing on the expected, or median, business condition, the probability for the expected gross income of the two subsidiaries being as high as $19.41 million has to take into account that there is one

Table 6.4
Subsidiary II: Gross Margin Range Limits

	BUSINESS CONDITIONS		
	WORST	EXPECTED	BEST
SUBSIDIARY II			
GROSS INCOME BEFORE DEPRECIATION, INTEREST AND TAXES			
HIGH	$1.10 MM	$3.95 MM	$9.10 MM
EXPECTED	-0.50	2.00	6.00
LOW	-1.90	0.15	3.10

Table 6.5
Subsidiaries I and II: Gross Margin Range Limits

	BUSINESS CONDITIONS		
	WORST	EXPECTED	BEST
SUBSIDIARY I & II			
GROSS INCOME BEFORE DEPRECIATION, INTEREST AND TAXES			
HIGH	$4.15 MM	$19.41 MM	$43.70 MM
EXPECTED	-0.50	11.20	23.50
LOW	-3.95	4.09	14.50

chance in a thousand that the gross income of Subsidiary I will be $15.46 and one chance in a thousand that the gross income of Subsidiary II will be $3.95 million. Therefore, the chance that both will occur simultaneously, which would be necessary for gross income to be $19.41 million, is one chance in a million. This does not mean, however, that there is virtually no probability that the gross income cannot be close to $19 million even if $19.41 million is a highly improbable event. That depends on the probability distribution of the gross income for both subsidiaries. Nevertheless, the tails of the combined probability distribution of the two subsidiaries should be thinner than the tails of the individual probability distribution, bearing in mind that the permissible range of gross income is widened when the values of gross income for the two subsidiaries are combined. Finally, there should be no great surprise if the probability distribution of combining both distributions peaks at the sum of the "peaks" of the two individual distributions.

The PEAK program in the appendix was written to examine the nature of the distribution of gross income for a single business condition: the expected or median assessment. Exhibit 6.1 shows the three probability distributions of gross income for the expected business condition of Subsidiary I, Subsidiary II, and the combination of the two.

The higher peaking of Subsidiary II in Exhibit 6.1 is a consequence of management's narrower assessments of the key variables. Gross income is restricted to a narrower range of possible values. The narrower the range of possible values, the higher the probability of occurrence for any particular value within that range. The higher the probability, the higher the peaking of the probability distribution. The peaking of the probability distribution associated with Subsidiary I is lower than that of Subsidiary II. The lower "height" reflects a wider range of possibilities. This means that the probability of the gross income taking on a particular value within the wider range of values has to be less. Nevertheless, the area under each of the two probability curves is the same, representing

Exhibit 6.1
Gross Income (Discrete Probability Distribution)

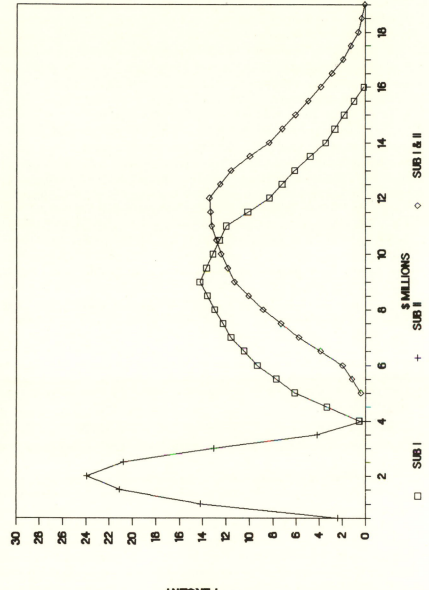

the totality (100 percent) of all occurrences of gross income within its prescribed range.

The greater range of possibilities for gross income for Subsidiary I is a consequence of management's relatively wide range on their assessments of price and volume. This, in turn, reflects their lack of confidence in their assessments, resulting in a lower height in the peaking of the discrete probability distribution. Thus the height of the discrete probability distribution becomes a measure of the confidence of management in its assessments. The higher the peaking of the discrete probability distribution, the greater the confidence. Exhibit 6.1 demonstrates that management of Subsidiary II has more confidence in its assessments of future values than the management of Subsidiary I.

The exhibit seems to confirm that the arithmetically determined gross income assessments of one subsidiary can be added to another, and that the results of the simulation of two subsidiaries is the same as the sum of the individual simulations. We can also see that the tails of the probability distribution associated with combining the two subsidiaries are thinner than either of the probability distributions of the individual subsidiaries, but, nevertheless, cover a wider range of possibilities. Table 6.6 compares the arithmetically derived expected and extreme values with those derived from running the simulation program. The simulation was run for each of the two individual subsidiaries for one specific level of business activity. Then the simulation was run combining the two subsidiaries for the same level of business activity.

The table was generated by running ten thousand simulations. When the simulations were run for a single subsidiary, the upper and lower limits were actually simulated, there being one chance in a thousand of this occurring. In

Table 6.6
Derivation of Gross Income Simulation versus Arithmetic Median Business Activity (Index Value, 50)

	SUBSIDIARY I	SUBSIDIARY II	SUBSIDIARY I & II
UPPER LIMIT			
ARITHMETIC	$15,460,000	$3,950,000	$19,410,000
SIMULATION	15,460,000	3,950,000	18,772,500
EXPECTED VALUE			
ARITHMETIC	$9,200,000	$2,000,000	$11,200,000
SIMULATION	9,196,340	1,999,873	11,191,960
LOWER LIMIT			
ARITHMETIC	$3,940,000	$150,000	$4,090,000
SIMULATION	3,940,000	150,000	4,615,000

running ten thousand simulations, there was a sufficient opportunity, so to speak, for the extreme values to occur at least once. No simulated result exceeded the extreme ends of the range. Had this happened, an investigation would have been initiated to determine whether there was a bug in the program or an error in the arithmetic calculations. The expected values were close to those derived from the arithmetic calculations.

When the simulation was run to obtain a combined gross income for the two subsidiaries, its expected value was close to the combined expected values of the two individual subsidiaries. The extreme points were not actually simulated, however. This reflects the point that the extremes represent the simultaneous occurrences of two very unlikely events. The lower probability of the extreme values can be seen in the narrower tails of the combined probability distribution in Exhibit 6.1.

A simulation need not be run for each of one hundred subsidiaries. All that is necessary is for each subsidiary to prepare the tables of assessments for sales volume, price, and variable and fixed costs or the tables of assessments for unit gross margin, and volume and fixed costs, for the three business conditions and forward them to the parent organization. It is at this point that a simulation program has to be called upon to create the probability distribution of the gross income of the conglomerate, or corporation, as a whole. This is the first step in the process of determining a safe, or perhaps, optimal level of debt in the capital structure of a corporation.

ASSESSING THE SAFE LOAD OF DEBT

Structures support weight. The more weight that is added to a structure, the greater the internal stress. Continual loading of a structure can increase the internal stress to a point where, suddenly, and often without warning, the structure collapses. The capital structure of a company is similar. A small loading of debt can be easily supported. Adding to the loading of debt increases the internal pressure on the cash flow to service the debt. At some point, the capital structure collapses under the weight of the debt load.

Financial officers are interested in determining the safe loading of debt. They cannot make this assessment without considering an unsafe loading of debt on the capital structure of a company. What are the signs that the load of debt is too heavy? The classic signs that there may be trouble on the financial horizon are when the cash reserves are exhausted, available credit lines have been drawn down, and there is still insufficient cash to make the amortization and interest payments on debt. The frequency and the magnitude of shortfalls of cash to satisfy financial obligations are the essence of judging the safe loading of debt in a company's financial structure.

For illustration purposes, suppose that the following set of circumstances fairly represents the situation for the chief financial officer of the conglomerate that consists only of these two subsidiaries. The fixed costs of operation of the parent is $1 million per year for median business conditions. This can be reduced to $0.8 million during the worst of times and is expected to expand to $1.2 million during the best of times. The chief financial officer has decided to maintain $1 million in a special account called cash reserves. This is above, and separate from, the minimum level of liquidity that is required to sustain the operations of the firm on a day by day basis.

The cash reserves of $1 million are segregated from the cash account and are invested in short-term government and corporate paper. The purpose of cash reserves is to cover the contingency of the firm not being able to make timely payments on interest and amortization. The minimum level of liquidity in the cash account covers the contingency of a cash shortage developing over timing differences between paying bills and collecting on receivables for the purpose of keeping the suppliers satisfied. The cash reserves are designed to cover a potential shortage of cash for the purpose of keeping the lenders satisfied.

Suppose that the chief financial officer has established lines of credit totaling $5 million. The average maturity of long-term debt is ten years with an average interest rate of 12 percent. New stock issues and new loans cannot be negotiated in a bad business climate. This can be simulated by defining such a climate when the index value of business activity is below 35. Moreover, when business conditions are conducive to acquiring new debt and issuing stock, a history of at least two years of increasing profitability is required.

The second program in the appendix, named DEBT, creates a thousand-year simulation of the gross income of the conglomerate of two subsidiaries. The gross income of the conglomerate utilizes the individual simulators of price, volume, and variable and fixed costs for Subsidiary I and the individual simulators of unit gross margin, volume, and fixed cost for Subsidiary II. The combined gross income of the two subsidiaries, less the overhead cost of the parent organization, is the gross income before taxes and financing charges for the conglomerate. An arbitrary century of gross income for the conglomerate is shown in Exhibit 6.2.

The gross income table of values for the two subsidiaries (Table 6.5) has an absolute worst case of −$3.95 million and an absolute best case of $43.7 million. Yet, during this hundred-year simulation, gross income varies from about $6 million to nearly $17 million. During the entire thousand-year simulation, the highest gross income is $16.9 million and the lowest is $3.6 million.

The extremes experienced in the simulation are nowhere near that indicated in the table of possible values. The reason for this is that the combining of the subsidiaries makes the probability of simultaneous occurrence of extreme values highly remote compared to the chances of their individual occurrence. The probability is further diminished by the fact that the business activity index itself is biased against the appearance of values near 1 or 100. Business index activity levels between 25 and 75 have a 70 percent probability of happening, while business activity levels less than an index value of 25 and more than an index value of 75 have only a 30 percent probability. Furthermore, business activity

Exhibit 6.2
Gross Income Before Taxes and Financing Charges

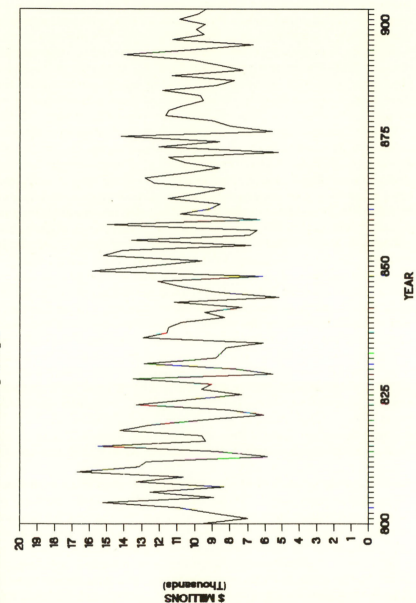

levels of 1 and 100 have the lowest probability of all the index values. Coupling the infrequent times that business activity levels are near the high and low limits of its range with the low probability of the extreme values of gross income of both subsidiaries occurring simultaneously means that gross income being as low as −$3.95 million or as high as $43.7 million are very rare events indeed. And this rarity may be somewhat overstated in that the SIMTWO generates simulators with "fat" tails in that there is one chance in ten of an extreme value in volume, price, or fixed costs being selected. If the SIMTWO generator were amended to have thinner tails, then the probability of simulating the extreme points in the table of gross income for the two combined subsidiaries becomes even more remote.

The fact that combining subsidiaries reduces the probability of occurrence of extreme values in gross income has a direct impact on the measure of risk in establishing a safe load of debt. The risk of default is associated with those times when the gross income is insufficient to support financial charges. If the probability of extremely poor levels of gross income of two individual subsidiaries can be reduced by joining them together in one conglomerate, then there is less risk in lending to a conglomerate with subsidiaries in different lines of business than in lending to the individual subsidiaries as independent companies. Put another way, it is safer to stand together than to stand alone.

The standard deviation is as measure of scatter on how the data points fall around a mean. The standard deviation is also a measure of risk in how much the gross income can vary with respect to the average gross income. When two normal distributions are combined, the resulting standard deviation is not the addition of the two individual standard deviations. Variance, which is the square of the standard deviation, is additive. If the standard deviation of one normal distribution is 2, and the other is 3, their respective variances are 4 and 9. The variance of combining the two distributions is 13. The square root of the combined variance of 13, or 3.6, is the standard deviation of the combination of the two distributions. The combined standard deviation of 3.6 is less than the sum of the two standard deviations of the original distributions.

However, the range of possibilities is additive. The combined worst gross income of the conglomerate is the sum of the two worst gross incomes of each subsidiary; and, similarly, the best combined gross income is the sum of the individual best gross incomes. However, the net effect of a slightly larger standard deviation with a relatively wider range representing all the possibilities of combining the two distributions is that values near the extremities of the combined range have a much smaller probability of occurrence.

The point of all this is that the chances of two subsidiaries each having a bust year is less when the two are combined than when each remains independent. This has been shown as the number of subsidiaries increased from one to two. This continues as subsidiaries are added to the conglomerate, particularly when they are in different lines of business. There is less of a chance of a conglomerate with many operating subsidiaries having the ultimate bust year than a conglomerate with a few operating subsidiaries. Hard times affect different companies in varying degrees. Subsidiaries that are suffering less support those that are suffering more.

This is the secret of diversification. The more subsidiaries there are, the less the chance of obtaining extreme values of gross income because such extremes can only occur when all the subsidiaries are simultaneously at the same end of the range of their gross incomes. A company with several diverse businesses is a safer investment than one that specializes because a really poor performance by one division can be counterbalanced by adequate performance by another. Studies in stock investments have shown that risk reduction, as measured by the probability of having a horrible return, can be achieved through diversification of holdings. Such risk reduction requires relatively few stocks in different industries. A conglomerate of one hundred subsidiaries may not have that much of an advantage over a conglomerate of ten subsidiaries with respect to the possibility of facing the worst of all possible worlds.

Naturally, the "cost" of reducing the risk of default through diversification is the lessening of the probability of the conglomerate making a great deal of money. The rarity of the event of every subsidiary performing extremely poorly is matched by the rarity of the event of every subsidiary performing extremely well. The fact that the gross income never approached −$3.95 million is matched by the fact that it also never approached $43.2 million.

The other matter of interest in Exhibit 6.2 is the average gross income. It appears that the average gross income is between $10 and $11 million. Over the thousand-year simulation, the average is $10.3 million. The three values associated with the expected gross income in Table 6.5 is a worst case of −$0.5 million, a median of $11.2 million, and a best case of $23.5 million. The average of these is $11.4 million, which net of the overhead of the parent organization of $1 million, is $10.4 million. The weighted average, counting the most expected value of $11.2 million four times to its upper and lower limits of −$0.5 million and $23.5 million, is $11.3 million, which net of $1 million in overhead, is $10.3 million. Any attempt to derive the average gross income from Table 6.5 using the extreme points of −$3.95 million or $43.7 million, when nothing close to these values occurs during the thousand-year simulation, provides a misleading indication of the average gross income. In other words, the estimation of the average gross income from a table of values can be distorted by the inclusion of the extremes associated with the worst and best of business conditions because of their highly remote chance of occurrence.

Management must satisfy the claims of tax collectors and bankers before they have access to the profits of the conglomerate. When things are going badly for a company, interest and depreciation usually provide a sufficient shield against a reduced level of operating income to significantly reduce taxes. Uncle Sam is willing to wait for a better day before taking his slice of the pie. Lenders, however, are not so amenable to any delay on the return of, and on, their investment in the company. Management cannot easily ask lenders to take a smaller slice of the pie using the feeble excuse that the sales were not as high as anticipated. Lenders expect the company to make its regular payment of interest and amortization without regard to market conditions. Lenders have a legal right to be paid and borrowers have the legal obligation to pay lenders their due or face the consequences. Assuming that taxes are being paid on a current basis, Uncle Sam does not drive companies to the wall. Lenders so. The more managers rely on debt as an external source of funding, the greater is their loss of independence.

When the gross income is insufficient to keep lenders happy, the chief financial officer can draw on the special cash reserves account, which was set up with this contingency in mind. Once that is exhausted, the chief financial officer can start drawing down on a line of credit established for such an exigency. If gross income jumps back to a level that covers financing charges, any surplus in funds after paying the lenders and Uncle Sam their due cannot be made available for dividends and capital expenditures until the line of credit has been paid off and the cash reserves account has been replenished. Then, any excess monies are available for the payment of dividends and the internal funding of capital expenditures. Exhibit 6.3 shows the funds available for dividends and capital expenditures with a long-term debt load of $30 million on the company's capital structure.

Exhibit 6.3 shows the internally generated funds that are available for dividends and capital expenditures after taxes and financing charges and after paying off the outstanding balance in the lines of credit and replenishing the cash reserves. Exhibit 6.4 shows the funds available for dividend distribution and for funding capital projects if the underlying financial structure contains $40 million in long-term debt.

The times when there are no funds available for dividends and capital expenditures are those times when the gross income of the company is dedicated to satisfying debt servicing needs, or liquidating the balance in the line of credit, or replenishing the cash reserves. Comparing these two exhibits demonstrates that the cost of supporting a higher debt load reduces the amount of internally generated funds available for dividends and capital expenditures. Exhibits 6.3 and 6.4 show only the internally generated funds from operations and do not reflect the impact of refinancing the debt during the good times back to a level of $30 or $40 million. The refinancing of debt up to the maximum prescribed level is a source of externally generated funds that can also be dedicated to capital expenditures.

In the simulation, long-term debt is amortized over ten years. The annual amortization for a maximum debt load of $30 million is $3 million per year. After three years, the conglomerate's debt has been reduced to $21 million. Suppose that conditions are right for the company to go to the financial well. Then the company can float an additional $9 million in debt, bringing its overall debt up to the maximum permissible ceiling of $30 million. The $9 million is a source of funds that is first used to pay off any outstanding balance in the line of credit and then to replenish the cash reserves, if necessary. After that, any remaining funds are considered to be externally generated funds that can be used

Exhibit 6.3
Funds Available (Dividends and Capital Expenditures)

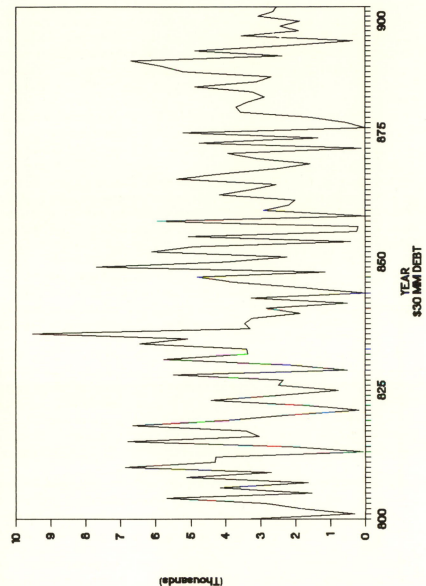

Exhibit 6.4
Funds Available (Dividends and Capital Expenditures)

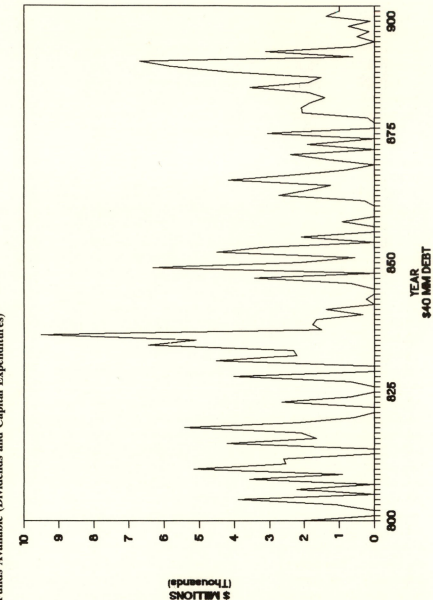

to fund capital projects. Externally generated funds are not included in Exhibits 6.3 and 6.4 except to the degree that refinancing debt has been used to pay off the line of credit and replenish the cash reserves. Any shortfall between what is needed to fund capital projects, and what is generated internally or externally by refinancing long-term debt, is satisfied by sales of shares of stock. If stock cannot be sold to the degree necessary to fund all the projects, then certain projects have to be culled from the wish list because the loading of debt cannot exceed the stipulated maximum debt.

The purpose of the simulation is to identify a safe load of debt. Capital demands above the safe load of debt are presumed to be raised by selling equity. The model is not concerned with the demand for capital expenditures other than this demand being greater than what a firm can generate internally.

The various loading of debt on the financial structure of the conglomerate is analyzed according to the following rules that have been incorporated in the DEBT program. If the gross income is insufficient to support debt servicing charges and the payment of taxes, the first source of funds to be drawn on is the cash reserves account that has an initial balance of $1 million. Once the cash reserves are liquidated, the company draws on its line of credit. From the point of view of the simulation, there is no limit to the line of credit. The company, however, has established a line of credit with the banks with an overall maximum limit of $5 million. Therefore, whenever the line of credit is in excess of $5 million, the company is in danger of being declared in default on its underlying debt. Exhibit 6.5 shows the excess drawdown of the line of credit above $5 million over the century under examination with $50 million of debt in its capital structure.

Drawdowns on the line of credit in excess of $5 million are, generally speaking, infrequent and not very large. Either expanding the cash reserves to $2 or $3 million, or alternatively, expanding the lines of credit to $6 or $7 million would cover many of these excess drawdowns. With either of these adaptations, there would be sufficient cash reserves or borrowing capacity in the line of credit to accommodate those relatively infrequent times when there is insufficient cash being generated by the operations of the conglomerate to satisfy the financing charges associated with a debt load of $50 million. Yet this condition of reasonable control during times of poor financial performance is totally lacking when the debt load on the capital structure of the firm is $60 million (see Exhibit 6.6).

Comparing Exhibits 6.5 and 6.6, it is apparent that $50 million is a safe load in debt requiring only a modest increase in either cash reserves or the line of credit to accommodate those times when the operating gross income is not quite up to expectations. This cannot be said when there is $60 million of debt in the capital structure. Excess drawdowns beyond modest levels are an open invitation to bankruptcy. An excess drawdown of $10 million means that the cash reserves have been drained dry and the line of credit totaling $5 million has been drawn down, and the company is still $10 million short in making interest and amortiza-

Exhibit 6.5
Excess Drawdown (Line of Credit)

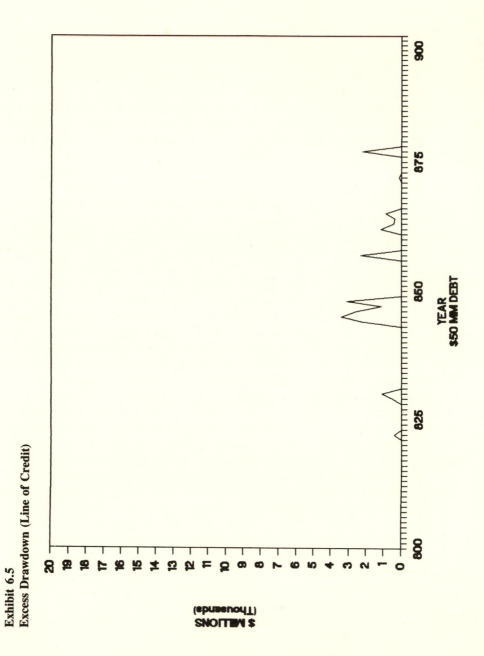

Exhibit 6.6
Excess Drawdown (Line of Credit)

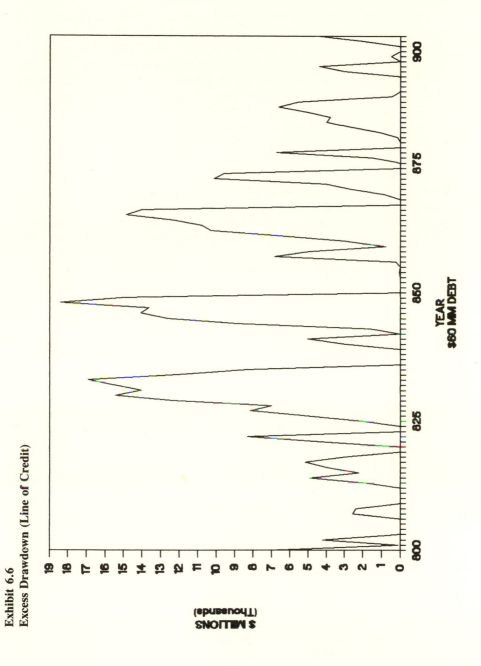

tion payments. Exhibit 6.7 illustrates the probability associated with the size of various excess drawdowns for the two levels of debt.

If the conglomerate had $50 million in long-term debt, the probability of excess drawdown on the line of credit is 11.9 percent, or 119 years in a millennium. From Exhibit 6.7, it can be seen that excess drawdowns of $3 million or less have an associated probability over the millennium of 10 percent. Therefore, expanding the cash reserve account and the lines of credit by $3 million reduces the probability of excess drawdowns from 11.9 percent to 1.9 percent, or 19 years in a millennium. Assuming that an excess drawdown of $5 to $9 million puts a firm on the endangered species list, there is a 1.1 percent chance of this happening if a company limits its long-term debt to $50 million. If an excess drawdown of $10 million or more is considered fatal to the continuance of the company as a solvent institution, then there is only a 0.4 percent chance of a financial fatality. Or alternatively, we can be 98.1 percent confident of not being either endangered or doomed to extinction with a maximum of $50 million debt in the financial structure of a company. We can also be 99.6 percent confident of not becoming a financial fatality if the long-term debt load is limited to $50 million.

Another $10 million in debt in the financial structure of the company paints quite a different picture. There is a 55.5 percent chance that there will be an excess drawdown in any particular year when the company assumes a debt burden of $60 million. Putting in another $3 million in lines of credit or cash reserves can reduce the probability of an excess drawdown to 32.5 percent, or 325 years every millennium. That means that the chief financial officer will have to deal with less than happy lenders one year in three.

With the same criteria as before of $5 to $9 million in excess drawdowns being injurious, but not necessarily fatal, to the financial health of a company whereas $10 million or more probably is fatal, then we can be only 74 percent confident of not being declared an endangered, or extinct, company. There is an 18 percent chance that the excess drawdown is between $5 and $9 million and another 8 percent chance that the excess drawdown is $10 or more million. No financial officer would relish the prospects of having essentially one chance in four in any given year of being called before a creditors' meeting to explain what is going to be done to prevent them from taking precipitous action against the company.

If for some reason the financial officer feels comfortable with an annual 75 percent survival rate, then the chances of surviving two consecutive years ought to be considered (56.25 percent: 75% × 75%). The chance of surviving three consecutive years is 42.1875 percent. If the financial officer dreams about working for a solvent company for the next ten years, until he can retire, the chances of this happening is all of 5.6 percent. Or, alternatively, the chances of his retirement program going down the drain along with the company at some point over the forthcoming decade is 94.4 percent. Overburdening the capital structure of a company with too much debt is injurious to the survival of the company as a

Exhibit 6.7
Discrete Probability (Excess Drawdown)

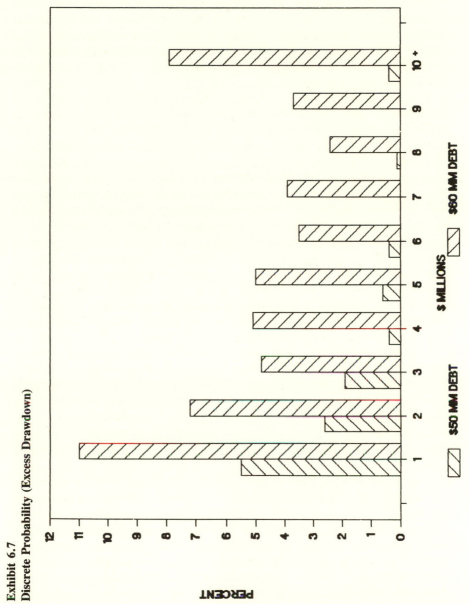

solvent institution, and to the professional longevity and retirement benefits of the chief financial officer.

The determination of the safe loading of debt on the corporate capital structure does not take the equity value of a firm into consideration. The only criterion for determining the safe load of debt is the ability of the firm to generate the cash needed to satisfy the financing charges. The methodology merely presumes that there is a need to garner external funds to support capital expenditures and provides a means of measuring the maximum loading of debt in the capital structure of the company.

If it is not necessary to seek external sources of funds to support capital expenditures, then the best use of internally generated funds in excess of capital expenditures and payment of dividends is the liquidation of debt. Shareholder value in the form of dividend payout can be maximized by reducing the amount of interest paid to the lender, even after taking into consideration the higher payment of taxes with reduced debt. If debt is not necessary because the firm can internally fund all projects, then every before tax dollar paid to the banker in interest is one less after tax dollar that cannot be paid out to shareholders. Comparing Exhibits 6.3 and 6.4 shows the wisdom of eliminating debt if it is not needed to fund capital expenditures. If the ultimate value of a share of stock is linked to the aggregate amount of dividends to be paid out over the lifetime of a company, then any reduction in dividend payout in having to pay interest on unnecessary debt must adversely affect the value of a share of stock.

If the tables of values generating gross income are valid, and if the financing of capital expenditures requires external sourcing of funds, then the conclusion of the simulation is to identify $50 million as the maximum safe loading of debt that the capital structure of the conglomerate can support. All other externally generated capital has to be in the form of equity—the sale of shares of stock. And, if for some reason, the requisite amount of stock cannot be sold, and if the company decides to rely more on debt financing, and if the company loads the capital structure with $60 million in debt, then the chief financial officer starts each fiscal year fairly confident that the survival rate for the following year is about three chances in four. There is, consequently, one chance in four of not making it through this year. And this means, in turn, that the company has a 95 percent chance of not surviving the next ten years.

The methodology provides an indication of the safe debt load independent of the amount of equity in a firm. Equity has little meaning other than in the collateral value backing a loan if the loan goes into default. Collateral value protects the lender, not the borrower. If the cash flow is insufficient to support the debt burden, and if cash can be raised by auctioning off large chunks of the company, the beneficiary is the lender. The borrower is merely being liquidated. A borrower who is looking to the equity value of a company to support a higher than safe load of debt is protecting the interests of the lender, not his own.

Although there are exceptions, the problem of relying on equity to support an excessive loading of debt evolves around the willingness of purchasers to pay $10 million for a company that is on the auction block for defaulting on a $10 million loan. And if there are people willing to bid $10 million for a business that cannot support a $10 million loan, then the next logical question concerns the wisdom of management's decision on loading the company with $10 million in debt. Equity may provide collateral value in case of a loan default, but it is cash flow that prevents the default. Equity provides protection to a lender's exposure to risk in case of a default. Management of a company, or the shareholders, are hardly comforted by making the lender whole if that means the liquidation of their jobs and investments. It is cash flow that keeps the lenders at bay, not equity.

Coverage of cash flow to interest payments is a common measure of the amount of debt that a financial institution is willing to lend a company. Suppose that a lending institution demands a two to one coverage of cash flow to interest. Using, for purposes of illustration, a gross income averaging $10.2 million, a two to one coverage means that the maximum loan exposure is one that generates $5.1 million in interest charges. The maximum loan exposure at 12 percent interest is $42.5 million because its interest charges are at the maximum permissible limit of $5.1 million. For three to one coverage, the maximum loan amount is $28.3 million.

Using debt to equity, or debt to total capitalization, guidelines, we can obtain a maximum loan exposure. Heuristic rules abound and there are as many assessments as to the maximum loading of debt as there are rules or guidelines. Yet, with some adjustments to the amount of cash reserves and the line of credit, the safe loading of debt is about $50 million. If lenders are willing to advance funds in excess of $50 million because their guidelines on debt to equity permit them to do so, the interests of borrowers are not being served because there is a real chance of their going into default. If lenders are willing to lend some amount below $50 million because of the application of a guideline concerning the ratio of cash flow to interest payments, the interests of the borrowers are also not being served if higher levels of debt are desired.

The optimal amount of debt in a firm that requires garnering of outside sources of funds to support its capital projects is generally, but not always, the maximum safe load of debt. Issuing stock is a relatively expensive source of financing capital projects. The more stock that has to be sold as an external means of raising capital, the greater the dilution of ownership for the existing shareholders. The issuing of more shares means a diminution in the value of a share of stock because its ultimate value is the aggregate discounting of all future dividend payments on a per share basis. As the number of shares increase for a given level of after tax profits, the value of a share of stock must decrease.

Furthermore, interest paid on debt is tax deductible. In essence, Uncle Sam is assuming some of the burden of financing a new project because he is willing to accept less in taxes as the debt load within a company increases in size. Dividends are paid out of after tax dollars. Dividends actually are subject to double taxation. Profits generate the cash to be paid out as dividends and profits are taxable. Dividends, once received by the shareholder, are again taxed as income.

As long as the capital expenditures are earning a rate of return in excess of the combined returns on equity and debt in a company's capital structure, then the optimal amount of debt, from the perspective of the shareholders, is usually the maximum safe load of debt that can be supported by the company's gross income. The safe load of debt is determined by the ability of the company to generate cash flow on a sustained—and sustainable—basis.

There are times, however, when the optimal level of debt may be less than the maximum safe loading of debt. For instance, suppose that the stock is grossly overpriced in relation to earnings. The optimal course of action might be to sell stock to the public rather than accumulate more debt. It is possible to construct a simulation model whose purpose is to select the optimal mix of equity and debt in the financial structure of a company. This would entail detailed modeling of major capital projects with regard to funding and their impact on volume, price, and variable and fixed costs. The price of stock would have to be modeled—a challenge in itself. This can be attempted by considering the historic spread in the multiple between the price of a share of stock and its earnings. The modeling of the price of the stock need only be done when there is a "window" for a new stock issue. Presumably, this would be the same window that permits refinancing debt. There is no purpose in modeling the price of stock if market conditions are such that a company is precluded from selling stock to the public. The objective of the simulation is to select a mix of equity and debt that maximizes the aggregate discounted value of all future dividends paid on a share of stock.

The present determination of the safe load of debt is based on a conventional analysis of ratios of debt to equity, cash flow to interest, and current assets to current liabilities. This is a static form of analysis. Simulation provides a dynamic view of a situation. But the simulation discussed herein is itself static. The assessments on gross income for a particular subsidiary should include the impact on price, volume, and variable and fixed costs of funding capital expenditures. Most capital expenditures result in a firm being able to sell a higher volume of goods at a lower variable cost of production.

This modification can be incorporated in a more complex simulation model by using different tables of gross income that are keyed to specified time periods relating to the completion of major capital projects. The model in this chapter merely supposes that capital expenditures exceed internally generated funds with no impact on the variables determining gross income. That is rarely the case. Capital expenditures normally improve the productivity of a company. A more sophisticated model would be tailor-made to a particular company containing the specific capital expenditures that have been approved for funding. One table of values for determining gross income might cover the first few years with other tables being used thereafter to account for the impact of the completion of the projects associated with capital expenditures. A more dynamic model would make the timing of the making of capital expenditures dependent on business conditions, if their timing has not yet been decided. A more comprehensive model might be more attentive to the optimal mix of debt and equity. Such a model might have a ten- or twenty-year time horizon because the discounted values of dividends paid beyond such a time horizon become minuscule.

More sophistication should be introduced to handle liquidity. Cash reserves are set aside for potential shortfalls in satisfying financing charges. Mismatches between the payment of receivables and payment of bills can lead to a liquidity crisis of another type. Although the same line of credit and the cash reserves can be used to keep the suppliers happy, this reduces the company's ability to keep the lenders happy. Furthermore, if a firm does not react fast enough to declining sales, inventories can expand, absorbing the liquidity of a company. Although inventories are considered a current asset, this does not mean that they can be easily liquidated. If the inventory of finished goods is expanding rapidly because marketing cannot sell what production is making, how can a huge overhang of finished goods inventory be considered a current asset? A current asset implies a certain degree of liquidity. Firms have failed, not because of a missed interest payment, but because of not being able to pay the suppliers what they were owed because the company could not sell what it was making from what was purchased from the suppliers. If products cannot be sold as they come off the assembly line, they cannot be sold from the warehouse. Under these conditions, finished goods inventory is not a current asset, but a liability that can destroy a company. A more realistic model simulating the safe loading of debt should take into consideration the impact on a firm's liquidity from changes in the timing of the payment of receivables and from changes in inventory levels as business activity shifts between good and bad times.

It is not the intent of this chapter to provide the final model for determining the safe loading of debt or the optimal mix of equity and debt. The intent is to introduce the concept of looking at the safe loading of debt in terms of cash flow, but not as an average value as flat as the surface of a millpond. The intent is to look at cash flow as waves on an ocean. At times, the surface of the ocean is calm; at other times it is tempestuous. Cash reserves and a line of credit act as stabilizers to keep the financial ship from capsizing in the midst of a storm. But stabilizers cannot save an overburdened vessel. Simulation can help in determining what is a safe load of debt for the safety of vessel and crew and what is the adequate sizing of cash reserves and a line of credit to stabilize the vessel in rough seas.

APPENDIX

There are two programs in this appendix. The first is named PEAK and its purpose is to investigate the nature of the probability distribution for gross income for Subsidiary I and Subsidiary II, both individually and combined. The purpose of the second program, DEBT, is to establish the safe level of debt in a conglomerate owning these two subsidiaries.

PEAK

Statements 40 to 140 feed in the simulators previously generated for prices, volume, and variable and fixed costs for both companies as described in the chapter. Note that the O array for Subsidiary I and the T array for Subsidiary II are three-dimensional to reduce the number of two-dimensional arrays that would have had to be used to contain all the variables. If a conglomerate consists of one hundred subsidiaries, then a four-dimensional array can be introduced, such as S(I,J,K,L), where I denotes the subsidiary, J denotes whether the variable is price, volume, or variable or fixed costs, and K and L are the two-dimensional array values associated with each variable.

The R(I,J) array stores the results of the three simulations. This array is the source of data for the discrete probability distributions in Exhibit 6.1. The Z(I,J) array records the extreme points and the expected results of the three simulations. Statements 150 to 160 initialize the values in these arrays. The simulation starts in statement 170, where, for each of ten thousand simulations, random numbers are drawn from 1 to 10 establishing the volume, price, and fixed costs for the applicable simulators for the expected, or median, business condition under investigation. Statements 180 to 230 perform this function for Subsidiary I, keeping track of the minimum, maximum, and average results. Statements 240 to 290 do the same for Subsidiary II. The process is repeated for each subsidiary, combining the gross income (statements 300–370). Statements 380 to 390 store the results during the running of the simulation. After the simulation is over, the final results are printed out, or stored, by statements 400 to 450.

```
10 REM NAME OF PROGRAM IS PEAK
20 DIM O(3,10,100):DIM T(3,10,100):DIM V(100)
30 DIM R(3,200):DIM Z(3,3)
40 FOR J=1 TO 3:ON J GOTO 50, 60, 70
50 OPEN "I",#1,"PRI1":GOTO 80
60 OPEN "I",#1,"VOL1":GOTO 80
70 OPEN "I",#1,"FIX1"
80 FOR I=1 TO 100:INPUT #1,O(J,1,I),O(J,2,I),O(J,3,I),O(J,4,I),
O(J,5,I),O(J,6,I),O(J,7,I),O(J,8,I),O(J,9,I),O(J,10,I):NEXT:
CLOSE #1:NEXT
90 FOR J=1 TO 3:ON J GOTO 100, 110, 120
100 OPEN "I",#1,"MAR2":GOTO 130
110 OPEN "I",#1,"VOL2":GOTO 130
120 OPEN "I",#1,"FIX2"
130 FOR I=1 TO 100:INPUT #1,T(J,1,I),T(J,2,I),T(J,3,I),T(J,4,I),
T(J,5,I),T(J,6,I),T(J,7,I),T(J,8,I),T(J,9,I),T(J,10,I):NEXT:CLOSE
#1:NEXT
140 OPEN "I",#1,"VAR1":FOR I=1 TO 100:INPUT #1,V(I):NEXT:CLOSE #1
150 FOR I=1 TO 3:FOR J=1 TO 200:R(I,J)=0:NEXT:NEXT
160 FOR I=1 TO 3:Z(I,1)=0:Z(I,2)=1000000!:Z(I,3)=0:NEXT
170 FOR S=1 TO 10000!
180 GOSUB 460:P=O(1,K,50):GOSUB 460:V=O(2,K,50)
190 GOSUB 460:F=O(3,K,50):G1=(P-V(50))*V-F:Z(1,3)=Z(1,3)+G1
200 IF G1>Z(1,1) THEN 210 ELSE 220
210 Z(1,1)=G1
220 IF G1<Z(1,2) THEN 230 ELSE 240
230 Z(1,2)=G1
240 GOSUB 460:P=T(1,K,50):GOSUB 460:V=T(2,K,50)
250 GOSUB 460:F=T(3,K,50):G2=P*V-F:Z(2,3)=Z(2,3)+G2
260 IF G2>Z(2,1) THEN 270 ELSE 280
270 Z(2,1)=G2
280 IF G2<Z(2,2) THEN 290 ELSE 300
290 Z(2,2)=G2
```

```
300 GOSUB 460:P=O(1,K,50):GOSUB 460:V=O(2,K,50)
310 GOSUB 460:F=O(3,K,50):H1=(P-V(50))*V-F
320 GOSUB 460:P=T(1,K,50):GOSUB 460:V=T(2,K,50)
330 GOSUB 460:F=T(3,K,50):H2=P*V-F:G3=H1+H2:Z(3,3)=Z(3,3)+G3
340 IF G3>Z(3,1) THEN 350 ELSE 360
350 Z(3,1)=G3
360 IF G3<Z(3,2) THEN 370 ELSE 380
370 Z(3,2)=G3
380 G1=INT(G1/100+.5):G2=INT(G2/100+.5):G3=INT(G3/100+.5)
390 R(1,G1)=R(1,G1)+1:R(2,G2)=R(2,G2)+1:R(3,G3)=R(3,G3)+1:NEXT:S=S-1
400 FOR J=1 TO 3:A=0:FOR I=1 TO 200:A=A+I*R(J,I):NEXT
410 PRINT "MAX GROSS INC SUB ";J,Z(J,1)
420 PRINT "EXPECTED VALUE SUB ";J,Z(J,3)/S
430 PRINT "MIN GROSS INC SUB ";J,Z(J,2):PRINT:NEXT
440 OPEN "O",#1,"RESULTS":FOR I=1 TO 200
450 WRITE #1,I,R(1,I),R(2,I),R(3,I):NEXT:CLOSE#1:END
460 X=RND(X):K=INT(10*X+.5)
470 IF K=O THEN 480 ELSE 490
480 K=10
490 RETURN
```

DEBT

This program is the source of Exhibits 6.2 and 6.7 for evaluating the safe load of debt. The same simulators used in the PEAK program are fed into this program, along with the business activity simulator and the overhead costs of the conglomerate, in statements 40 to 160. Statement 170 initializes the values in the R(I,J) array that record the results of the simulation. Statements 180 to 200 determine the initial business condition. The input statements 210 to 230 permit the examination of different cash reserves, total lines of credit, and long-term debt.

The thousand-year simulation begins in statement 240. Business conditions have a 75 percent probability of being the same in a given year as they were the previous year with a limit of twelve consecutive years of either good or bad times (statements 250–360). New debt can be added to bring the total debt back up to the maximum allowable limit only if business activity has an index value over 35 and there are at least two consecutive years of positive and increasing gross income before taxes and financing charges (statements 370–420). If these conditions are satisfied, then additional loans are made that bring the total debt up to the limit under consideration. It is presumed that any equity in the form of selling shares to generate the external funds required in addition to the new loans is also accomplished at this time. New loans first replenish the cash reserves account and pay off the balance in the lines of credit before being available for funding capital projects.

The program does not specify dividend payout policies or delineate capital projects that are to be funded. Required funding is completed by internally and externally generated funds without specifying the amount of the requirement. The purpose of the program is to judge the ability of the conglomerate with two subsidiaries to carry various loads of debt independent of funding specific capital projects for the assessments of gross income set forth in the chapter.

Statements 430 to 460 simulate the generation of gross income by the two subsidiaries net of corporate overhead. The aggregate depreciation for the conglomerate is assumed to be $3 million per year throughout the simulation. The depreciation in an actual situation would be linked to current depreciation schedules plus the impact on depreciation from funding specific capital projects. Taxes to be paid. or to be carried forward, are calculated in statements 470 to 530.

The cash reserves account earns a rate of interest of 9 percent; the line of credit is charged an interest rate of 11 percent; and the long-term debt is charged an interest rate of 12 percent. Long-term debt is amortized over ten years. The cash flow net of taxes and interest and amortization payments is determined in statements 540 to 580. Statement 590 checks to see if the cash flow is positive or negative. If the cash flow is positive, any balance in the line of credit is first paid off and any remainder is applied against any shortage of funds in cash reserves. If there are still funds available, these are considered to be internally generated funds for dividend payouts and supporting of capital expenditures (statements 600–670).

If statement 590 detects a negative cash flow, the cash reserves are first tapped (statements 680 to 710). If there is still a deficit, the line of credit is drawn down (statement 720). The amount of the line of credit drawn down in excess of the prescribed limit of $5 million is recorded by statements 730 to 750. Internal checking of the program is performed by statements 760 to 780, that can be activated by removing the REM in each statement. The external storing of the gross income before taxes and financing charges, the amount of funds available for dividends and capital expenditures, and the excess drawdowns of the line of credit are performed by statements 800 and 810.

```
10 REM NAME OF PROGRAM IS DEBT
20 DIM O(3,10,100):DIM T(3,10,100):DIM V(100)
30 DIM R(3,1000):DIM Z(100):DIM B(100)
40 FOR J=1 TO 3:ON J GOTO 50, 60, 70
50 OPEN "I",#1,"PRI1":GOTO 80
60 OPEN "I",#1,"VOL1":GOTO 80
70 OPEN "I",#1,"FIX1"
80 FOR I=1 TO 100:INPUT #1,O(J,1,I),O(J,2,I),O(J,3,I),O(J,4,I),
O(J,5,I),O(J,6,I),O(J,7,I),O(J,8,I),O(J,9,I),O(J,10,I):NEXT:CLOSE
#1:NEXT
90 FOR J=1 TO 3:ON J GOTO 100, 110, 120
100 OPEN "I",#1,"MAR2":GOTO 130
110 OPEN "I",#1,"VOL2":GOTO 130
120 OPEN "I",#1,"FIX2"
130 FOR I=1 TO 100:INPUT #1,T(J,1,I),T(J,2,I),T(J,3,I),T(J,4,I),
T(J,5,I),T(J,6,I),T(J,7,I),T(J,8,I),T(J,9,I),T(J,10,I):NEXT:CLOSE
#1:NEXT
140 OPEN "I",#1,"VAR1":FOR I=1 TO 100:INPUT #1,V(I):NEXT:CLOSE #1
150 OPEN "I",#1,"BUS":FOR I=1 TO 100:INPUT #1,B(I):NEXT:CLOSE #1
160 OPEN "I",#1,"OVER":FOR I=1 TO 100:INPUT #1,Z(I):NEXT:CLOSE #1
170 FOR I=1 TO 3:FOR J=1 TO 1000:R(I,J)=0:NEXT:NEXT
180 X=RND(X):IF X<.5 THEN 190 ELSE 200
190 Z=1:GOTO 210
200 Z=2
210 PRINT:INPUT "CASH RESERVE ACCOUNT:    ";C:C1=C
220 PRINT:INPUT "TOTAL LINES OF CREDIT:   ";L:L1=0
230 PRINT:INPUT "LOAD OF LONG TERM DEBT: ";D:D1=D:D2=D/10
240 Y1=0:FOR Y=1 TO 1000
250 X=RND(X):IF X>.75 THEN 260 ELSE 290
260 Y1=0:ON Z GOTO 270, 280
270 Z=2:GOTO 290
280 Z=1
290 Y1=Y1+1:IF Y1=12 THEN 300 ELSE 330
300 IF Z=1 THEN 310 ELSE 320
310 Y1=0:Z=2:GOTO 330
320 Y1=0:Z=1
```

```
330 GOSUB 860:B=B(T)
340 ON Z GOTO 350, 360
350 IF B<50 THEN 330 ELSE 370
360 IF B>50 THEN 330
370 IF B>35 THEN 380 ELSE 420
380 Z2=Z1:Z1=R(1,Y-1)
390 IF Z2>0 THEN 400 ELSE 430
400 IF Z1>Z2 THEN 410 ELSE 430
410 D1=D:C1=C:L1=0:GOTO 430
420 Z2=0:Z1=0
430 GOSUB 820:P=O(1,K,50):GOSUB 820:V=O(2,K,50)
440 GOSUB 820:F=O(3,K,50):G1=(P-V(50))*V-F
450 GOSUB 820:P=T(1,K,50):GOSUB 820:V=T(2,K,50)
460 GOSUB 820:F=T(3,K,50):G2=P*V-F:R(1,Y)=G1+G2-Z(B)
470 T=.35*(R(1,Y)+9*C1/100-11*L1/100-12*D1/100-3000)
480 IF T<0 THEN 490 ELSE 500
490 T1=T1-T:T=0:GOTO 540
500 IF T1=0 THEN 540
510 IF T<T1 THEN 520 ELSE 530
520 T1=T1-T:T=0:GOTO 540
530 T=T-T1:T1=0
540 R(2,Y)=R(1,Y)+9*C1/100-11*L1/100-12*D1/100-T
550 IF D1>0 THEN 560 ELSE 590
560 D1=D1-D2:IF D1<0 THEN 570 ELSE 580
570 D1=0:PRINT "NEG DEBT YEAR ";Y
580 R(2,Y)=R(2,Y)-D2
590 IF R(2,Y)>0 THEN 600 ELSE 680
600 IF L1>0 THEN 610 ELSE 640
610 IF R(2,Y)>L1 THEN 620 ELSE 630
620 R(2,Y)=R(2,Y)-L1:L1=0:GOTO 640
630 L1=L1-R(2,Y):R(2,Y)=0:GOTO 730
640 IF C1<C THEN 650 ELSE 730
650 C2=C-C1:IF R(2,Y)>C2 THEN 660 ELSE 670
660 C1=C:R(2,Y)=R(2,Y)-C2:GOTO 730
670 C1=C1+R(2,Y):R(2,Y)=0:GOTO 730
680 E=-R(2,Y):R(2,Y)=0:IF C1>0 THEN 690 ELSE 720
690 IF E>C1 THEN 700 ELSE 710
700 E=E-C1:C1=0:L1=L1+E:GOTO 730
710 C1=C1-E:E=0:GOTO 730
720 L1=L1+E
730 IF L1>L THEN 740 ELSE 750
740 R(3,Y)=L1-L:GOTO 760
750 R(3,Y)=0
760 REM PRINT Y;R(1,Y),R(2,Y),R(3,Y)
770 REM PRINT T;T1,C;C1,L;L1
780 REM PRINT B;Y1;D,D1:PRINT:INPUT Z$
790 NEXT
800 OPEN "O",#1,"RESULTS":FOR I=1 TO 1000
810 WRITE #1,I,R(1,I),R(2,I),R(3,I):NEXT:CLOSE#1:END
820 X=RND(X):K=INT(10*X+.5)
830 IF K=0 THEN 840 ELSE 850
840 K=10
850 RETURN
860 X=RND(X):T=INT(100*X+.5)
870 IF T=0 THEN 880 ELSE 890
880 T=100
890 RETURN
```

7

Hedging and the Futures Market

All businesses operate in an environment where prices for goods and services are subject to change without notice. An individual company has little control over price because price is set by the aggregate decisions of many individual companies, each believing that they are acting independently of one another. The same can be said for volume of sales. Aggregate volume is in the hands of overall economic activity and consumer preferences, hardly matters under the control of an individual businessman.

Price and volume of sales are the risks of the marketplace. There may be yet another dimension to market risk in the form of timing. A manufactured item, such as a tractor, has a current price, which is known by the manager of a tractor factory. The manager also knows the cost of manufacture in fairly precise terms. There is a lapse in time between acquiring the steel, the motor, and other bits and pieces to manufacture a tractor, and its delivery to a dealership. A tractor cannot be sold to a farmer until it is a finished product. The moment of its sale sets the price, and consequently, determines the profit, in manufacturing the tractor. Therefore, the manager of the tractor-making plant does not know the profit in the making of another tractor on the day that the material for the building of the tractor is acquired even though the cost of manufacture and the current price of tractors are known.

The time lag between the day that sets the cost of manufacture and the day that sets the price represents a risk. The manufacturer must bear the risk of a price decline between the time of purchase of the raw materials and component parts and the sale of the finished product. There is no way for the tractor manufacturer to cover this risk of a potential price decline once the required material for production is purchased because there is no futures market for tractors.

Many, if not most, industries do not have a futures market in order to lay off the risk of an adverse price fluctuation. A futures market provides the opportunity for an industry to sell its output before it is produced or manufactured. If there were a futures market for tractors, and the manufacturer was worried about the repercussions of a decline in the price of a tractor that had not yet been built, then the manufacturer could sell a futures contract on the tractor. Then, at some point in the future, the manufacturer would deliver the tractor in fulfillment of the obligation generated by selling a tractor futures contract. The price received in selling the tractor is the price stipulated in the futures contract.

For purposes of illustrating the usefulness of a futures market, suppose that a manufacturer has purchased all the parts necessary for the making of a tractor. There is a lapse of two months from the time the component parts are ordered, which establishes the cost of the tractor, until the finished tractor is shipped to a dealership and sold to a farmer. The manufacturer does not know the profit in the production of the tractor even though there is a market price for tractors at the time the parts are ordered. Ordering the steel and parts, and throwing in the cost of labor and overhead expenses, determines the cost. Profit is not derived from the price of tractors on the day the steel and component parts are ordered, but from the price of tractors on the day the tractor is sold. That day is about two months after its cost has been established. The company is at risk as to its ultimate profit because of possible price fluctuations during the production cycle of the tractor.

If, for some reason, the tractor company manager thinks that the price of tractors is apt to fall over the next two months, the risk of a price decline may be averted by selling a futures contract on the tractor. Who buys a futures contract on a tractor before it is made? A farmer may if he intends to buy a tractor in two months and thinks that the price of tractors at that time is apt to be higher than what it is now. One may wonder why a farmer, looking at the same set of economic data, concludes that tractor prices will be higher in the future while another individual, the tractor manufacturer, arrives at the opposite conclusion.

All that can be said is that this phenomenon of one party thinking that prices will increase at the same time another party thinks they will decline happens all the time. On a given day, there are hundreds of millions of shares of stock traded on the world's stock exchanges. For each and every one of these transactions, one individual feels he is receiving the best price possible considering that the future price is bound to decline. That is why he is selling the stock. On the other side of the transaction, another individual feels he is paying the best price possible considering that the future price is bound to rise. A buyer feels that he has the advantage over the seller at the moment the transaction is completed. The irony is that the seller feels the same way. This is the commercial fact of life: a buyer will not purchase something if he feels confident that he can wait and obtain a lower price. Nor will a seller consummate a transaction if he feels he can wait and obtain a higher price. It is a miracle that there is so much buying and selling when one realizes the dichotomy of expectations that accompany each transaction.

THE ROLE OF SPECULATORS

To complicate matters, or add a bit of spice to the mundane act of buying and selling tractors, a futures market in tractors allows for a third party to enter the scene. This mysterious third party neither makes nor uses tractors, and is not a tractor manufacturer or a farmer. All he knows is that he has a gut feeling that the price of tractors is going up. He enters into the transaction by buying a nonexistent tractor today that he intends to sell to a farmer after it is manufactured and delivered into his hands two months in the future. If the price of tractors has indeed risen, he buys the tractor at a price stipulated in the futures contract and sells the tractor to the farmer at the higher market price and pockets the difference. If the price of tractors has declined, and since the third party has no need for a tractor, he still intends to sell it to a farmer at the market price and racks up the difference as a loss. It is possible for the third party to take delivery of the tractor and wait until the market improves before selling it to the farmer. In this case, he may have to get rid of his kids' backyard swing set to make room for parking a tractor.

The mysterious third party is a speculator. The speculator wants to take advantage of a price move in tractors and can do so because the price of the futures contract on a tractor is a small portion of its actual value since the tractor is not yet manufactured. When the futures contract expires, however, the speculator must purchase the tractor from the manufacturer at the stipulated price. Having no interest in owning a tractor, the speculator completes the transaction by selling the tractor to a farmer. The last thing he wants parked in his backyard is a spanking new tractor. The profit or loss is the difference between the price of the tractor purchased from the manufacturer and the proceeds from its sale to the farmer two months later.

The manufacturer is averse to the risk of a price decline. By entering into the futures arrangement, the manufacturer knows what is going to be received for making a tractor. Another party assumes the risk of a price decline that adversely affects profit between the time of purchase of the component parts of a tractor and its eventual sale as a completed product to a farmer. The manufacturer no longer cares if the price moves up or down; profit is established at the sale of the futures contract.

Actually, he does care, but it is an emotional care. He does care if the price of tractors goes up because he is going to regret entering into the transaction. This is profit foregone. He does care if the price of tractors declines because this confirms his business acumen in understanding the dynamic forces that mold, shape, and form tractor prices. But there is one care that is no longer a care: the care about how much he earns in manufacturing a tractor. That is set the moment he sells the futures contract to either a farmer or speculator.

The position of the farmer is straightforward. The farmer is in the market for a tractor. Rather than buying the tractor in March, the farmer purchases a futures contract from the manufacturer in January. The futures contract is an obligation to buy the tractor in March, at a price agreed upon in January. The farmer enters into the contract because the agreed price stated in the contract in January is, in his mind, less than the anticipated March price. The farmer's motivation for entering into the futures contract, and the manufacturer's motivation, are clear regardless of who is proven right or wrong by events that affect the price of tractors between January and March.

The mysterious third party, the speculator, is another matter. The speculator does not use tractors, has no intention of owning a tractor, and might not be able to recognize a tractor if it ran over him; at least, not in the moments before contact. He is in the transaction only because the price of tractors fluctuates. He is speculating on a price rise in tractors when he buys a futures contract. He is speculating on a price decline when he sells a futures contract. Buying and selling futures contracts is a way of effectualizing speculation on future price moves. The speculator is seeking risk, not trying to avert it. A speculator seeks out risk while other participants in the futures market are trying to avoid it.

THE FUTURES GAME

There are three participants in the futures market for tractors. One is the manufacturer, who, in entering into a futures contract, is attempting to lay off the risk of a price decline between the time a tractor is manufactured, which establishes costs, and the time the tractor is sold as a finished product. The second is the normal purchaser of tractors, a farmer, who is attempting to avoid the risk of a price hike in tractors by buying the tractor before it is built. These are legitimate players in the sense that they are the suppliers and consumers of a product. Their interest is in disposing of or acquiring an asset. The game can be played by these two players exclusively, both of whom are attempting to reduce the risk of an adverse price fluctuation.

The third player is the speculator who knows only one thing: the price of tractors fluctuates. By putting up 5 percent of the stipulated cost of a tractor, the speculator can double money, or lose it all, on a 5 percent move in the price of tractors. The speculator is participating simply to take advantage of a price move—a price move that he himself feels is a sure thing. What that price happens to represent is purely incidental.

A futures market can be established around anything if four criteria can be satisfied. First, the price must be easily verified as the authentic price for the product. One reason there is no futures market in tractors is because there are too many makes and models, which change over the years, to obtain an agreed upon price for a "commodity tractor." This problem has been overcome in other areas by the participants agreeing to an index that creates a single commodity out of something that is diverse in nature. If there were a demand for trading futures in tractors, someone would come up with an ingenious solution by creating a "commodity tractor" index linked to the price and volume of sales of an assortment of tractor makes and models. The expiration value of a "commodity trac-tor" index future would be derived by a panel of respected experts based on the applicable prices of an agreed assortment of tractor makes and models. The speculators, tractor manufacturers, and tractor users would enter into transactions based on the "commodity tractor" index. Their buying and selling establish the current cash value of the futures contract. The panel sets the value of the contract on the day of expiration by applying the applicable tractor prices to an agreed formula. This is a critical function in order to sort the winners on the day of settlement or the losers on the day of reckoning.

The second requirement is a desire on the part of suppliers and consumers to be the "legitimate" participants in the futures market. The suppliers and users are attempting to lay off risk. They can do it between themselves or pass it on to the speculators, who are seeking risk. Risk seekers with a common train of thought on the future trend in prices are going to find it difficult to establish their positions if there is no one willing to transfer the risk that they so desperately seek. A futures market functions best when all three participants are present.

The third requirement is a sufficient number of participants to generate the volume necessary to sustain a market in the futures. Commissions are based on price and volume. The higher the volume, the less of a commission that has to be charged to pay the expenses of having a futures market. Speculators, by the magnitude of the volume of transactions, generate the necessary commission revenue to sustain the expense of having a market. The speculators' trading volume adds depth to the market. This allows the two legitimate players, so to speak, to move in and out of the market, transferring with relative ease the risk they want to shed to those who seek its thrill.

The fourth requirement is the necessity of volatility of price. A futures market cannot be established for anything if its price is stable. Price volatility is the drawing card for suppliers, consumers, and speculators to participate in a futures market. It is the raison d'être of a futures market. It is the sine qua non of its existence. There is no futures market in tractors because price volatility is not sufficient for suppliers and consumers of tractors to seek protection from adverse price swings. Nor are the swings in prices sufficient for speculators to make a killing, or, for that matter, get killed.

Speculators have a legitimate role to play in any futures market by sustaining the market by the volume of their transactions. Their continual buying and selling of futures contracts establish a market price for futures. The futures contract allows suppliers to lock in a price for whatever they produce before it is produced. The futures contract sets the price that consumers pay for the product that is to be delivered at some future point in time. The activity of speculators generates the volume that allows suppliers to sell a futures contract when there are no consumers willing to buy one. The activity of speculators also allows consumers to purchase a futures contract when there are no suppliers willing to offer one.

This leads to an interesting situation where speculators are, in effect, creating futures in a commodity by virtue of selling a contract in something that does not physically exist. When suppliers sell a futures contract, they know that they will have the product to deliver to purchasers of the futures contract at the expiration date. When speculators sell a futures contract, they have no intention, or means, of honoring the contract, that is, delivering the goods. Their selling of a contract creates an obligation to produce something that they are incapable of doing—and certainly have no intention of doing. One might conclude that there is an element of fraud in speculators selling a contract that contains an obligation that they cannot honor.

At some point before futures contracts expire, speculators must get rid of their obligation of having to supply something that is beyond their capability by buying futures contracts back. If speculators do not buy these contracts back, they are obligated to deliver something to purchasers that is beyond their means to accomplish. It has been estimated that about 90 percent of all futures contracts have been created out of thin air by speculators selling a contract on something they do not own or produce, nor intend to own or produce, nor are capable of owning or producing. The obligation to deliver the goods is on the day the contract expires. If speculators buy contracts back before they expire, then they have voided the obligation to deliver something that they are incapable of delivering. As long as the buying and selling of futures contracts are matched on a one for one basis, then the difference in what speculators pay for futures contracts and what they receive in selling them is their profit or loss, and that ends the matter.

For the most part, futures do not represent warehouse receipts where the asset sits waiting to be claimed by the holder of a futures contract. Most of the time, the entire tangible value of a futures contract is the paper it is written on. But the written obligation on these slips of paper is real. A speculator circumvents the obligation of delivering the goods represented by the futures contract by eventually matching every buy order with a sell order, and every sell order with a buy order, before the expiration date of the contracts.

Although the role of speculators in the commodity markets has been criticized, their activity in selling something that does not physically exist and buying something that they have no intention of acquiring does create a market. This market establishes a price for the futures contract. The volume of futures contracts being exchanged in this market allows the supplier and consumer of a commodity to enter into transactions that reduce the risk of being exposed to adverse price fluctuations. The risk of price fluctuations does not go away when suppliers, consumers, and speculators enter into futures contracts. The risk is merely transferred from those with an aversion to risk to those seeking its pleasures. This is the function of the futures market.

The lack of warehouse receipts for what is being traded should not be alarming. If warehouse receipts were required, there would be no way for a farmer to sell a crop before it is planted, or for a copper producer to sell his output before it is mined, or for a forest products company to sell its lumber before the trees are cut down. This is the purpose of the futures market: to provide a mechanism for those who produce goods to hedge against a price decline between the time they plant the seeds, or mine the ore, or cut down the trees, and the time they sell the crops, or the metal, or the lumber. The futures market provides a mechanism for those who consume goods, such as flour merchants, copper wire manufacturers, and homebuilders to hedge against a potential price rise in a product that is near and dear to them.

There is no futures market for most manufactured goods. There is a futures market for agricultural products, industrial and precious metals, basic raw materials, and energy (oil). Futures are also actively traded in nonphysical commodities such as treasury bonds for those who desire to protect themselves against adverse movements in interest rates, stock market indices for those who desire to lay off some of the risk of an adverse movement in stock prices, and currency futures for those who do not want to be squeezed to death when the pound declines in relation to the deutschmark. Most of those participating in these markets are speculators who hope to be on the right side of a price move. The activity of speculators allows suppliers and users of a physical commodity, or bankers, portfolio managers, and international traders, to enter into futures contracts that reduce the risk of an adverse change in the prices of commodities, money (interest rates), stocks, and currencies.

Let us focus on the oil industry's use of the futures market to reduce the risk of adverse price swings on sales and to hedge, or protect, the value of an inventory. The week-ending cash prices of heating oil, gasoline, and crude oil, expressed in cents per gallon, and the closing two months' futures contract prices, were collected at the beginning of April 1990, for the period from January 1987 through March 1990. Exhibit 7.1 is the price history of heating oil and gasoline for the last fifteen months of this period of time.

Oil prices fluctuate along with the prices of anything else that is exposed to the vagaries of supply and demand. In addition to unpredictable fluctuations, there is a seasonal tendency for gasoline prices to rise during the summer as America goes on vacation and for heating oil prices to rise during the winter as America keeps its homes snug and warm. Even during the seasonal lulls for these products, prices of gasoline and heating oil fluctuate.

The level of prices in absolute terms, however, is not of primary interest to refinery operators. Their interest is in the difference in the price of products and the cost of crude oil. This is the refiner's margin, that, at the end of the day, determines profitability. Exhibit 7.2 shows the difference in price between heating oil and gasoline in New York, and the cost of West Texas crude.

The interpretation of Exhibit 7.2 is one of perspective. One perspective is that of a political demagogue who focuses on the obscene profits the oil industry made in December 1989 when the refiner's margin in heating oil rose to 60 cents per gallon. The fact that the profits lasted one week and that the whole episode of high heating oil prices was over in a month's time is simply ignored. Obviously, the insatiable greed of oil company executives which leads to high heating oil prices in the middle of the winter makes for good press.

Exhibit 7.1
Oil Product Prices

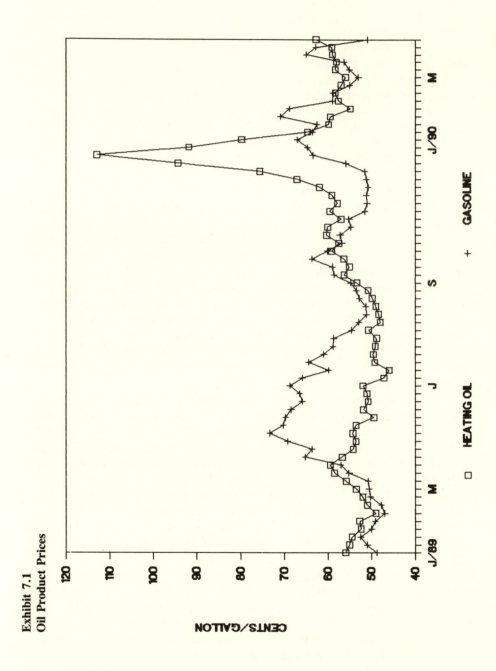

Exhibit 7.2
Refiner's Margin

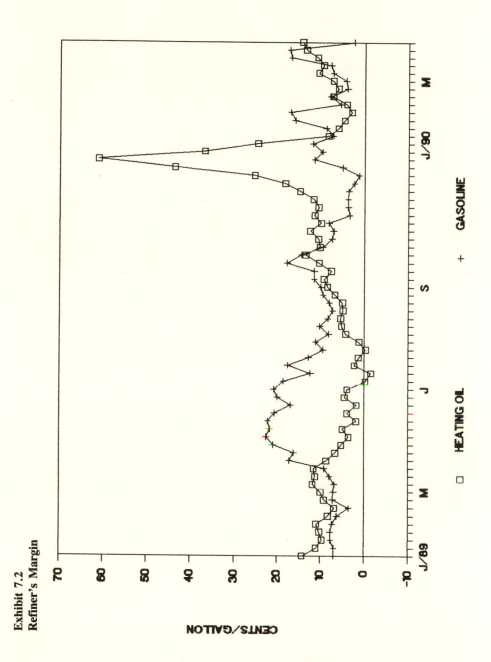

CENTS/GALLON

□ HEATING OIL   + GASOLINE

207

To be fair to the oil companies, which no self-effacing demagogue would dare to be, December has to be balanced with June when there was a negligible, if not negative, spread between the cost of the raw material and the price of the finished product. One can counter that the sales volume of heating oil is much higher in December than in June, which means that the profits during December were much greater than the losses in June. A point to keep in mind is that heating oil for homes and diesel fuel are essentially the same product. Therefore, trucking firms and railroads were purchasing diesel fuel at a price that was barely above the cost of crude oil. Certainly times of depressed margins ought to be considered along with those times when the oil companies are making a killing. From time to time, a robust December market in heating oil is required to balance the doldrums of the June market. What counts is not a spike in heating oil prices in December, but the volume-weighted average margin throughout the year.

Furthermore, the refiner's margin does not take into account any variable costs other than the cost of West Texas crude. Usually gross margin is net of variable costs. The refiner's margin does not include the variable cost of transport of crude to the refinery nor the variable cost of transport of the product to the consumer. The refiner's margin does not take into account the variable cost of the refining process, which of itself, absorbs about 7 percent of a barrel of crude to fuel the process of transforming crude oil to useful products. Nor does the refiner's margin reflect the point that heating oil and gasoline make up only a portion of a barrel of crude. The residue of refining crude oil for heating oil, gasoline, and other so-called high-end products is fit for paving roads or being burned as a low-grade fuel in ships and power plants. The margin on these low-end products leaves much to be desired. Profits come from the high end of the barrel, not the low end. Therefore, the true refiner's margin, taking into account the relatively low value of products from the bottom of the barrel, the crude lost in fueling the operations of the refinery, the variable costs of transport and refinery operation, is much less than that indicated in Exhibit 7.2.

The profit made by oil companies does not lie in the magnitude of the margin itself on a cents per gallon basis as it does on the sheer enormity of the volume of output. A small unit margin multiplied by a huge output can generate large profits. Low unit margin and high volume is as much the source of profits for oil companies as it was for Henry Ford and his Model T.

However, Exhibit 7.2 does not show the actual refiner's margin even with the inclusion of the items just discussed. Refinery operators buy crude now to be sold as gasoline and heating oil tomorrow. There is a lag between contracting for the purchase of a barrel of crude oil and the sale of gasoline and heating oil made from that barrel of crude. The crude oil has to be transported from its source to the refinery. It sits in crude oil tanks waiting to be refined. After it is refined, the products sit in other tanks waiting shipment to a distributor. The sale of oil products is made some time after the purchase of the crude oil. Therefore, the actual refiner's margin ought to take into consideration the lapse in time between the purchase of the crude oil and the sale of the oil products made from that crude oil. Exhibit 7.3 shows the relationship between the price of gasoline and crude oil with an eight-week lag between the purchase of the crude oil and the sale of the crude oil in the form of gasoline.

Concentrating on the cash-only curve, the refiner's margin based on the price of gasoline during the first week in January 1989 with the price of crude oil eight weeks before is just under 9 cents per gallon. When the refiner purchased the crude oil during the first week of November 1988, he did not know what he would receive for the actual price of the gasoline until it was sold during the first week in January 1989. The refiner's margin of just under 9 cents per gallon was not known, nor could it be known, at the time of purchase of the crude oil. It was established when the gasoline was sold, which was eight weeks after the purchase of the crude oil.

This eight-week lag in not knowing the refiner's margin on gasoline is demonstrated by the cash-only curve ending in February 1990. The data for the exhibits were collected at the beginning of April. Most of April and all of May was in the future. The refiner's margin was not known for crude oil purchased in February and March because the gasoline produced from this crude oil would not be sold until April and May. The refinery operator was "flying in the dark" because the products made from crude oil purchased during February and March were to be sold at a point beyond April 1. Therefore, it was impossible to know the refiner's margin in the cash market for crude purchased during February and March. This is the reason why the cash-only curve could not be completed.

The refinery operator could sell futures contracts for delivery of gasoline two months after the purchase of the crude oil. Had this been done during each week of February and March to cover purchases of crude oil, the margin would be certain, as indicated in Exhibit 7.3. The refiner's margin, and hence profit, is established with the sale of the futures contracts. All a refinery operator has to do is adjust the futures curve in Exhibit 7.3 for the remaining variable costs to obtain the gross margin on a gallon, or barrel, of crude oil. The gross margin, multiplied by the output of the refinery in gallons, or barrels, per day, less the fixed costs, is the profitability of operations during February and March.

The right-hand side of Exhibit 7.3 shows the quandary of the refinery operator. If the refiner stays in the cash market only, the gross margin for February and March is unknown. Only the cost of crude oil during this period of time is known. The gross margin for crude purchased in February and March is not known until April and May when the gasoline, heating oil, and other products are sold. Then, and only then, can the refiner's margin curve in Exhibit 7.3 for remaining in the cash market be completed. On the other hand, the refinery operator can sell futures each week during this period of time and lock in the refiner's margin. He may be right, or wrong, in taking such action, but the consequence of selling futures rather than staying in the cash market is that he has established his margin of profitability. By selling futures, the refinery oper-

Exhibit 7.3
Refiner's Margin on Gasoline (Eight-Week Lag)

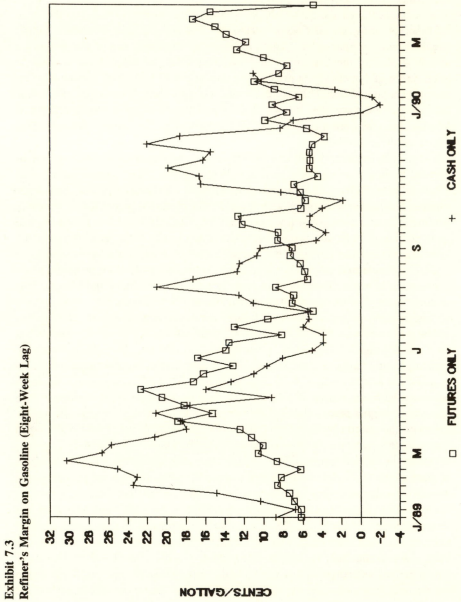

CENTS/GALLON

□ FUTURES ONLY   + CASH ONLY

ator is no longer exposed to the vagaries of the market, particularly adverse price swings.

The risk of adverse price fluctuations has been transferred, or laid off, to a third party. The cost of taking such an action is giving up the opportunity to profit from a favorable price fluctuation. The risk of an adverse price fluctuation has not been obviated when the refinery operator enters into a futures contract. It has merely been shifted from one party to another. The party may be a risk seeker willing to take on the risk in order to become the beneficiary of any favorable price move above the price in the futures contract. The seller of the futures contract (in this case the refinery operator) is not concerned about the speculator benefiting if the price of gasoline or heating oil increases. The refinery operator worries about the consequences of an adverse price fluctuation—a price decline, which can wipe out the profit margin and cause the red ink to flow. The selling of a futures contract removes that worry for at least the volume of production that is covered by the futures contract.

In a futures contract, the risk of an adverse price fluctuation has merely been transferred from one person to another. If those assuming the risk are speculators, they now worry about an adverse price fluctuation—in this case, also a price decline because they are going to have to pay the difference between the cash market and the futures price before, or at, the time the futures contract expires. Speculators, as risk seekers, have freely accepted a risk that someone else wishes to avoid. The compensation for seeking out a risk that is not in the normal course of business is the capture of the entire gain in the value of the contract should the price of gasoline advance rather than decline.

The purchaser of a refinery operator's futures contract may be a consumer, or user, of the commodity, such as a heating oil or gasoline distributor. Interestingly, this buyer of the futures contract may also be risk averse, attempting to avoid the consequences of an adverse price change. The buyer's view of an adverse price change is opposite that of the refinery operator's. To reduce the risk of paying a higher price in the future, the gasoline distributor fixes the price of a portion of his needs by buying a two-month futures contract from the refinery operator. If prices go up, the distributor allows the contract to expire which obligates the refinery operator to ship gasoline at the stipulated price. If the price of gasoline declines, the distributor is obligated to buy gasoline at a higher than market price at the time of the expiration of the futures contract.

One might argue that the gasoline distributor has really only changed the nature of his exposure to risk and has not really laid it off to a third party. He has reduced the negative consequences of a price rise only to have to pay the piper if there is a price decline. He has merely exchanged one risk for another. But in so doing, he has exchanged one risk that he abhors for one that he can endure. He fears a price rise and acts to protect himself against this risk by buying a futures contract. If he is wrong and the price declines, the part of his gasoline purchases covered by the expiration of the futures contract will be above the market price. But the market price for the rest of his gasoline purchases has declined. The risk of paying more for some portion of his gasoline requirements is something he can endure. It is the cost of the insurance policy to protect himself against a risk he abhors—the risk of rising prices. From this, one can conclude that the futures market allows suppliers and consumers to exchange a risk that is abhorred for one that can be endured.

Regardless if the buyers and sellers of futures contracts are averse to risk, or seekers of risk, or simply changing the nature of their exposure to risk, the futures market merely redistributes the risk. The risk does not disappear in the transfer process. Who bears the risk, or the nature of the risk, is what is being exchanged.

In Exhibit 7.3, a refinery operator was much better off selling gasoline in the cash market for the first three months in 1989 than in fixing revenue by entering into futures contracts two months before when he purchased the crude oil. The cash curve is above the futures curve indicating a wider refiner's margin in avoiding the futures market. However, the curves reverse in the second quarter of 1989 where the refinery operator would have been better off selling futures contracts as soon as the crude oil was purchased rather than waiting two months to see what the cash market offered for a gallon of gasoline. The curve on top of the other indicates the optimal strategy because it represents the course of action that enhances, or widens, the refiner's margin. Exhibit 7.4 is the same as Exhibit 7.3 except that it pertains to heating oil.

The closeness of the two curves representing different courses of action indicates that, for most of the year, it does not matter if the refinery operator hedges risk by selling futures in heating oil at the time of the purchase of the crude oil or waits eight weeks to sell the heating oil in the open market at some unknown price from the point in time of acquiring the crude oil. With all the benefit of hindsight, however, the refinery operator will greatly regret hedging risks in October. For crude oil purchased in October, and in selling two-month futures in heating oil, locks in a refiner's margin of about 10 cents. Had the refiner waited two months, the gross margin would have been three or four times greater. Once the refinery operator locks in the profit by selling a futures contract, the buyer of the contract as either a rank speculator, or a concerned consumer of heating oil such as a distributor, has also locked in the cost. The profit of the price rising above this cost belongs to the buyer of the futures contract. Again, the risk of adverse price fluctuations has not been eliminated, but merely redistributed among the participants in the futures game.

In reviewing Exhibits 7.3 and 7.4, the preferred strategy is indicated by whichever curve is above the other as it represents the greater profit potential for the refinery operator. Sometimes it pays for the refinery operator to have sold futures; sometimes it pays to avoid the futures market. And, as anyone in business knows, there is no rhyme or reason for whose on first and what's on second. Although the patterns are such to make any speculator salivate over buying futures before their price spirals upward and in selling futures just as their prices

Exhibit 7.4
Refiner's Margin on Heating Oil (Eight-Week Lag)

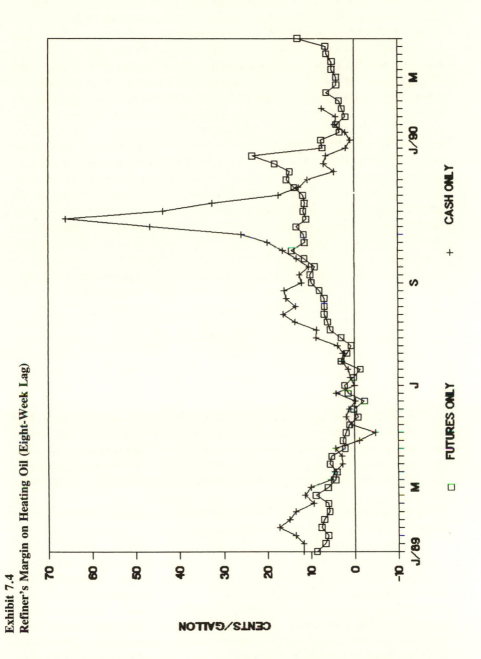

peak, the patterns themselves have no apparent predictive property other than they go up and down with highly irregular regularity. Despite advice on what to do with the soybean complex, the customers seem to own few yachts.

The apparent lack of customers' yachts is not the central issue. The issue is what should a refinery operator do: Sell futures and lock in profit, or be daring and wait eight weeks and see how things turn out in the cash market? The latter strategy is the only strategy for businessmen who operate in an environment where there is no futures market. Refinery operators, and other managers of businesses, either real or financial, that have a futures market, do have a choice. The refinery operator can have pure strategies of only selling in the cash market eight weeks after the purchase of the crude oil or of only selling futures at the time of purchase of the crude oil. Both of these strategies can be considered "do-nothing" strategies because there is no consideration of changing the strategy once the decision is made as to which to follow—once in cash, always in cash; once in futures, always in futures. The refiner's aggregate margin on a weekly output of one hundred gallons from January 1987 to February 1990 for these two strategies is as follows.

**Total Refiner's Margin on Output of 100 Gallons/Week,
January 1986–February 1990**

	STRATEGY I	STRATEGY II
	100% Futures Sales 0% Cash Sales	0% Futures Sales 100% Cash Sales
Heating oil	$1,117	$1,446
Gasoline	$1,290	$1,612

The conclusion of looking back in time and judging the two strategies is that there is no advantage in selling exclusively in the futures market. The refinery operator is better off ignoring the futures market and taking his chances on what the cash market will be eight weeks after the purchase of the crude oil. Although Exhibits 7.3 and 7.4 clearly show that there are periods of time when one is better off selling futures rather than waiting two months to sell the products, the "do-nothing" strategy of single-minded dedication to one approach is best effected by ignoring the futures market.

We might be tempted to wonder where the profit differential between an all futures and an all cash strategy went to since the futures market merely redistributes risk. Whether a refinery operator sells directly into the cash market or sells into the futures market and the buyer of the futures sells into the cash market is immaterial. The gasoline and heating oil eventually end up being sold in the cash market. The difference in the profits of these two strategies does not disappear. For end users who resort to the futures market to establish the cost basis for their purchases of heating oil and gasoline, and for speculators who take positions in these markets to profit, or lose, from the shifting change in price levels, the conclusion can only be that the end users and speculators, in the aggregate, are net beneficiaries. Perhaps this is a necessary requirement for a futures market to exist. The participants, in the aggregate, have to earn a living. For this to happen, the oil companies, in selling futures, have to leave a little on the table for the participants to survive. Perhaps, there may even be a few customers' yachts.

Another strategy to pursue, other than selling exclusively in the cash or futures market, is to sell futures when they are higher than the current cash price. If the futures price is higher than the current price, sell a futures contract; if not, wait eight weeks and sell in the cash market when the heating oil and gasoline are produced and are ready to be marketed. This would be considered an easy strategy to follow because an oil products marketing manager can readily justify such a strategy to his superiors. If the current price of gasoline is 70 cents per gallon (wholesale) and the current futures price is 72 cents per gallon, sell a futures contract rather than wait eight weeks for the gasoline to be ready for sale. The justification for such a decision is that the futures price is higher than the current price. This can turn out to be a wrong decision if the price of gasoline in eight weeks is higher than 72 cents per gallon. However, it appears reasonable to assume that the marketing manager would have more trouble justifying selling a futures contract when the futures price is 68 cents per gallon and the current market price is 70 cents per gallon.

Unfortunately, test runs performed incorporating the relatively easy strategy of selling into the futures market whenever the futures price is higher than the current price failed to increase the profitability above that indicated for selling all the products in the cash market. No benefit was achieved in comparison to the do-nothing strategy of simply selling the heating oil and the gasoline at the time it was ready for sale, that is, eight weeks after the crude oil was purchased.

A search was then made for a set of blind rules that might beat the profit inherent in selling exclusively in the cash market eight weeks after the purchase of the crude oil in order that this chapter not be written in vain. Exploration for the elixir of higher profits did result in discovering one set of blind rules that generated profits higher than selling exclusively in the cash market over the three-year period under scrutiny. The blind rules, which are applied with no forethought to the actual situation in the oil markets, are as follows.

Compare the current price of gasoline, or heating oil, with what it was W weeks before. If the price is higher, then apply rule 1, otherwise apply rule 2.

Rule 1: Compare the futures price with the current price. If the difference is above K cents per gallon, where K can be a negative value, then wait eight weeks and sell the product in the cash market. If the difference is below K cents per gallon, sell a futures contract immediately.

Rule 2: Compare the futures price with the current price. If the difference is above L cents per gallon, where L can be a negative value, then wait eight weeks and sell the product in the cash market. If the difference is below L cents per gallon, sell a futures contract immediately.

Before considering the results of this strategy, it should be noted that this strategy goes completely against the vein of what one would naturally do. This is because the values of K and L turn out to be negative. Therefore, the strategy is basically saying that one sells futures only when there is a significant negative difference between the futures price and the current price. In effect, futures are sold only when there is a sharp discount between the futures price and the current cash price. This is not a "natural act" on the part of the oil products marketing manager. It is much easier to sell futures when they have a higher price than the current cash price. It is going to be difficult to justify selling futures in heating oil and gasoline on the basis that the price in the futures market has dropped so low in comparison to the current cash market that the thing to do is to sell futures. Yet that is what this strategy demands.

This strategy was a winning strategy for all values of W from two to twenty weeks that were tested, although different intervals for measuring rising and falling prices gave different results. The best run was obtained using seven weeks as the interval for determining whether prices were higher or lower. The strategy improved the refiner's margin on heating oil by 3.5 percent, and on gasoline by 5.1 percent, over selling exclusively in the cash market during the three-year period under consideration. These gains resulted from following these blind rules:

If this week's price on heating oil or gasoline is higher than it was seven weeks ago, and if the difference between the current futures price and the current cash price is greater than −2 cents per gallon, then sell the products made by crude oil now entering the refining process eight weeks later in the cash market. Otherwise, sell a futures contract now. As noted, this is an unnatural act. Futures contracts are sold only when the futures contract is more than 2 cents per gallon less than the current cash price.

To complete the picture, if this week's price of heating oil or gasoline is lower than it was seven weeks ago, and if the difference between the current futures price and the current cash price is greater than −5 cents per gallon, then sell the products in the cash market. Only when the futures prices is more than 5 cents per gallon less than the current price does one sell a futures contract.

This strategy resulted in 76 percent exposure to the cash market and 24 percent exposure to the futures market for sales of heating oil. The respective exposure of gasoline sales was 68 percent to the cash market and 32 percent to the futures market. In examining the results, it seems that a plausible explanation for being able to improve the refiner's margin for such an implausible set of rules is that the futures market underestimates the fall in prices when everyone fully expects a fall in the price of gasoline and heating oil. Trends do not last forever, particularly seasonal trends. It is no secret that gasoline prices fall after the summer driving season is over and that heating oil prices fall after the worst of the wintry blasts are gone. The exact timing may be in question, but not the eventuality. As more and more participants expect the market to fall, the spread between the futures price and the current cash price becomes steadily more negative.

Marketing managers may be hesitant to sell futures when there is such a large negative disparity with current prices because it would be a difficult decision to justify to their superiors. Yet this is exactly what they should be doing because the discount, no matter how negative, seems, on balance, to underestimate the subsequent decline in cash prices. Therefore, the refinery operator is better off, on balance, to be selling futures at the very time that most participants in the market believe that the price of heating oil or gasoline is sure to decline. Because the buyers of futures contracts appear to be underestimating the true extent of the fall in prices, the price of the futures contract turns out to be higher than the actual price eight weeks later—despite the negative difference with current prices. If this is the case, then the refinery operator can take advantage of this market anomaly by selling futures during the beginning phase of a seasonal downswing in prices rather than remaining in the cash market.

This same condition might hold true during the initial phases of the seasonal upturn in prices, although a cursory review of the results seems to indicate that an anomaly between futures prices and subsequent cash prices is more closely associated with the initial phase of a seasonal downturn in prices. A different set of rules might be better able to take advantage of a corresponding anomaly during the early stages of the seasonal upswing of heating oil and gasoline prices if such an anomaly exists. It is not the intent of this chapter to present the optimal set of rules, but to suggest that there might be an opportunity for oil companies to improve their refiner's margin by judicious use of the futures market.

Following blind rules blindly should not be considered judicious use of the futures market. Nevertheless, in following blind rules blindly, the futures market provides an opportunity for those responsible for the marketing of gasoline and heating oil to hedge against an anticipated price decline, and in so doing, improve the margin of profitability.

Other rules followed less blindly may yield better results, but that is not important. What is important is a caveat. The arrival at an optimal set of rules that worked best between January 1987 and March 1990 should not be construed to mean that this set of rules will necessarily work best between April 1990 and some distant point in the future. The simulation of various rules with past data is no guarantee of future performance other than for the case where the past and future patterns of refiner's margins bear a general semblance to one another. The rules work only to the extent that there is some degree of similarity of the pattern of past data that identifies the optimal set of rules, and the pattern of future data that determines the efficacy of following those rules. One should not have a great deal of confidence in replicating the results of rules on future data whose derivation has been based on past data.

One other caveat is in order. This one is even more painful than the success ratio of replicating the results of blind rules derived from past data on future data. Even if the elixir of a wider refiner's margin through the use of an optimal set of rules based on past data is working perfectly well, it is absolutely essential that the rules be kept a secret. If it becomes generally known that there may be an anomaly between futures prices and actual prices as one approaches major anticipated turning points in prices, then the pursuit of all to take advantage of this anomaly will obliterate its existence. Nothing can relegate an anomaly to a historic footnote faster than a massive response by the participants in a futures market trying to take advantage of its existence.

HEDGING THE VALUATION OF AN INVENTORY

Every firm has a minimum working inventory or safety stock. In the case of a refinery, there is gasoline and heating oil in the system that cannot be sold. Part of this inventory keeps the pipelines full and prevents the tanks from being completely emptied. Some inventory is always in transit and the rest, known as safety stock, is required to satisfy the vagaries of demand in time and place. This inventory is necessary for the smooth operation of the company and is not considered salable.

Gasoline in a pipeline cannot be sold. The pipeline must be kept full for it to be capable of moving gasoline between two locations. Nevertheless, this gasoline is considered part of inventory and accountants have their own rules as to how to value this inventory for book-keeping purposes. Of concern to refinery operators, and managers in general, are inventory writedowns caused by a falloff in prices.

Without a futures market, there is no way to hedge, or protect, the value of an inventory. With a futures market, inventory managers can sell futures if they feel that prices will decline. They can sell futures, but they cannot deliver the inventory required for the smooth functioning of the operations of the company. Therefore, if inventory managers sell futures because they fear a downtrend in prices will result in a writedown of the value of the inventory, and if they are right, they cannot physically deliver products to those who purchased contracts without adversely affecting the operations of the company. If they do deliver the inventory to the purchaser of contracts, they must buy an equivalent amount of the product to replace what they sold on a one-for-one basis. Therefore, it is much easier to buy back futures contracts before they expire. The profit in buying back contracts acts as a hedge to protect the value of the inventory as prices decline. If a sufficient number of futures contracts are sold, the accountants would not be in a position to make managers write down the value of the inventory because of a severe drop in prices. The inventory lost value when prices declined, but this risk was hedged by the sale of the futures contracts that generated a profit each time the price of the goods in inventory dropped.

On the other hand, if prices rise, the value of the inventory is enhanced except to the degree that futures contracts were sold to hedge against a price decline. We might argue that the futures market is actually exchanging the nature of the risk that an inventory manager must face rather than laying it off to a third party. A hedging position against a price decline means that a loss will be suffered if there is a rise in prices proportionate to the number of futures contracts sold.

Nevertheless, the sale of the futures contracts provides a hedge to protect the inventory manager against the risk of a writedown of the valuation of the inventory from a potential price decline. The cost of the protection is that the manager does not fully accrue the benefit of a rise in inventory value if prices increase because the futures contracts are generating a loss. This is something the inventory manager must endure: it is the cost of insuring against something abhorred.

A simulation was run on the historic data to evaluate a simple blind rule for a variety of relationships between the current price and the futures price. If the price of a unit of inventory, for example, a gallon of heating oil or a gallon of gasoline, is less than it was W weeks ago, then sell a futures contract; otherwise do nothing. This means that the inventory manager is acting on the basis that prices have already declined from where they were W weeks before, and is attempting to manage the risk of the inventory falling further in value by selling a futures contract.

A comparison can be made between the price of the futures contract and the actual cash price eight weeks in the future. The cash price eight weeks hence completes the transaction of selling a futures contract now. It also is a measure of the effectiveness of selling the futures contract. If the cash price eight weeks after the purchase of the futures contract is higher than the futures price, the inventory manager erred in attempting to protect the value of the inventory. The futures contract is going to be liquidated with a loss. If the cash price eight weeks in the future is less than the price stipulated in the futures contract, then the futures contract has generated a profit which acts as a hedge in protecting the value of the inventory. Blind rules can be easily evaluated on the basis that their application over a three-year period generates a net profit or loss.

No blind rule seemed to work if the criterion for taking action involved the fact that the value of the inventory had already declined. Hedging did generate profits, however, which means hedging was successful in protecting the inventory from a decline in prices, if the hedge was put in place while prices were rising. This is an unnatural act but one that works. The blind rule that seemed to provide consistently beneficial results in hedging inventory value for both gasoline and heating oil was to hedge only if prices were higher than what they were eight weeks previously and if the difference between the futures price and the current price was less than -2 cents per gallon. For a certain number of week intervals, and for the respective products, -1 or -3 cents per gallon provided marginally better results.

Nevertheless, it appears that the same anomaly is at work. The longer an uptrend continues, the more negative is the spread between futures and current prices as more and more participants look forward to a price decline. They are right in their expectation, but wrong in their anticipation of the magnitude of the price decline. They are underestimating the degree of fall in prices and the simulation is identifying this anomaly.

Again, the two caveats still stand. What works on past data may not work on future data and market anomalies do not remain anomalous when everyone knows about them.

APPENDIX

There are two programs in this chapter. The OIL program evaluates three strategies. One is the "do-nothing" strategy of remaining solely in the futures and cash markets, selling futures only if their price is higher than the current price, and selling futures if their price is less than the current price of gasoline and heating oil. The OILINV program evaluates hedging operations in a falling and rising market environment.

OIL

The data base on prices, taken from the financial press, is stored in a DATAFF file and fed into the program in statements 30 to 50. Statements 70 to 120 evaluates the single strategy of remaining either fully committed to the cash or futures market. The array $D(1,I)$ contains the cash price of heating oil; $D(2,I)$, the two-month futures price of heating oil; $D(3,I)$, the cash price of gasoline; $D(4,I)$, the two-month futures price of gasoline; and $D(5,I)$, the cash price of crude oil. All figures are in cents per gallon. The strategy of selling only in the futures market is measured by taking the cumulative total of the differences between the futures price of heating oil or gasoline and the crude price (statements 70–90) over the period of time under scrutiny. The strategy of selling only in the cash market is measured by taking the cumulative total of the differences between the cash price eight weeks in the future compared to the current price of crude oil over the same period of time (statements 100–120).

Statements 130 to 240 examine the strategy of selling futures only when there is a positive $(K > 0)$ difference between the futures price and the current price. This strategy does not generate any improvement over the cash-only strategy.

Statements 250 to 710 evaluate the third strategy of bringing in the point of whether prices are higher or lower than they were W weeks before. Statements 300 and 370 measure the price difference for heating oil and gasoline, respectively. Rule 1, as described in the chapter, is contained in statements 310 to 330 for heating oil and statements 380 to 400 for gasoline. Rule 2 is carried out in statements 340 to 360 and statements 410 to 430 for heating oil and gasoline, respectively. Printouts are limited only to those instances where performance is better than the all-cash strategy, as determined in statements 650 to 700, or where a new record is established (statements 450–480).

```
10 REM NAME OF PROGRAM IS OIL
20 DIM D(5,200)
30 OPEN "I",#1,"DATAFF"
40 FOR I=1 TO 172:INPUT #1,D(1,I),D(2,I),D(3,I),D(4,I),D(5,I):NEXT
50 CLOSE #1
60 GOTO 250
70 PRINT:PRINT "STRATEGY OF 100% FUTURES    NO CASH":PRINT
80 A=0:B=0:FOR I=1 TO 164:A=A+D(2,I)-D(5,I):B=B+D(4,I)-D(5,I):NEXT
90 PRINT "HEATING OIL: ";A:PRINT "GASOLINE:     ";B:PRINT:INPUT Z$
100 PRINT:PRINT "STRATEGY OF NO FUTURES    100% CASH":PRINT
110 A=0:B=0:FOR I=1 TO 164:A=A+D(1,I+8)-D(5,I):B=B+D(3,I+8)-D(5,I):NEXT
120 PRINT "HEATING OIL: ";A:PRINT "GASOLINE:     ";B:PRINT:INPUT Z$
130 FOR K=-2 TO 5 STEP .5
```

```
140 A=0:FOR I=1 TO 164:K1=D(2,I)-D(1,I):IF K1>K THEN 150 ELSE 160
150 A=A+D(2,I)-D(5,I):GOTO 170
160 A=A+D(1,I+8)-D(5,I)
170 NEXT
180 B=0:FOR I=1 TO 164:K1=D(4,I)-D(3,I):IF K1>K THEN 190 ELSE 200
190 B=B+D(4,I)-D(5,I):GOTO 210
200 B=B+D(3,I+8)-D(5,I)
210 NEXT
220 PRINT "DIFFERENCE BET FUTURES AND CASH IS: ";K
230 PRINT "HEATING OIL: ";A:PRINT "GASOLINE:    ";B
240 PRINT:PRINT:INPUT Z$:NEXT
250 FOR W=2 TO 20
260 LPRINT:LPRINT:LPRINT:LPRINT ".........................":LPRINT
270 GOSUB 570
280 FOR K=-10 TO 2:FOR L=-10 TO 2:A=0:B=0:N1=0:N2=0:N3=0:N4=0
290 N=0:FOR I=W+1 TO 164:N=N+1
300 IF D(1,I-W)<D(1,I) THEN 310 ELSE 340
310 IF D(2,I)-D(1,I)>=K THEN 330 ELSE 320
320 N1=N1+1:A=A+D(2,I)-D(5,I):GOTO 370
330 N2=N2+1:A=A+D(1,I+8)-D(5,I):GOTO 370
340 IF D(2,I)-D(1,I)>=L THEN 360 ELSE 350
350 N1=N1+1:A=A+D(2,I)-D(5,I):GOTO 370
360 N2=N2+1:A=A+D(1,I+8)-D(5,I)
370 IF D(3,I-W)<D(3,I) THEN 380 ELSE 410
380 IF D(4,I)-D(3,I)>=K THEN 400 ELSE 390
390 N3=N3+1:B=B+D(4,I)-D(5,I):GOTO 440
400 N4=N4+1:B=B+D(3,I+8)-D(5,I):GOTO 440
410 IF D(4,I)-D(3,I)>=L THEN 430 ELSE 420
420 N3=N3+1:B=B+D(4,I)-D(5,I):GOTO 440
430 N4=N4+1:B=B+D(3,I+8)-D(5,I)
440 NEXT
450 IF A>H THEN 460 ELSE 470
460 H=A:GOTO 490
470 IF B>G THEN 480 ELSE 560
480 G=B
490 LPRINT "WEEKS RISING/FALLING PRICES: ";W
500 LPRINT "DIFFERENCE BET FUTURES/CASH RISING PRICES:   ";K
510 LPRINT "DIFFERENCE BET FUTURES/CASH FALLING PRICES: ";L
520 A=INT(A+.5):B=INT(B+.5):N1=INT(N1*100/N+.5):N2=INT(N2*100/N+.5)
530 N3=INT(N3*100/N+.5):N4=INT(N4*100/N+.5)
540 LPRINT "HEATING OIL: ";A;" %CASH: ";N2;" %FUT: ";N1
550 LPRINT "GASOLINE   : ";B;" %CASH: ";N4;" %FUT: ";N3:LPRINT
560 NEXT:NEXT:NEXT:END
570 LPRINT:LPRINT "WEEKS RISING/FALLING PRICES: ";W
580 LPRINT "STRATEGY OF 100% FUTURES    NO CASH"
590 A=0:B=0:FOR I=W+1 TO 164:A=A+D(2,I)-D(5,I):B=B+D(4,I)-D(5,I):NEXT
600 LPRINT "HEATING OIL: ";A:LPRINT "GASOLINE:    ";B:LPRINT:A1=A:B1=B
610 LPRINT:LPRINT "WEEKS RISING/FALLING PRICES: ";W
620 LPRINT "STRATEGY OF NO FUTURES    100% CASH"
630 A=0:B=0:FOR I=W+1 TO 164:A=A+D(1,I+8)-D(5,I):B=B+D(3,I+8)-D(5,I):NEXT
640 LPRINT "HEATING OIL: ";A:LPRINT "GASOLINE:    ";B:LPRINT:A2=A:B2=B
650 IF A1>A2 THEN 660 ELSE 670
660 H=A1:GOTO 680
670 H=A2
680 IF B1>B2 THEN 690 ELSE 700
690 G=B1:GOTO 710
700 G=B2
710 RETURN
```

OILINV

The database is entered in statements 30 to 50. Statements 90 and 120 determine whether prices are rising for heating oil and gasoline, respectively. If so, then a comparison is made between the difference between the futures and the present price for heating oil (statement 100) and gasoline (statement 130). If the difference is less than the L value, a futures contract is sold.

The profit or loss over the period under investigation of entering into the transaction is the cumulative difference between the futures price and the cash price eight weeks after the futures contract is sold. This is determined in statement 110 for heating oil and 140 for gasoline along with the number of times that futures contracts are sold. Statements 160 to 170 limit printouts only to those times when there was net profitability in entering into futures transactions.

Changing the less than ($<$) to greater than ($>$) in statements 90 and 120 evaluates the original strategy of selling futures only in a falling market. To avoid confusion in reviewing the results, "falling" should be substituted for "rising" in the applicable PRINT statements.

```
10 REM NAME OF PROGRAM IS OILINV
20 DIM D(5,200)
30 OPEN "I",#1,"DATAFF"
40 FOR I=1 TO 172:INPUT #1,D(1,I),D(2,I),D(3,I),D(4,I),D(5,I):NEXT
50 CLOSE #1
60 FOR W=2 TO 20:PRINT W
70 FOR L=-10 TO 10:A=0:B=0:N1=0:N3=0
80 N=0:FOR I=W+1 TO 164:N=N+1
90 IF D(1,I-W)>D(1,I) THEN 120 ELSE 100
100 IF D(2,I)-D(1,I)<=L THEN 110 ELSE 120
110 N1=N1+1:A=A+D(2,I)-D(1,I+8)
120 IF D(3,I-W)>D(3,I) THEN 150 ELSE 130
130 IF D(4,I)-D(3,I)<=L THEN 140 ELSE 150
140 N3=N3+1:B=B+D(4,I)-D(3,I+8)
150 NEXT
160 IF A<=0 THEN 170 ELSE 180
170 IF B<=0 THEN 230 ELSE 180
180 PRINT "WEEKS RISING PRICES: ";W
190 PRINT "DIFFERENCE BET FUTURES&CASH RISING PRICES <: ";L
200 A=INT(A+.5):B=INT(B+.5):N1=INT(N1*100/N+.5):N3=INT(N3*100/N+.5)
210 PRINT "HEATING OIL: ";A;" %FUT: ";N1
220 PRINT "GASOLINE   : ";B;" %FUT: ";N3:PRINT:INPUT Z$
230 NEXT:NEXT:END
```

Index

Actuaries, 123
Adjustors, 126–131, 147–148
Anomaly, 217–220
Artificial intelligence, 145, 158, 169
Assessments, 7, 13–18, 34–36, 40, 47, 55, 97, 163–170, 174–176
@RISK, 12

Banking, 85–91
Bankruptcy, 33–34, 56–57, 72–73, 129, 148–149, 158, 188
Blind rules, 215–217, 219
Business activity, 12, 28–33, 44–47, 52–53, 56, 130, 169

Capital, 65, 155–163, 167, 185
Captive company, 125–126
Central tendency, 7, 10
Collateral, 84–86, 90, 96, 148, 190–191
Computer integrated manufacturing, 92–93
Credit, 84–86, 96, 102, 117, 125–126, 128, 156
Credit cards, 147–148
Cumulative probability, 6, 8, 10, 21, 27–28, 48

Debt, 98, 111, 115, 177
Discounted value, 60–62, 65

Discrete probability, 6, 8, 27–28, 176
Discrete values, 11, 16, 40, 59–60, 163, 170
Diversification, 181
Dividend, 56, 65, 159–160, 191

Equity, 98, 111, 115, 130, 190
Escrow, 64, 66, 70–73, 106
Exhibit construction, 48–49
Expected value, 8–10

Financial analysis, 5–6, 156, 162, 172
Fixed costs, 57–58, 93, 162–163, 166
Flexible manufacturing systems, 92–93
Forecasting, 165, 169–170
Futures, 199–205

Generalists, 3–4
Gross income, 102, 107, 163, 170, 172, 178
Gross margin, 57–58, 66–67, 107, 165, 172

Hedging, 161, 205, 218–220
Hurdle rate, 6–7, 10, 56, 65–66

Insolvency, 56–57, 66, 69, 72–73, 107
Internal rate of return, 60–64, 110

Intuition, xiii, 2–4, 11, 66, 72, 88, 156, 170
Inventory, 158, 193, 205, 218–220

Judgment calls. *See* Intuition
Junk bonds, 146–147

Line of credit, 107, 111–112, 157, 178, 182, 185
Liquidity, 56–57, 64, 66, 72, 131, 139, 148–149, 157–159, 164, 178, 193
Loss reserves, 124–125, 138–146
LOTUS, 49–50, 83

Mean, 8–10, 18–19
Median, 8, 10, 18–19, 39
Mode, 8, 10
Models, 55, 104, 123

Negative cash flows, 62, 64
Net present value, 62

Oil industry, 13–14, 148–149, 165, 205–209

Payment. *See* Credit
Present value, 60–62
Probability distributions, 174–177, 190
Project investment fund, 62–64
Protection. *See* Collateral
Purchasing, 91–95

Range, 7, 10–11, 16
Reserves, 123–124, 178, 182
Residual value, 59–60
Retained earnings, 159–160
Risk premium, 105, 107, 123–124, 138–145, 147, 155, 211–212, 219

Savings and loan industry, 148–149
Self-insurance, 91, 123–126, 146
SIMONE, 47–50, 52–53, 81, 117, 150, 166, 172
SIMTWO, 39–44, 47, 50–53, 128, 131, 134, 149, 166, 171–172, 180
Simulation games, 1–2
Single sourcing, 92–95, 99–101
Solvency. *See* Liquidity
Speculation, 201–205
Standard deviation, 10, 180
Steel industry, 160–161

Taxes, 69–70, 152

Underwriters, 126–128, 147–148, 155, 157

Validation, 13–15, 55
Variable costs, 57–58, 162
Variance, 180

"What If," 11–12, 56, 67, 79
Wild card, 148
Workout team, 128–129

About the Author

ROY L. NERSESIAN chairs the Management Department at the Monmouth College School of Business in West Long Branch, N.J. He is the author of *Corporate Planning, Human Behavior, and Computer Simulation* (Quorum Books, 1990) and *Computer Simulation in Business Decision Making* (Quorum Books, 1989).